MORE ADVANCE PRAISE FOR *SPEECHLESS*

"Barry explains how we lose our freedom of speech every day when we go to work. This is a must-read for anyone who cares about free speech."

—**Lewis Maltby**, President, The National Workrights Institute

"A generation of Americans growing up in the age of networking, blogging, and instant messaging will be surprised to learn they park most of their rights to free speech, expression, and association at the door of their workplace. Barry's thorough analysis demonstrates how out of touch this is with our democratic values and suggests reforms that would allow us to be both good citizens and loyal, productive workers. A very good book."

—**Thomas A. Kochan**, George M. Bunker Professor of Management and Co-Director, MIT Workplace Center, and author of *Restoring the American Dream: A Working Families' Agenda for America*

"Bruce Barry documents in telling detail how workplace strictures on free expression can adversely affect morale, productivity, and profit. He argues persuasively that too often court rulings have helped enforce a management muzzle to a degree that the law has permitted the evolution of a corporate ethos that offends the political and cultural commitment to free speech in a democratic society."

—**John Seigenthaler**, founding Editorial Director, *USA Today*; former President, The American Society of Newspaper Editors; and Founder, The Freedom Forum First Amendment Center

"*Speechless* is a new and important contribution to the literature on free speech. For over 200 years Americans have held onto the myth that unrestricted free expression is a right that should be and is respected and protected everywhere in our country. Barry has the audacity to bring into question that myth both theoretically and with a series of examples that challenge our ungrounded beliefs."

—**Patricia Werhane**, Ruffin Professor of Business Ethics, University of Virginia; Wicklander Chair in Business Ethics and Director of the Institute for Business and Professional Ethics, DePaul University; author of *Employment and Employee Rights* and *Moral Imagination and Management Decision-Making*

"A pioneering, fresh, and thorough analysis of the subtle erosion of American expressive rights. *Speechless* concludes with a set of bold and sensible steps that legislatures, courts, managers, and workers can take to refashion workplace communities for putting America back on the track toward deliberative democracy."

—**Daniel B. Cornfield**, Editor, *Work and Occupations*

Speechless

Speechless

THE EROSION OF FREE EXPRESSION IN THE AMERICAN WORKPLACE

BRUCE BARRY

BERRETT-KOEHLER PUBLISHERS, INC.
San Francisco
a BK Currents book

Berrett-Koehler Publishers, Inc.
235 Montgomery Street, Suite 650
San Francisco, CA 94104-2916
Tel: (415) 288-0260; Fax: (415) 362-2512; www.bkconnection.com

ORDERING INFORMATION

Quantity sales. Special discounts are available on quantity purchases by corporations, associations, and others. For details, contact the "Special Sales Department" at the Berrett-Koehler address above.

Individual sales. Berrett-Koehler publications are available through most bookstores. They can also be ordered directly from Berrett-Koehler: Tel: (800) 929-2929; Fax: (802) 864-7626; www.bkconnection.com

Orders for college textbook/course adoption use. Please contact Berrett-Koehler: Tel: (800) 929-2929; Fax: (802) 864-7626.

Orders by U.S. trade bookstores and wholesalers. Please contact Ingram Publisher Services, Tel: (800) 509-4887; Fax: (800) 838-1149; E-mail: customer.service@ingrampublisherservices .com; or visit www.ingrampublisherservices.com/Ordering for details about electronic ordering.

Berrett-Koehler and the BK logo are registered trademarks of Berrett-Koehler Publishers, Inc.

Printed in the United States of America

Berrett-Koehler books are printed on long-lasting acid-free paper. When it is available, we choose paper that has been manufactured by environmentally responsible processes. These may include using trees grown in sustainable forests, incorporating recycled paper, minimizing chlorine in bleaching, or recycling the energy produced at the paper mill.

Library of Congress Cataloging-in-Publication Data

Barry, Bruce, 1958-
    Speechless : the erosion of free expression in the American workplace / Bruce Barry.
      p.   cm.
    Includes bibliographical references and index.
    ISBN-13: 978-1-57675-397-2 (hardcover)
    1. Freedom of speech—United States. 2. Communication in organizations—United States. I. Title.
    JC599.U5B29 2007
    323.44'30973—dc22   2007002007

First Edition
11 10 09 08 07   10 9 8 7 6 5 4 3 2 1

Book management, design, and production by BookMatters; copyedited by Mike Mollett; proofed by Anne Friedman; indexed by Leonard Rosenbaum *for Megan and Max*

Always the eyes watching you and the voice enveloping you. Asleep or awake, working or eating, indoors or out of doors, in the bath or in bed—no escape. Nothing was your own except the few cubic centimetres inside your skull.

—George Orwell, *Nineteen Eighty-Four*

Contents

Speechless at Work in America

IMAGINE IT'S THE FALL OF 2004. You arrive at the office building where you work and park in the parking lot. As you get out of your car and head to the building, you see your boss getting out of her car nearby and exchange a wave. Later that day she asks you to stop by her office, where she says, "Hey, I noticed when you pulled in this morning that Bush-for-President sticker on your car. I don't know anything about your politics, but frankly I can't cope with having someone work for me who thinks Bush should be reelected. I'm sorry it's come to this, but you're fired. I need you to clear out by the end of the day."

Is this restriction on freedom of speech legal? Ethical? Reasonable? Outrageous?

What it isn't is far-fetched. It happened, with some minor variations, to Lynne Gobbell, an Alabama factory worker.[1] Gobbell had a John Kerry bumper sticker. Her boss informed her that the owner of the factory, Phil Geddes, had demanded that she remove the sticker or be fired; he also told her, "you could either work for him or John Kerry." Geddes had on a previous occasion inserted a flyer in employee paycheck envelopes pointing out the positive effects that Bush's policies as president were having on them. "It upset me and made me mad," said Gobbell, "that he could put a letter in my check expressing his political opinion, but I can't put something on my car expressing mine."

Lynne Gobbell's experience, although striking and lamentable, is uncommon. If it were an everyday occurrence, she probably wouldn't have received a sympathetic phone call a few days later from John Kerry and an offer of a paid position with the Kerry campaign.[2] Few people, even among those generally sympathetic to the management side of workplace issues, would likely view this as a great moment in the annals of employment or a wise use of managerial discretion. Even fewer would see it as a highlight in the history of free speech and the First Amendment.

Americans take freedom of speech for granted. This attitude begins at an early age, in elementary and middle school, when students are first exposed to core principles of liberty embedded within the Constitution and the Bill of Rights. "Hey, it's a free country," we learn to say reflexively when others say or do harmlessly objectionable things. The term "free speech" becomes an easy defensive gambit when self-expression is challenged or silenced. After all, it's not just any individual right; it's at the heart of the *First* Amendment and the first of four "essential human freedoms" Franklin D. Roosevelt famously listed in his 1941 State of the Union speech.[3] Justice Benjamin Cardozo in a 1937 Supreme Court opinion called it "the matrix, the indispensable condition, of nearly every other form of freedom."[4] Writing more recently (if with similar extravagance), constitutional scholar David Strauss of the University of Chicago dubbed the First Amendment "the most celebrated text in all of American law."[5]

We don't, for the most part, think much about why free speech matters, nor do we spend a lot of time thinking about the limits of free speech; we tend to leave that to lawyers and judges. Every so often, though, free speech comes center stage in the collective American mind for a while, usually when some national event or high-profile court case makes headlines. The aftermath of September 11, 2001, is a powerful example: A sudden onset of belligerence against a largely unseen "enemy" ignited a national conversation about the tension between liberty and security. Free speech is an important part of that conversation, as we learned painfully on September 26, 2001, shortly after 9/11. White House press secretary Ari Fleischer, near the end of his regular press briefing, was asked for a reaction to an acerbic statement that the liberal comedian and provocateur Bill Maher had made about terrorists and the U.S. military. With an apparently contemptuous sneer at the First Amendment, Fleischer characterized Maher's comment as a reminder "to all Americans that they need to watch what they say, watch what they do. This is not a time for remarks like that; there never is."[6]

The First Amendment does not, of course, generally require that people "watch what they say," even in times of military engagement, and Fleischer's comment was rightly pilloried. (So was the shabby attempt by

Fleischer's office to rewrite history by initially leaving the words "watch what they say" out of the White House's official briefing transcript.)[7] The reality, though, is that people frequently do watch what they say, not because the law requires it, but because life requires it. The great thing about our constitutional system of free speech is that personal expression is presumptively safe from government interference. But the flip side is that personal expression is safe *only* from government interference. Our system of constitutional law generally fails to protect civil liberties, including free speech, from actions that threaten or infringe upon them when those actions are committed by private parties. Employers in the private sector have no obligation to respect the expressive rights or impulses of those who work for them. Even in public-sector jobs, where government is the employer, the reach of the First Amendment is quite limited. At work, Fleischer's dictum is fully realized: we must watch what we say.

Although what happened to Lynne Gobbell—losing a job over a bumper sticker—may not be typical, it is one of the extreme cases that define the subject because they vividly illustrate the abundant power available to employers for controlling the expressive activities of employees. Extreme cases also establish the boundaries within which the middle ground—the everyday terrain of employee rights and denials of rights—plays out in workplaces and court cases. Measures that seem unusually severe, like punishing speech on a bumper sticker in an employee parking lot, make less extreme reactions by employers advancing their economic interests seem almost reasonable in comparison. It's hard to see how the interests of Phil Geddes and his firm were served by firing a factory worker because of a political message on her car, but there are plenty of situations where employers censor or punish employee speech because they do see strategic advantage in doing so.

Take the case of Edward Blum, who in the late 1990s was a stockbroker at Paine Webber in Houston. Blum's off-work "hobby" was political activism in opposition to affirmative action; he served in his spare time as president of a nonprofit organization devoted to this cause. In 1997 he led a campaign for a local ballot initiative that would have barred the city of Houston from hiring and contracting based on race and sex, an initiative strongly opposed by Houston's mayor at the time, Bob Lanier. Blum resigned from his job in mid-1998, charging that Paine Webber, which did a lot of bond underwriting business for the city, had pressured him to curtail his off-work political activity. Blum said a senior city official intervened with Paine Webber to try to silence him and added that the firm told him it was losing city business because of his political activities.[8]

Mayor Lanier vehemently denied threatening Paine Webber with a loss of city contracts, but he did admit that he had complained about Blum to the firm in the run-up to the (unsuccessful) referendum on the initiative. Paine Webber, noting that Blum was not fired, said he was "asked to refrain from publishing articles with a point of view that reflected negatively on the firm's reputation and led to client complaints and a loss of business."[9] A few months earlier, Blum had been reprimanded by Paine Webber for submitting anti–affirmative action op-ed articles to business publications. The company had a policy requiring articles written by employees to be cleared in advance, and Blum was pointedly told that "the firm will not clear for publication articles or other press contacts in which you espouse an anti–affirmative action position."[10] (After leaving Paine Webber, Blum managed to turn his "hobby" into a career, holding positions at various conservative organizations, including most recently the American Enterprise Institute, where he spent some of his time arguing that the Voting Rights Act has outlived its usefulness.[11] Paine Webber, incidentally, has since merged with and disappeared into the Swiss financial conglomerate UBS.)

Blum's approach to racial politics in America may appeal to some people more than others, but Paine Webber's approach to Blum comes off as an equal-opportunity affront to the very idea of free speech. Like the Alabama factory owner who fired Lynne Gobbell for her political bumper sticker, Paine Webber had a legal right to disapprove of its employees' political activities and to leverage that disapproval with terms and conditions of employment. I hasten to add here, as we will see in more detail in Chapter 5, that some states have laws protecting political activity by employees working for private companies, although these laws typically balance the employee's right to political speech against an employer's right to conduct business without excessive interference. Under such a law, it's hard to imagine that Gobbell wouldn't prevail, while Blum's situation seems to present more of an unpredictable collision between employee rights and employer interests.

Freedom of speech in the workplace doesn't mean that a firm like Paine

Webber has to put up with any and all employee expression on any subject at any time. Nor does it mean that an employer must allow itself to be associated with speech that contradicts its business philosophy or strategy or that departs from key principles held by its leaders. This book is not motivated by a hidden desire to turn every workplace into a Hyde Park Speakers' Corner,[12] where those trying to run an enterprise must always yield to those within the organization trying to run their mouths.

This book is motivated by alarm that situations like those that Gobbell and Blum experienced can occur without meaningful recourse for those whose speech is silenced, and without significant consequences for employers doing the silencing. A toxic combination of law, conventional economic wisdom, and accepted managerial practice has created an American workplace where freedom of speech—that most crucial of civil liberties in a healthy democracy—is something you do after work, on your own time, and even then (for many), only if your employer approves. As we'll see throughout much of the book, the role of law is especially important: constitutional law erects formidable potential barriers to free speech in workplaces, while employment law gives employers wide latitude to use those barriers to suppress expressive activity with impunity. The law, however, doesn't account by itself for the repressive state of free expression in the American workplace. Our legal system gives employers a great deal of discretion to manage the workplace, including employee speech, as they see fit and imposes few limits on how that discretion is exercised.

That discretion is where conventional wisdom and customary practice come in. At the risk of a bit of overgeneralization (a liberty one can take in an introduction), the civil religion that underpins work and employment in the United States is the religion of markets. In other words, we view our lives at work—the relationship between employer and worker—through a lens of property rights and contracts. The system works well, by this view, when employers are given the right of "property" ownership over not just *what* they manage but *how* they manage. Employees, in the strict market view, either accept a given employer's conditions of work or move on in the marketplace for their labor to something preferable. U.S. law, as we'll see later, is more dedicated to the unbridled worship of market forces in employment, and less protective of employee rights, than the laws of other democracies with advanced economies.

But employers escape more than legal difficulties when they come down hard on employee speech; they appear just as likely to escape moral consequences. In the field of business ethics—undeniably a growth industry over the past decade—some argue that when corporations assert rights to economic autonomy in the way they do business, they incur commensurate obligations to act in moral ways toward employees and other stakeholders.[13] In other words, a "right" to do business as you see fit doesn't operate in moral vacuum; it comes with an obligation to respect the rights of others as moral equals, including those who work for you.[14]

Americans may not generally agree with ethicists that rights are as important as markets. In a recent twenty-country poll of attitudes toward corporations and free markets, Americans endorsed the virtues of a free-market economy to a greater degree than respondents from all but two other countries in the poll (China and the Philippines). Americans in the poll were also less likely than those in most other countries to agree that a free market economy works best when accompanied by strong government regulation.[15] This belief doesn't, however, translate into much confidence that employers act with moral integrity, at least as measured by attitudes toward business leaders. A Gallup poll in 2005 found only 16 percent of Americans willing to rate the honesty and ethical standards of business executives as "high" or "very high."[16]

It all adds up to a kind of perfect storm for limiting free expression on or off the job. The law gives employers broad control and wide discretion. Prevailing market-focused attitudes about our economy and system of work leave employers free to be regarded as property owners who can (largely) make and enforce rules for workers as they see fit. Americans don't think highly of the moral rectitude of those who run corporations, but they aren't clamoring for more regulation to rein in the worst impulses of business leaders. (As we'll see in Chapter 2, workers have a severely inflated sense of their existing workplace rights.) So, many employers hew to a default view that even mild infringements on operational efficiency and organizational harmony are to be frowned upon and, if necessary, halted with (economic and legal) force.

Employers, then, possess not just the legal ability to repress employee speech but also all too frequently a reflexive impulse to do so. Free speech that doesn't in any serious way jeopardize the employer's interests is viewed as a potential threat, and these views are given far more weight than First Amendment rights. As an employer, I have the right to be free of even the slightest risk that your behavior will compromise my interests, even if your behavior happens to be the kind that would otherwise merit First Amendment protection.

This impulse to treat expressive behavior as threatening leads to many examples of employer overreaction, such as when DuPont fired an engineer who had sixteen years with the company for writing a book of satire about an imaginary corporation and its imaginary employees.[17] Or when the Nationwide Insurance Company fired an employee of fifteen years who preferred not to participate in the company's effort to lobby the state legislature for a bill that went against his personal beliefs.[18] Or when Goodwill Industries fired a sewing-machine operator because of his off-work activities as a member of the Socialist Workers Party.[19] Or when a defense contractor in Connecticut fired a worker who declined to participate cheerfully in a Gulf War celebration.[20] Or when the social networking firm Friendster fired a Web developer for mentioning her employer in writings posted to her personal blog.[21]

This overreaction to what is essentially harmless employee speech on or off the job hides the effect it has on everyone else—the chill that it puts on other forms of expression by employees. This book is peppered with cases where speech by employees at or outside of work has come under the scrutiny of their employers. I will not make the indefensible claim that there is a rampant movement afoot in the American workplace to silence and punish every outbreak of non-work-related speech. I do contend, however, that a generally inhospitable workplace climate for free expression by employees puts workers on notice and at risk of consequences for their speech.

Limits on free speech at work go hand in hand with an absence of due-process rights and just-cause protections in the American workplace. Unlike the systems of work in most advanced nations, ours gives employers near-absolute discretion to fire employees for just about any reason, or for no reason. A person disciplined or fired for her speech enjoys no assurance of a fair process (or, for that matter, any process) for challenging that outcome. Yes, many employers elect to tolerate a wide range of speech by their workers, but there is no obligation to do so, and the lack of an inherent right to due process on the job inevitably chills employee free speech. As we will discover, workers punished for their expressive activity can in limited circumstances seek due process in the courts, but at high personal and financial cost and with little chance of success.

The natural (if frequently subconscious) apprehension that results diminishes not just our rights as employees but our effectiveness as citizens—as participants in the civic conversations that make democracy work. Work is where most adults devote significant portions of their waking lives, and where many forge the personal ties with other adults through which they construct their civic selves. Yet work in America is a place where civil liberties, including but not limited to freedom of speech, are significantly constrained, even when the exercise of those liberties poses little or no threat to the genuine interests of the employer.

Let me say a few words about the structure of the book. My purpose is to examine expressive activity in and around the workplace from legal, managerial, and moral perspectives. I include within the ambit of my analysis any and all speech that draws employer interest and disapproval, whether it occurs at work or away from work, happens during work hours or afterward, and addresses audiences inside or outside the firm. All employers, of course, restrict at least some speech in the sense that virtually none of them would allow absolutely any utterance or expressive act at any time. Certainly employers prefer to, and are entitled to, do something about expression that markedly disrupts workplace objectives or that places the firm at legitimate legal risk. However, even if we assume no inherent right to free expression at work, it is likely in practice that tolerance for expression varies significantly from employer to employer. It is this variation—arising from differences not just in policies but also in organizational cultures and customary practices—that stimulates my approach to this subject.

The first three chapters set the stage for the discussion of the specific legal and managerial status of workplace expression that follows. In Chapter 1, I explain what I mean by "expression" and "workplace expression," describe the various forms that workplace expression can take, and discuss why the subject of speech at work is not just of enduring importance but of increasing importance. Chapters 2 and 3 each examine a crucial background piece of American law that is critical for understanding limits on workplace expression. Chapter 2 looks at a key principle of constitutional law: the "state action" doctrine, which defines how constitutional rights, including freedom of speech, apply differently in public and private settings. Chapter 3 explores in depth the fundamental basis for U.S. employment law: the "employment-at-will" system, which gives employers vast control over expressive activity on and off the job.

With these key principles in place, I then tackle the central question of how much free speech actually exists by law in the American workplace, and I consider how that law squares with theoretical ideas of the meaning and value of free speech. The divide between public- and private-sector employment is basic to understanding the reach of individual rights at work, so this division guides my approach. Chapter 4 looks at the evolution and status of free expression at work in *government* employment, where rights are more expansive than in the private sector. Chapter 5 focuses on the *private-sector* workplace, where there are some (limited) rights to expression. I then turn to questions of how and when free speech matters, questions that have occupied the attention of legal and political theorists and philosophers for the better part of a century. In Chapter 6 I draw upon these theorists' ideas about the value of free speech as a way to shed light on the opportunities and limitations of expression in the workplace.

The chapters that follow move beyond (although not entirely away from) the law, exploring specific ways that expression actually operates in and around contemporary workplaces. Some of the most contentious situations involving speech at work arise with matters of discrimination and harassment—the hot-button workplace issues of race, sex, religion, disability, national origin, and so forth. Chapter 7 examines this intersection between civil rights and workplace speech, focusing on how and when employers have to accommodate speech on these issues and examining the fine line that separates free speech from harassment. Chapter 8 takes on advances in information technology and their consequences for workplace expression, describing what these changes are and how they affect the issues that have been developed from a legal perspective in preceding chapters. I then turn in Chapter 9 to how employers handle issues of speech and expression in managerial terms. This discussion is fueled partly by social science research on behaviors and systems in organizations that bear on connections between expression and performance and partly by how corporations themselves are setting policy on workplace issues that involve expressive activity.

In the Conclusion, I pull together the legal, managerial, and ethical issues that have been raised in earlier chapters in order to flesh out the argument that free expression on and off the job is overly constrained. I contend that an erosion of free expression at work isn't a problem just for workplace culture and individual liberty; it poses risks for the health of civil society and deliberative democracy.[22] I offer recommendations for changes to both law and management practice and suggest that the consequences of these changes would be far from dire for the employer's economic efficiency.

Pressed to come up with a list of critical issues facing the contemporary American workplace, one thinks quickly of job insecurity, stagnant wages, health care costs, downsizing, offshoring, workplace safety, and retirement worries. Freedom of expression for employees might seem less urgent than these issues, but it is precisely the freedom to speak about these and other issues at the intersection of work, economy, democracy, and society that is at stake. Thirty years ago, David Ewing of the Harvard Business School condemned the U.S. system of employment as a "black hole" in our civil liberties universe, "with rights so compacted, so imploded by the gravitational forces of legal tradition, that, like the giant black stars in the physical universe, light can scarcely escape."[23] Today, as we will see in the chapters to come, employers are controlling workers and their lives on and off the job just as much, if not more than, they did thirty years ago. The result for employees is an erosion of freedom to express themselves, an impairment of their ability to participate fully as citizens in our collective social and political enterprise.

ONE

When Work and Speech Collide

If you want to be absolutely literal, all human life is speech. Every
time a person goes to work all he does is speak. Or write. Or listen
to other people speaking. Or eat lunch.

—Supreme Court Justice Stephen Breyer[1]

THIS BOOK IS ABOUT FREEDOM OF EXPRESSION at work and after
work—how expression is exercised by employees, regulated by law, and
encouraged, punished, or censored by employers. The necessary place to
begin is with a brief excursion into the meaning of "speech" and "expression."

If I walk into your office carrying a cup of coffee and spill some of it on
your new handmade Nepalese rug, you might see that as a careless act but
probably not as an expressive act. But suppose I come to your office, notice
your new Nepalese rug, and voice my disgust at the prevalence of child
labor in Nepal's hand-knotted rug industry.[2] I then state my intention to
spill coffee on the rug to protest your consumer support for Nepal's hand-
knotted rug economy, and I proceed to spill as announced. Is the spill now
an expressive act? Surely yes, because it is specifically intended to convey a
viewpoint. (It wouldn't, of course, be a legally protected act, since courts are
unlikely to forgive the destruction of someone else's property in the name
of free speech.)

We can accept with little difficulty that "freedom of speech" (as the First
Amendment phrases it) refers fundamentally to verbal communication—
messages conveyed with words, whether oral or written. Expressive behavior doesn't require words, however, and there are many ways to express an
idea or a viewpoint nonverbally or symbolically. Justice Breyer's (sarcastic)
observation is one way to imagine the reach of symbolic expression: any
action can potentially be perceived or understood as a form of communication, which means that everything we do has some conceivable form of
expressive value. Although philosophically interesting, this approach to

"expression" is hardly practical: if any and every nonverbal action can be painted as a form of communication with free speech value, then we'll have people claiming First Amendment protection for criminal behavior and courts trying to sort out whose expressive conduct is sincere and whose isn't.[3] Besides, as Stephen Breyer conceded in his next sentence, "The First Amendment cannot possibly allow you to run to the court with a First Amendment case every time you open your mouth."[4]

Figuring out whether nonverbal conduct qualifies as "speech" or "expression" is an ongoing First Amendment dilemma. Courts have wrestled with the boundary between conduct (doing something that may have expressive value) and speech (expressive value that earns legal protection) for the better part of a century. The U.S. Supreme Court seems especially apt to involve itself in symbolic speech cases when people burn things, like draft cards and flags. The issue of "desecration" of the American flag, in particular, is one that seems to recycle politically every so often.[5] Flag burning itself is obviously not a pressing issue in the arena of workplace expression, but expressive activity that amounts to symbolic protest is as relevant to work as to any other social setting. The legal history of symbolic speech is worth a quick digression because it sheds light on the meaning of speech and expression, and on the divide between verbal and symbolic expression.

That history is dominated by the flag. By the early 1900s, at the behest of veterans' organizations and other patriotic lobby groups, most states had laws on the books making it illegal to mar, mutilate, deface, or alter any object that resembled the U.S. flag, or to use the flag for advertising purposes.[6] A test of one of these laws—Nebraska's—reached the U.S. Supreme Court in 1907 when the owners of a beer bottling company were convicted of a misdemeanor and fined fifty dollars for selling Stars and Stripes beer with a flag on the label. Ruling against them (and their beer), the Court said that a state is entitled to cultivate patriotism by regulating uses of the flag and that no "right of personal liberty is violated" when a state forbids the use of the flag as an advertisement on a bottle of beer.[7]

Eventually—it took over a half century—the Supreme Court came to treat the symbolic act of altering or destroying a flag, when done in the service of delivering a political message, as speech worthy of First Amendment protection. But that conclusion was embedded in a larger Court struggle with the boundary between illegal "conduct" and legally protected "expression." (The Court didn't even view labor union picketing as a form of speech until the late 1930s.)[8] In a famous Vietnam-era case, a man named David O'Brien burned his draft card—a violation of federal law—to convey an antiwar message and argued that the law he violated was unconstitutional because the act of burning his draft card is protected symbolic speech. O'Brien lost in the Supreme Court, which in 1968 rejected the notion that "an apparently limitless variety of conduct can be labeled 'speech' whenever the person engaging in the conduct intends thereby to express an idea."[9]

But the Court in 1974 sided with a college student in Seattle who flew a U.S. flag upside down from his apartment window with a peace sign affixed to it in an effort, he said, to associate the flag with peace instead of war. The Court ruled that this kind of communication "through the use of symbols" with "intent to convey a particularized message" merits constitutional protection.[10] Full recognition of the link between symbolic protest and free speech came in the case of a protestor at the 1984 Republican National Convention in Dallas who burned a flag and was prosecuted under a Texas law. Deciding for the protestor, the Supreme Court rejected the state of Texas' claim that destroying a flag is not expressive conduct and asserted that it doesn't matter whether legitimate expression takes a verbal or nonverbal form. The distinction between verbal and symbolic conduct, said the Court, "is of no moment where the nonverbal conduct is expressive, as it is here, and where the regulation of that conduct is related to expression, as it is here."[11]

Having now made it clear that flag burning is protected free speech, the Court triggered numerous attempts to amend the U.S. Constitution to "protect" the flag—efforts that over the years have found lawmakers and others struggling with the tension between "conduct" and "speech." In Senate floor debate on a flag amendment in 2006, Pennsylvania's Arlen Specter asserted that "flag burning is a form of expression that is spiteful or vengeful. It is designed to hurt. It is not designed to persuade."[12] Dianne Feinstein of California called burning a flag "conduct, not speech" because the flag is "the symbol of our democracy, our shared values, our commitment to justice, our remembrance to those who have sacrificed to defend these principles."[13] You don't have to be opinionated one way or the other about flag "desecration" to see the hair-splitting illogic in both senators' comments. Each makes a tortured effort to differentiate flag burning from other types of symbolic political expression because of the kind of expression involved (it's vengeful or spiteful or not designed to persuade or about shared values). Neither, however, succeeds in defeating the reality that flag burning in the service of political protest is inescapably expressive.

People may not be burning flags on the job, but they are engaging in other forms of symbolic expression that raise workplace speech concerns. And as with flag burning, sometimes the expression makes people uncomfortable. But is it protected free speech? Baltimore police office Robert Berger put this question to the courts back in the 1980s when his employer (the city police department) tried to force him to cease his after-work activity: giving, at bars and taverns, musical performances that featured an Al Jolson impersonation in blackface makeup and a black wig. Berger argued that the police department's actions violated his First Amendment rights to free speech. As we'll see in more detail in Chapter 4, a government employee has free speech rights an employer cannot infringe, as long as the "speech" is on a matter of public interest (and is not disruptive to employer interests). A federal appeals court said Berger's performances qualified as artistic expression that met the standard, being "of obvious public interest to those considerable segments of the community who willingly attended and sometimes paid to see and hear them."[14] Audiences may regard Berger's performances as entertainment rather than as an expression of political or social views, said the court, but the First Amendment still applies.

A decade later, in the case of an Arkansas police officer named Kevin Tindle, who was suspended after wearing blackface makeup (and other racially provocative costume accoutrements) to a Halloween party, another appeals court reached the opposite conclusion. Artistic expression in front of a public audience and a costume worn to a private party are two very different things, said the court: "Here there were no public performances, and there is little in the record to suggest there was much entertainment value in Tindle's appearance."[15] This distinction between public performance and private expression might seem reasonable at first glance as a benchmark for First Amendment protection, but applied to employee speech and employer punishment it feels arbitrary and illogical. A government employer must tolerate provocative expression after hours by a worker as long as it occurs in public before an audience, but the employer can punish that same expression with impunity when it occurs in private.

We'll see in later chapters that an individual's ability to express himself or herself without paying a price on the job depends in various ways on the content and context of speech. The specific details of the situations I have just described, where workers engaged in racially insensitive symbolic (non-verbal) expression, may not seem routine or commonplace, but they do raise typical—and difficult—questions about what we mean by "speech" and "expression," and what kinds of expressive activity fall under the umbrella of "workplace expression," which is my focus throughout the book. I will spend the rest of this chapter answering these questions and will say a few words about why the subject of workplace expression deserves a new and detailed examination now.

There is a temptation to use the words "speech" and "expression" inter-changeably, and I find it convenient to do so at many points in the book,[16] but it is worth taking a moment to distinguish them, at least at the outset. I start with the text of the First Amendment, which mentions "speech" but not "expression":

> Congress shall make no law respecting an establishment of religion,
> or prohibiting the free exercise thereof; or abridging the freedom of
> speech, or of the press; or the right of the people peaceably to assemble,
> and to petition the government for a redress of grievances.

Thomas Emerson, one of the twentieth century's major theorists of the First Amendment, says "the root purpose of the First Amendment is to assure an effective system of freedom of expression in a democratic society."[17] The key word here is "system." The First Amendment brings together a constellation of behaviors related to the cultivation and communication of ideas—religious belief and practice, speech, a free press, assembly and free association, and petition for redress—and taken as a package they form (in Emerson's usage) a system of freedom of expression.

Free speech, in this view, is not synonymous with free expression but is instead a piece of it. An act of "speech" might be regarded as the act of conveying to someone else an idea or an attitude, using communication methods that might be verbal or nonverbal, oral or written, published or unpublished. It can happen through an artistic performance rather than a straightforward message and can involve an overt act of communication or the absence of such an act. We have to be careful, however, with the assumption that "speech" necessarily involves communicating to an audience. C. Edwin Baker, another prominent free speech theorist, cautions that many uses of speech do not involve communicating ideas or attitudes to others. Baker calls them the "solitary" uses of speech—diary writing, prayer, self-direction, and creative self-expression, to name a few—that "contribute to self-fulfillment and often to individual or social change."[18]

"Speech" covers a lot of territory but represents only part of the larger idea of "expression." Freedom of *speech* is the freedom to say what one wishes to say in the form, and to an audience, of one's choosing (including an audience of oneself only). Freedom of *expression* is the broader ability not just to speak freely but also to believe what one wishes, to associate with those of one's choosing, and to live in a society where a free press and the right to petition government are guaranteed. The First Amendment, then, protects free speech and these other key freedoms as well, and taken as a whole it defines an overall system of free expression.

FREE SPEECH AND EXPRESSION IN THE WORKPLACE

Freedom of speech is fundamental to effective democracy and a healthy civil society. Work is where many adults develop and maintain the social ties that make up civil society. Work is also how people create for themselves economic independence—a necessity if social and political rights are to have much meaning. Yet the intersection between free speech and work has not been widely explored. Legal issues around employee speech—especially in public-sector jobs—have been percolating in courts and legislatures for many years. When the connection between work and speech does come up, the focus tends to be limited to speech *at work* or *about work*. For example, law professor Cynthia Estlund describes "freedom of speech in the workplace" as "the freedom to speak out *at or about the workplace* free from the threat of discharge or serious discipline."[19] Richard Lippke, a professor of philosophy and religion, sees "work-related speech" as "speech that occurs within the workplace, but also speech which is sufficiently *about work* so that though it occurs outside the workplace, it is subject to employer sanction."[20]

I take a more expansive view. As some of the examples I mentioned in the Introduction make abundantly clear, speech with little or no connection to one's job can still attract an employer's attention and disapproval. My treatment of speech and work in this book, therefore, encompasses the full range of expressive acts that an employer might be inclined to discourage, punish, or regulate. Expression, as I suggested earlier, involves more than just the acts of verbal and symbolic communication that we think of as "speech." Expression includes the larger set of principles that come together in the First Amendment: the freedom to believe, the freedom to speak, the freedom to publish, and the freedom to associate with like-minded others. To these freedoms to act, I hasten to add the freedom *not* to act—the ability to be free from compelled or coerced belief, speech, or association. Freedom of expression, then, includes discretion both to act and to not act in expressive ways.

My approach to *workplace* in relation to expression is also expansive. I am interested in expressive activity that happens both on and off an employers' physical premises, that occurs both during and after normal working or business hours, and that involves communication with others both internal and external to the employer's organization. In drawing a boundary around what is and isn't workplace-related speech, it doesn't really matter where, when, how, or why expression occurs. If it is expressive activity, and if it arouses the nontrivial attention of one's employer leading to good, bad, or indifferent outcomes, then it qualifies as workplace-related expression.

Thus far I have been referring enigmatically to free speech in and around the workplace without being specific or precise about the kinds of expression involved. Here I wish to reduce this abstraction by describing some specific ways that expressive actions, topics, and contexts vary. With *expression* and *workplace* both framed in such broad terms, there is potentially a wide range of actions and situations that could be construed as workplace-related expression and that could give rise to infringements on freedom of expression. To make sense of the possibilities, it will help first to impose some conceptual order—categories—on things. I suggest here six ways to imagine variations in workplace-related expressive activity.[21]

The first is *location*—drawing a distinction between expression that occurs at the physical site of the employer's workplace and expression that occurs elsewhere. The boundary between workplace and off-site is not always clearly drawn; for many people the actual location of one's place of work is not necessarily defined by concrete physical space falling within the property rights of an employer. Examples are many: the salesperson or consultant who spends time in the field with clients; the telecommuter who works from home; the police officer on patrol; the journalist covering a story; and the traveling executive who spends "working" time in airplanes, airports, and taxis. Communication technology blurs the distinction further: It can be hard to decide if the "location" where speech occurs is on-site or off-site when communication is electronic and possibly transmitted through employer-owned devices and networks. Is private expression contained in email sent from a coffeehouse using the company's laptop off-work speech? Or a call made on a home phone to a colleague at the office?

Second is *time*—whether some particular expressive activity occurs during or after the "workday." As with venue, there is plenty of room here for uncertainty, given that in many occupations the temporal boundaries of work are unclear. If, as an employed academic, I took a quick break between writing that last sentence and this one to send an email to my congressman to urge an upcoming vote, have I engaged in speech on or off the clock? What about the delivery person who happens upon a political rally in progress and pulls over and joins in for a while? Or the traveling employee who wears a campaign button on the flight to Cleveland?

The location and timing of speech are important because many would say that employers ought to be able to regulate expression at the workplace and/or during work hours but not otherwise. But given how hard it can be to figure out when and where work ends and life begins in the modern workplace, drawing the necessary boundaries is challenging as a practical matter. Location and time also matter because courts have seen fit to treat them as important. In a case where employees at a Wyoming newspaper lost their jobs after refusing to wear antiunion buttons, the court said, "Terminating an at-will employee for exercising his right to free speech by refusing to follow a legal directive of an employer *on the employer's premises during working hours* does not violate public policy."[22] Similarly, in a Tennessee case where an employee refused to wear company-issued garb opposing a takeover attempt, an appeals court said, "We do not think firing an at will employee for exercising his right to free speech *on his employer's premises during working hours* violates the public policy of this state."[23]

Third, workplace expression varies by *topic*, and although that can mean any number of things, the distinction of interest here is between speech about the organization itself and speech about the world beyond it.[24] This, too, has its gray areas. A book editor can speak about how the publishing industry works or about how her publishing house handles manuscripts. A physician can talk about health insurance industry practices or about how his physician group handles insurance billing. Many employers prefer that workers avoid discussing their salaries,[25] but conversations about salary trends in an industry or profession are something else entirely. These complications aside, it makes sense to condition some judgments of the appropriateness of workplace speech, and the legitimacy of the law's reaction to it, on whether the expressive topic is specifically related to one's job, employer, or workplace.

Fourth, an effort to catalog forms of workplace expression should take into account *audience*, which I think of in two ways. One is, again, an inside/outside divide: is someone's expression directed at listeners inside the organization or at listeners who are not co-employed? Another is the distinction between expression directed at a narrow, confined audience of listeners (one-to-one or one-to-few) and expression that uses vehicles for expression that reach broader, unconstrained audiences (one-to-many channels or mass media).

Fifth, we can distinguish expressive activity that is freely offered by the speaker from expression that is *compelled* by employer mandate or coercion. The significance of compelled speech as a sinister counterweight to free expression goes back more than two centuries to Thomas Jefferson's assertion that "to compel a man to furnish contributions of money for the propagation of opinions which he disbelieves, is sinful and tyrannical."[26] In the modern era of free speech law, it originates with Justice Robert H. Jackson's famous sentence in the landmark 1943 Supreme Court ruling that schoolchildren cannot be forced to pledge allegiance to the flag:

If there is any fixed star in our constitutional constellation, it is that no
official, high or petty, can prescribe what shall be orthodox in politics,
nationalism, religion, or other matters of opinion or force citizens to
confess by word or act their faith therein.[27]

Perhaps no public official can compel speech, but it's a different story for
private employers. There have been many situations where a worker is punished or fired for refusing to participate in conveying an employer's preferred message. Employees have used the courts to try to escape compelled
speech in situations where the coerced message was both workplace-related
(for instance, newspaper employees refusing to wear antiunion buttons)[28]
and unrelated to work (such as a factory worker wishing not to participate in
an on-site Gulf War celebration).[29] In Chapter 9, I will discuss corporate
participation in the political process through political action committees
(PACs) that collect funds from employees and donate to campaigns. Donor
participation in these efforts, as we will see, is typically pitched as voluntary
but in practice is often perceived by workers as compulsory. Politics aside,
employers commonly put words in employees' mouths regarding the firm,
its culture, or its products and services and are free to punish nonconformity.

Finally, an inventory of expressive forms would be incomplete without a
mention of situations where expression takes the form of *association* with
some group or cause rather than specific communication. Questions involving freedom of association with political causes figured prominently in
the development of free speech law during the twentieth century. Although
freedom of association is not an explicit right spelled out in the Constitution, it is well accepted as falling within the protections of the First Amendment. The Supreme Court made this clear in 1984 when it said that freedom to speak, worship, and petition "could not be vigorously protected
from interference by the State unless a correlative freedom to engage in
group effort toward those ends" was also in place.[30] Rights to "expressive
association" (as they are known when organizing is for the purpose of
speech or worship) are protected in a variety of settings, but cases involving
public-sector employees have produced mixed results, so the reach of associational rights to speech in the workplace remains uncertain.[31]

To recap, employee expression can occur at work or somewhere else. It
can happen during work hours or at some other time. It can be about the
job or workplace or not. It can be directed at an audience that is inside the

organization for which the speaker works or at an outside audience. Expression can serve communication aims that are intimate or can be conveyed through channels that reach mass audiences. It can be freely offered or coerced. And it can entail specific message-driven communication or mere association. I could—but I won't—combine these various characteristics of speech to create unique profiles of expressive behavior; there would be dozens of them, even allowing that several combinations are unlikely or uninteresting. (For example, employer-coerced mass communication that occurs after work and off the premises about matters unrelated to the job is something we probably don't need to worry about.) My aim is not to count up the different flavors of employee speech; it is to emphasize that the canvas here is a broad one and that particular expressive acts have a number of attributes that help to explain how employee speech works, both in law and in practice.

WHY CARE ABOUT WORKPLACE EXPRESSION? AND WHY NOW?

Free speech on and off the job has been a topic of some interest to attorneys, especially employment lawyers, who wrestle routinely with the legalities involved in circumstances where people are disciplined or fired for their actions. But the reality of freedom of expression at work is not just a matter of legalities; it is also about the discretionary choices that individual employers make about employee freedom, managerial discipline, and workplace culture.

As a management issue, free speech in the workplace drew some interest from writers on employment rights during the 1970s and 1980s, but little since then. An early and important account of rights at work was David Ewing's 1977 book *Freedom Inside the Organization*. Ewing observes that "a right to free speech is resisted more stubbornly by management than any other concession it can make to employees."[32] Business ethicist Patricia Werhane proposes in her important 1985 book *Persons, Rights, and Corporations* that employee speech rights are necessary for moral equivalence between worker and employer.[33] If corporations have rights to free speech and due process, says Werhane, then moral consistency requires granting similar rights, including rights to free expression (within limits), in the workplace to individual employees. Ewing and Werhane both argue for greater protections for employee whistleblowers and for freedom from employer interference with activities outside of work, including expressive activities.

The time is right to take a new look at free expression in the workplace for several reasons. First, the nature of work is changing in ways that render rights to expression both more threatened and more important.[34] Employment over the course a working lifetime is less stable and more transitional than in the past, which means less individual economic security and more workplace docility and self-censorship. Fearing the consequences (or even the loss of a job), employees develop survival instincts that make them more inclined to curry favor than to speak out about management or corporate practices.

Second, the precipitous drop in the size of the unionized workforce in the United States means fewer workers who can expect due-process protections when they speak out about workplace issues (or anything else).[35] Although unions have stepped up organizing efforts in recent years, the climate for organized labor and collective bargaining continues to deteriorate. In an important ruling in late 2006, the National Labor Relations Board decided that workers with merely occasional supervisory responsibilities are ineligible for union representation.[36] Critics see the ruling as undermining the rights of millions of workers to organize,[37] which means diminished opportunities for due process at work and more risks associated with expressive activity.

Third, we have seen in recent decades a marked increase in political partisanship by corporations, including involvement in hot-button issues that play to social, cultural, and political divisions in society. One result, as the Alabama factory worker with the political bumper sticker discovered, can be a chill on employee expression that departs from an employer's preferred point of view. As corporations expand their visibility as players in regional, national, and international politics, they are more apt to regard unregulated free speech by corporate employees as a threat to their economic and political interests.

Fourth, employee speech is implicated in the ascending priority that firms give to the value associated with their corporate brands.[38] Workers are increasingly called upon to buy in to that priority, avoiding words or deeds on or off the job that would undermine brand equity. As one brand management consultant puts it, protecting the brand means engaging "the entire organization in reinforcing the brand's promise through every action taken by the organization—internally and externally."[39] The evolving mentality of "brand stewardship" creates new opportunities for conflict between management aims and employee expression.

Fifth, some of the most dramatic changes to work and to workplaces over the past generation have come from developments in information technology and digital networks—advances that alter the landscape for workplace expression in complex ways. Digital information technology can be said to promote free expression at work by making easy-to-use, low-cost communication networks widely available. The Internet allows individuals who are not professional pundits or journalists to reach large and diffuse audiences with little effort. As I will discuss at some length in Chapter 8, many employers are struggling to figure out how to cope with this changing digital terrain—blogs, wikis, listservs, instant messaging, and all the rest—while keeping control of operational efficiency, brand image, and the firm's reputation.

It is important to keep in mind that the same technology giving workers new avenues for expression is giving employers new ways to police it. Improvements in information and biomedical technology will continue to create additional opportunities for employers to track the activities and conduct of workers. Electronic monitoring and other forms of surveillance are commonly treated as privacy issues,[40] but they raise free speech concerns to the extent that the content of monitored communications can be grounds for discipline or termination. "It is not a great leap," observes employment law expert David Yamada of Suffolk University, "to conclude that electronic surveillance in the workplace severely chills employee free speech."[41]

New attention to free speech at work is also warranted by changes we've seen in the study and practice of organizational management over the past couple of decades. Researchers and many managers are more attuned to employee involvement and self-direction, to team-based structures that de-emphasize hierarchy, and to the role of rank-and-file input into operational and strategic decision making. As management theory and practice have grown comfortable with flatter organizational designs, more worker involvement through group decision-making mechanisms, and more flexible processes, structures, and reward systems, the importance of employee participation and by extension employee expression, inevitably grows. I will explore the connection between these management issues and free expression in Chapter 9.

Finally, people are simply spending more time at work than in the past.[42] With less free time away from the job, people may forfeit opportunities to do expressive things outside the workplace. But the role of free speech here goes beyond just the sheer amount of time we spend at work. As we spend more of our waking hours interacting with work colleagues, the workplace takes on added importance as a place for developing citizenship and building community engagement.[43] When people spend more time at work, their conversations with co-workers increasingly represent opportunities to exchange personal, social, and political views on issues of the day. Close to half of all employed adults in a national poll a few years ago said that co-workers express fear or anxiety about national and world events in the workplace at least several times a week.[44]

Work, in other words, is where civic discourse happens for many people.[45] The quantity and quality of that discourse gives meaning to the idea of citizenship in a free society and helps to define the success of democratic institutions. A key theme of this book, accordingly, is the link between expressive rights on the job and the health of a self-governing democratic society. Democracy isn't something that happens just at night and on weekends; work and democracy go hand in hand. As Yale professor Vicki Schultz observes, it's no accident that democracies are inevitably "employment societies." Paid work, she writes, is democracy's foundation, providing "one of the few arenas—perhaps the only one—in which diverse groups of people can come together and develop respect for each other through shared experience."[46] But there's more than mutual respect going on. For many people, work is where ideas and opinions are shared with other adults and where people make connections that build friendships and community. The workplace thus serves as a vital breeding ground for the development of social ties that give life to the idea of civil society.

Opportunities to speak freely without employer interference are therefore more than just managerial niceties that make the experience of work feel a little less tyrannical. Workplaces are important venues for shared experience and public discourse, so workplace speech rights matter for advancing citizenship, community, and democracy in a free society. But if it's so important for people to be able to express themselves, what's stopping them? Employers in the United States have immense power to discourage or punish speech by employees and frequently are willing to do so, even when the speech involved has little or nothing to do with work.

Why do we grant so much control over the raw materials of democracy to employers? And why are employers eager to exercise that control? The answers to the first question are found in the American legal system—the system of constitutional law that governs free speech and the system of employment law that defines the American workplace. In the next two chapters I show how these strands of law give employers the power to silence employee speech. Later, in the book's final chapters, I'll come to the second question: how and why employers make repressive choices about employee speech and what can be done about it.

TWO

Constitutional Rights in Public and Private

IN A SPEECH IN THE HOUSE OF REPRESENTATIVES on June 9, 1789, proposing that a bill of rights be added to the Constitution, James Madison cautioned:

> The prescriptions in favor of liberty, ought to be levelled against that quarter where the greatest danger lies, namely, that which possesses the highest prerogative of power: But this [is] not found in either the executive or legislative departments of government, but in the body of the people, operating by the majority against the minority.[1]

Madison had a point, as history has confirmed on so many tragic occasions. But the bill of rights that Madison offered, and the one we ended up with, restrains what government can do to individuals, not what individuals can do to one another. The First Amendment and the rest of the Bill of Rights safeguard the powerless from the powerful in public life, not, for the most part, from the powerful in private life.

Yes, we learned all this back in secondary school, but apparently it didn't stick. We like to celebrate (and self-congratulate) our vigorous collective allegiance to individual rights—free speech among them—as the heart and soul of the American experiment. Alongside this civic pride, or perhaps because of it, we harbor some serious misconceptions about the reach of our rights, especially where the workplace is concerned. Americans cling to a stubborn, if noble, delusion that a right to speak freely trumps an employer's right to control the expressive activity of its workers. In a national opinion survey on rights in the workplace commissioned in 2001 by the AFL-CIO, fully 80 percent of respondents said that it is illegal to fire an employee for expressing political views with which the employer disagrees.[2] Unfortunately, those respondents were wrong—some states have laws protecting employees from being punished for political activity, but most workers enjoy no such protection. In any event, for the person whose neck is on the business end of a falling workplace ax, it is difficult to prove that political views are the reason. Employers, it turns out, enjoy what one labor law expert calls "nearly untrammeled power to censor and punish the speech of their employees."[3]

How can this be true in the land of free speech? And just how limited are an individual's expressive rights in the face of employer power and discretion? Chapters 4 and 5 will take on the second question with a detailed look at the legal status of free expression in and around the workplace. Before we go there, however, we need a clear sense of the core legal ideas that erect a foundation for this "nearly untrammeled power." To set the stage, I focus in this chapter and the next on two critical legal principles, or "doctrines" (the preferred term for basic rules of law that arise through judicial decisions over time). This chapter tackles a cardinal element of American constitutional law—the principle of *state action*. Chapter 3 will look at the basic rule in American labor law known as *employment at will*. Separately these principles erect limits to rights at work, especially (but not, as we will see later, exclusively) in the private sector. Together, they make it difficult to view the American workplace as anything other than hostile to the idea of free speech.

In broad terms, *state action* is shorthand for the basic idea that the reach of the U.S. Constitution, and in particular the rights and privileges it grants, extends only to situations where government is involved—where the "state acts." The flip side of state action is private action—when a private individual or organization is responsible for some outcome. It's often easy enough to divide workplaces into the right piles here. You either work for the government or you don't. Your employer is either a public agency or a private corporation. We can say in general that constitutional rights apply in a government job but not in a private-sector job, and as we'll see in Chapters 4 and 5, there are important differences in employee speech rights across the public-private divide.

A government worker who thinks his employer violated his constitutional rights—say, he was demoted for exercising free speech rights—can go to court seeking a remedy.[4] To win, he'll have to prove several things: that the employer is a state actor *and* that an infringement of free speech rights occurred *and* that some negative employment outcome (like being demoted) occurred *and* that the speech is the actual cause of the demotion.[5] He may or may not win the case, but he can at least be confident that state action is present: the government agency that employs him is clearly a state actor engaged in the conduct of official business. A similar lawsuit by a private-sector worker would fail from the outset because the employer isn't a state actor.

But the nature of the employer isn't always so clear: think of government-created corporations, quasi-public agencies, privatized public services, subcontractors retained by governments, and private businesses operating on public property, to name just a few. Here the line between public and private can be a knotty abstraction rather than a clear division. When a worker at an organization that straddles the public-private divide charges that her employer has violated her constitutional rights, the court has to make a judgment about whether or not state action is present—whether the employer is acting "under color of law," as a key federal statute puts it.[6] Courts and legal scholars have struggled for decades with how and where to draw the line in making this judgment.[7] With governments increasingly privatizing services or managing them through public-private partnerships, the reach of constitutional rights in the workplace is riding on these judgments—on whether an employer is or isn't a state actor.

Although the term "state action" wasn't coined until much later, a form of it is explicit in the First Amendment: "*Congress shall make no law* . . . abridging the freedom of speech, or of the press.*" What the First Amendment creates is not an affirmative right to speak freely but a protective right against congressional action—state action, if you will—that might otherwise curtail one's expression. Indeed, for most of the nineteenth century that's all the First Amendment was: a limit on the ability of the Congress to restrain speech. There was little to stop state legislatures from passing laws restricting free expression. Even at the federal level, prevailing ideas about speech deserving protection were a bit more provincial, to judge by Congress' willingness to prohibit "writing, printing, uttering, or publishing any false, scandalous, and malicious writing or writings against the government of the United States" in the notorious Sedition Act of 1798.[8]

What looks like a state-action requirement in the "Congress shall make no law" language of the First Amendment is only dimly related to the development of the lasting legal doctrine known as "state action" in constitutional law. That's because the principle of state action arose not from controversies over free speech but from laws and cases about civil rights and race discrimination following the Civil War. It's a compelling piece of legal and political history that profoundly affects how constitutional law works on this country, with ramifications that stretch far beyond the narrow context of racial discrimination from which it emerged.

THE CIVIL RIGHTS CASES

A short version of this history begins with the 1868 ratification of the Fourteenth Amendment, which stopped states from enforcing laws that "abridge the privileges and immunities of citizens." Translation: the liberty guarantees contained in the Bill of Rights—regarding free speech, due process, search and seizure, cruel and unusual punishment, and so forth— which originally applied only to actions by the federal government ("*Congress* shall make no law . . .") now applied to the states as well. The Fourteenth Amendment also barred states from denying any person "equal protection of the laws" and granted to Congress the power to enforce the amendment's provisions with appropriate legislation. An energized Congress responded by passing various measures during the early 1870s that forced the states to protect black voting rights, improve voter registration practices, and crack down on racial intimidation.[9]

One particular act of Congress—a civil rights measure adopted in 1875—put in motion events leading to the Supreme Court's creation of a state-action doctrine. This 1875 law, formally titled An Act to Protect All Citizens in Their Civil and Legal Rights, made it both a civil and criminal offense to deny anyone "the full and equal enjoyment of the accommodations, facilities, and privileges of inns, public conveyances on land or water, theaters, and other places of public amusement."[10] For the first time, Congress had used its power to make actions of *private* discrimination illegal. You can see where this is going from a state-action perspective. If the basic liberty assumption of the Constitution is that we safeguard rights against abuses by *government*, then is it legitimate for the Congress to pass a law criminalizing infringements on rights that occur through the actions of *private* parties, such as hotels, theaters, and other public accommodations operated by private individuals?

Eight years after the act's passage, that very question was before the Supreme Court in the form of a collection of five separate cases, each involving discrimination against a black person in violation of the 1875 act. Two of the cases involved denial of accommodation at an inn or hotel, two involved access to theater seats, and one involved seating privileges on a passenger railroad. Consolidated as *The Civil Rights Cases*, the five cases were argued before the Supreme Court in the spring of 1883, and a ruling came in October of that year.[11] The basic question before the Court was whether Congress had acted within the Constitution when it criminalized *private* discrimination in the 1875 act. In a resounding defeat for federally enforced civil rights, the Court said no.

The decision, written by Justice Joseph P. Bradley, an appointee of President Grant in 1870, put the principle of state action as a basic legal doctrine into historical motion.[12] Bradley argued that the Constitution isn't supposed to stop any and all actions that infringe on someone's rights, only those that result from actions by the state. His explanation of the difference between incivilities that individuals inflict and those caused by actions of government was an early, seminal statement of the state-action doctrine:

> Civil rights, such as are guaranteed by the constitution against state aggression, cannot be impaired by the wrongful acts of individuals, un-supported by state authority in the shape of laws, customs, or judicial or executive proceedings. The wrongful act of an individual, unsupported by any such authority, is simply a private wrong, or a crime of that indi-vidual; an invasion of the rights of the injured party, it is true, whether they affect his person, his property, or his reputation; but if not sanc-tioned in some way by the state, or not done under state authority, his rights remain in full force.[13]

There was one contrary vote on the Court in *The Civil Rights Cases*— Justice John Marshall Harlan. In a compelling dissent, Harlan conceded that private parties generally can't be charged with violating constitutional rights, but he argued that the private actors involved in these particular cases should be treated differently because they provide public accommo-dations. "In every material sense," wrote Harlan, railroads, innkeepers, and managers of public amusements "are agents of the state," which means they perform public functions that make them subject to public regulation. Otherwise, he said, if these kinds of businesses were allowed to discriminate based on race, "then that race is left, in respect of the civil rights under discussion, practically at the mercy of corporations and individuals wielding power under public authority."[14] With this argument, Harlan was anticipating the legal battles to come in the twentieth century over gray-area distinctions between public functions and private actors on matters of free speech.

As for the Reconstruction-era evolution of civil rights in America, the ruling in *The Civil Rights Cases* struck a forceful blow against the power of the federal government to expand and enforce equal protection. As a practical matter, the decision launched a grim future for civil rights protections, which would languish in American law for the next eighty years. Had the Court instead left standing the key provisions of the 1875 act, the notorious 1896 case *Plessy v. Ferguson* accepting the doctrine of separate but equal might have been differently decided, and the Jim Crow laws (many of them, anyway) might not have survived constitutional scrutiny. (Justice Harlan was again the lone dissenter in *Plessy*!) Law professor Jack Balkin puts it this way: "By invoking the shibboleth of states' rights to limit Congressional power, the Supreme Court helped crush equal opportunity for blacks for generations."[15]

STATE ACTION AND FREE SPEECH

As the historical excursion in the last section reveals, the state-action requirement became a central piece of constitutional law because of nineteenth-century controversies over civil rights and equal protection, not because of controversies over free speech or the First Amendment. Nonetheless, state action persists as a core principle that applies to all federal constitutional rights, including those contained within the First Amendment. The basic principle is that when the behavior of a private party interferes with my constitutional rights, I typically cannot seek legal remedies through the courts. I might have an available remedy *if* there happens to be a law—an act of Congress—authorizing a legal remedy of some sort against the particular action that infringed on my rights. For example, a restaurant that refuses to serve me because of my race is not a state actor so cannot be sued for a constitutional violation, but it can be called to account for illegal discrimination under legislatively created civil rights laws. However, when that same restaurant refuses to allow me to exercise my free speech "rights" by handing out antiwar leaflets to my fellow diners on the premises, I have no recourse because there is neither state action nor any other legal basis for me to take action.

Cases involving free speech with a state-action flavor didn't show up in the courts until well into the twentieth century. In fact, as an intriguing historical aside, cases involving free expression of any flavor didn't really show up on the Supreme Court's agenda until the time of World War I. In a timeline of First Amendment history that appears in a key legal textbook, there is an entry for the Sedition Act of 1798 and an entry for an 1879 case regarding free exercise of religion (a Mormon convicted for bigamy).[16] Those two are the only First Amendment legal highlights during the first 130 years of the republic, until a series of cases beginning in 1917 led the Supreme Court to grapple with issues of protest and dissident speech related to wartime activities.[17]

Beginning in the 1940s and running through the 1980s, the Supreme Court wrestled with the intersection of free speech and state action in a number of cases. These cases mainly involved people engaging in expressive behavior on private property (such as leafleting at a shopping center) who were stopped by the property owner from doing so and went to court asserting an infringement of First Amendment rights. The key question in these cases typically boils down to whether the actions of a private party should be somehow construed as state action because of the nature of the private party and that party's relationship with government. We will look briefly at a few of the key cases that reached the Supreme Court to get a feel for how the law regarding speech on private property (which has everything to do with workplace-related expression) has come to be where it is.

Among the earliest of these is a 1946 case involving a woman named Grace Marsh, a Jehovah's Witness who was arrested for handing out religious literature on a sidewalk in the town of Chickasaw, Alabama. Ordinarily this might be a free speech no-brainer, but the town of Chickasaw, a suburb of Mobile, was actually private property—a company town owned entirely by the Gulf Shipbuilding Corporation. It had the usual features of a town: residential buildings, streets and sidewalks, a sewer system, and a business district—all company owned. There were no obvious divisions or barriers between Chickasaw and its surrounding area; the town like any other was freely accessible to the general traveling public. When Grace Marsh took to the sidewalk to hand out literature, she was warned that she needed a permit to do this and that none would be forthcoming. When asked to leave, she refused and was arrested and later convicted for violating a state trespassing law. Marsh lost on appeal in the Alabama courts, but her First Amendment claim won the day in the U.S. Supreme Court, which ruled that Gulf Shipbuilding's property rights interest "is not sufficient to justify the State's permitting a corporation to govern a community of citizens so as to restrict their fundamental liberties."[18]

The Marsh case is important because it was among the first to be based on the idea that a private actor can be held responsible for infringements of individual civil liberties—in other words, be treated as a state actor—when it has responsibility for performing a vital public function. But what qualifies as a vital public function? In a later case the Court explained that this involves "the exercise by a private entity of powers traditionally exclusively reserved to the State."[19] It's easy to see how this principle applies in Chickasaw, a wholly owned company town. But while it might be a clean example of a private entity performing a public function, it's an unusual one in present-day terms, company towns having largely disappeared from the municipal landscape.[20] Even so, the case of *Marsh v. State of Alabama* remains a notable one because it was the first to define what has come to be known as the "public function test" for the presence of state action.

The Court in some other cases has identified a few specific functions that turn private parties into state actors. One is participation in elections: on several occasions the Court has found it constitutionally unacceptable for a political party—ostensibly a voluntary private association—to erect barriers to participation by race in elections (such as primaries) that are conducted by the party.[21] Another is the management of a public facility: the Court in 1966 refused to allow a city park in Macon, Georgia, that was overseen by a private trust to be operated as a racially segregated facility.[22] Even where a private party is not performing a vital public function, in some situations sufficient state involvement in the private party's (objectionable) behavior creates state action. The famous (in legal precedent terms) example here is a 1961 case involving a privately owned restaurant in Delaware that leased its space in a public building and refused service to a customer because of his race. Because the incident occurred before passage of the Civil Rights Act of 1964, this kind of discrimination by a privately owned business was generally legal. Given the restaurant's location in a public building, however, the Supreme Court ruled that the entanglement between the restaurant and the agency that managed the building amounted to state action: "The State has so far insinuated itself into a position of interdependence with Eagle [the restaurant] that it must be recognized as a joint participant in the challenged activity."[23] In these cases the courts didn't dismantle the usual requirement for government action; they just carved out narrow exceptions to it.

The Civil Rights Act of 1964 was an important development because it made discrimination a concrete legal wrong regardless of whether the person or the organization doing the discriminating was "public" or "private." By outlawing all discrimination in employment, education, and public accommodations, the act essentially took the state-action issue out of the picture where discrimination is involved. With a law in place barring discrimination by any kind of employer, there is no need to convince a court that there was state action.

That's where free speech took over as a battleground for state-action controversies. Beginning in the late 1960s, we find a string of cases over the span of several years that brought the Supreme Court back to the collision between state action and the First Amendment—between private property and free speech—for the first time since the Chickasaw, Alabama, case in the 1940s. The Court meandered through these new cases with something short of a consistent approach, although by the end of its run its position on the issue of free speech on private property had become clear—and clearly unsympathetic to those doing the speaking.

First up was a 1968 case known as *Logan Valley*, involving union members picketing peacefully at a Pennsylvania shopping center to protest the opening of a nonunion supermarket. The owners of the shopping center and the supermarket obtained a court injunction preventing the picketers from trespassing on their property. Claiming that they were exercising First Amendment rights, the union members challenged the injunction. They lost in the Pennsylvania state courts but prevailed in the U.S. Supreme Court, which found that the shopping center served as the functional equivalent of a business district, freely accessible to the public. Trespassing laws, the Court said, should not be used "to exclude those members of the public wishing to exercise their First Amendment rights on the premises," although it did grant property owners some latitude to make reasonable rules governing free speech on their property.[24] If this sounds like a reprise of the outcome in the Alabama company-town case, it's because, in a sense, it was: the Court relied heavily on the Alabama case in its reasoning, drawing an analogy between the shopping center and the company town's business district.

The tide shifted markedly four years later when the Court took up another shopping center case, this one in Oregon involving antiwar protestors distributing handbills. Security guards forced the protesters off the premises (under threat of arrest), leading the protesters to file a federal lawsuit claiming infringement of free speech rights. The protestors were successful in the lower courts, but the Supreme Court by a close 5–4 margin rejected their First Amendment claim.[25] How do we explain this apparent reversal, even though the circumstances appear similar to the Pennsylvania shopping center case? This case was different, said the Court, because the earlier Pennsylvania case involved speech (union member picketing) that was specifically directed at patrons of a specific store on the property, whereas the antiwar protest in the Oregon case was unrelated to any shopping center activity, leaving protestors with ample alternative options for spreading their message. In a dissenting opinion, Justice Thurgood Marshall stated forcefully his view of the tension between free speech and state action: "We must remember that it is a balance that we are striking—a balance between the freedom to speak, a freedom that is given a preferred place in our hierarchy of values, and the freedom of a private property owner to control his property. When the competing interests are fairly weighed, the balance can only be struck in favor of speech."[26]

The court found itself swimming in these waters again in 1976 with a case known as *Hudgens*. This one involved striking union members picketing their employer's store at—yes, you guessed it—a privately owned shopping center in suburban Atlanta, until they were forced to leave under threat of arrest. The case wound up in the Supreme Court after the National Labor Relations Board sided with the picketers, relying, not surprisingly, on that earlier Pennsylvania shopping center case involving labor pickets. Departing again from its ruling in the strikingly similar Pennsylvania case, however, the Court ruled here for the shopping center, and in doing so made it clear that the ruling wasn't about the nature of the speech (as suggested in the Oregon antiwar protest case ruling); it was simply about the rights of property owners to control speech on their property.[27] By now the Court had completely repudiated its earlier view that for First Amendment purposes a privately owned shopping center is like the business district of a privately owned (company) town. A corporation that owns and runs a town might need to respect the First Amendment rights of its occupants, the Court now believed, but a corporation that owns a shopping center need not do so. Thurgood Marshall again dissented with gusto, arguing that private spaces that serve public purposes are important venues for First Amendment activity in modern society:

> The owner of the modern shopping center complex, by dedicating his property to public use as a business district, to some extent displaces the "State" from control of historical First Amendment forums, and may acquire a virtual monopoly of places suitable for effective communication. The roadways, parking lots, and walkways of the modern shopping center may be as essential for effective speech as the streets and sidewalks in the municipal or company-owned town.[28]

Then in 1980 came *Pruneyard*, an important coda within the expansive symphony of shopping center–based free speech litigation. By now the Supreme Court, with its ruling in the *Hudgens* case, had made clear its very limited tolerance for attempts to assert free speech rights on private property. The *Pruneyard* case involved some California high school students who went to a privately owned shopping center (called, it will not shock you to learn, "the Pruneyard") to hand out leaflets and collect signatures on a petition opposing a U.N. resolution. As with "speakers" in the earlier shopping center cases, the students were forced to leave and filed a lawsuit. What makes this one different is that the students sued in *state* court asserting free speech rights under the California state constitution, not First Amendment rights in federal court, and they won in the California Supreme Court.

The shopping center owner appealed to the U.S. Supreme Court, which sided with the students as well.[29] At the U.S. Supreme Court, the issue was not whether the First Amendment protects free speech at a privately owned shopping center. By this time, after *Hudgens*, it was clear the Supreme

Court didn't think so, and the students would probably have lost had they brought their lawsuit in federal court in the first place. The issue was whether the state of California could interpret its own constitution as granting free speech rights at a privately owned shopping center. In ruling for the students, the U.S. Supreme Court said that a state is at liberty to grant expressive rights that are *more* generous than those guaranteed by the U.S. Constitution.

The *Pruneyard* outcome raises an important side issue about free speech and the state-action requirement. In this case speech was permitted because the California court saw in its *state* constitution a more expansive view of free speech on private property than the federal courts found in the *U.S. Constitution*. Other states besides California mention free speech in their state constitutions. So have other states followed California's lead, allowing free speech on private property? And does that mean that the state-action requirement isn't really an obstacle to free speech? The short answers are no and no. With respect to shopping centers and malls, where many of these speech-on-private-property cases play out, only a handful of states offer more protection than we find at the federal level, and those that do tend to have laws that are confined to narrow circumstances.[30] To cite one example, in New Jersey visitors to certain kinds of shopping centers have a right to expression that is confined to "leafleting and associated speech in support of, or in opposition to, causes, candidates, and parties—political and societal free speech."[31] So presumably you can leaflet against the war, but not against the quality of the pizza.

Returning to the U.S. Supreme Court, we look at a final example that takes us out of the mall and into the workplace, where the speech at issue cost people their jobs. Five teachers and a staff member were fired by a private school in Massachusetts after voicing sympathy with student protests against decisions by the school's director. The fired educators saw potential state action here because even though it was a private school, public funds accounted for more than 90 percent of the school's operating budget (it was a tuition-free nonprofit school primarily enrolling students with drug, alcohol, or behavioral problems or other special needs). The educators argued in court that the school was performing a public function and was involved in a close symbiotic relationship with the state, making the dismissals a form of state action in violation of their constitutional rights. The U.S.

Supreme Court rejected these arguments out of hand, noting, "that a private entity performs a function which serves the public does not make its acts state action" and observing that "the school's fiscal relationship with the State is not different from that of many contractors performing services for the government."[32] Translation: it's not a public function just because it serves the public.

THE CURRENT STATE OF STATE ACTION

The outcomes of all these cases can be distilled into a few concise points. An action by a private party that limits my constitutional rights (to free speech, due process, equal protection, etc.) cannot be legally challenged unless I can convince a court that the private party should be construed as a state actor. The situations where a private party "becomes" a state actor can be boiled down to a couple of categories.[33] The first category is when the private party's activity is sufficiently public in nature that the state assumes responsibility for it. Lawyers call this the "public function test," and it requires that the private party is engaged in an activity that is normally reserved to government. The second category includes situations where connections between the private actor and the government make them symbiotic or inseparable; lawyers refer to this as the "nexus test." As the Massachusetts private school case illustrates, financial ties between the government and a private actor are not sufficient to meet the test.

Both of these tests are highly subjective, so it comes as little surprise that they are not as easily applied as the word "test" might suggest. "Subjective" is my label for them. "Hopelessly indeterminate" is law professor John Fee's; he says it's "impossible to develop any set rules for determining when a private person should be fairly considered a state actor, so instead they [the courts] have created a list of criteria that are highly flexible and easily manipulated."[34] The result is a frustrating state of affairs in which it can be difficult to know if a private party is or is not a state actor. Fuzzy though the rules may be, it does appear that the Supreme Court over the last few decades has grown less willing to find state action in private behavior.[35] That means fewer rights for workers in private-sector jobs.

Given the importance of state action to our constitutional system, combined with the messiness involved in its application to actual situations, we should not be too surprised that legal scholars have been dissecting, analyzing, and criticizing the state-action doctrine for decades. Writing forty years ago, the influential constitutional scholar Charles L. Black called state action "the most important problem in American law."[36] Thirty years later, another influential scholar, Julian Eule, wrote, "Almost no one seriously defends the [state-action] doctrine in its present form."[37] The arguments in its defense focus on its value as a protection of private liberty that safeguards private individuals' freedom of action.[38] Critics see it as not just inconsistent in application but also perplexing as an instrument of liberty. Why, they ask, should a free society tolerate violations of basic constitutional freedoms just because they are perpetrated by a private party rather than the government?[39]

Another objection to the doctrine of state action rests on an internal contradiction. We can usually figure out without much difficulty whether some action is taken by a public or a private party. But keep in mind that just about every private action has a *public* aspect to it. What I mean here is that someone's ability to do something as a "private party" may well rely on the "public" system of laws and rights that we live in. Here's an illustration: Suppose I run a private company, you work for me, and I decide to fire you because I don't like the political bumper sticker on your car out in the parking lot. Since I'm a private employer, the act of firing you seems like a private act. However, it is our system of employment and property law—a *public* system—that makes it possible for me to enforce my wishes, or to defend myself against your efforts to violate my wishes. Employment law (as we will explore in the next chapter) lets me tie your job to your politics. Trespassing law lets me call in the authorities to have you removed if you won't go willingly.

The division between private action and state action is built on a kind of myth. As a private employer, I need not respect your free speech rights because there is no state action in what I do, so at my workplace you have no rights. But to say that there is no state action in my private behavior is to ignore how government makes it possible for me to pursue my private behavior. Pondering this paradox, law professors Gary Peller and Mark Tushnet observe that "every exercise of 'private' rights in a liberal legal order depends on the potential exercise of state power to prevent other private actors from interfering with the rights holder."[40] Cass Sunstein puts it more succinctly: "State action is always present."[41]

A less ethereal and more practical concern is that state action might be outdated in the sense that it hasn't sufficiently adapted to our present-day economic realities. There are a couple of angles to this criticism. One is the expanding trend toward privatizing activities that were traditionally undertaken in the public sector.[42] We see this on a variety of fronts, with governments now routinely farming out services related to welfare, public health, education, corrections, and public works, to name a few.[43] What does it mean to say that state action applies to private behavior that would ordinarily be a government function, when the very nature of government function is changing? The second angle asks how we square state action with the expansion of large institutions in the private sector that exert significant control over our everyday lives as individuals. Charles Reich develops this argument in a provocative 1991 article, declaring the state-action doctrine "obsolete":

> Large organizations are governmental in nature, and government itself
> is just another large organization. The interests of these two kinds of
> large organizations are far more similar than they are different. . . . We
> should, therefore, interpret any constitutional guarantee against harm
> coming from the "state" to mean harm from any organization that possesses sufficient power to be "governmental" in its ability to dominate
> and control individuals.[44]

The public-private distinction that drives the state-action principle, Reich contends, is inconsistent with what the framers of the Constitution had in mind—they could not anticipate the rise of large quasi-public organizations we find now, nor could they anticipate the adverse effects of these organizations on individual liberty.

Perhaps the state-action principle has outlived its usefulness, but it isn't going anywhere anytime soon. Forceful critiques of it by legal academics have been around for decades, but there is no indication that the U.S. Supreme Court has been or is likely to be influenced by them. This means that constitutional rights, including freedom of speech, will continue to be imaginary rights in private settings. Private corporations and organizations grow ever more powerful in relation to the daily lives of individual Americans, and the law fails to adjust, leaving citizens with fewer opportunities to exercise basic rights. For workers holding private sector jobs—which is to say most of us—this situation means hanging up your constitutional rights along with your coat at the start of a workday. You get them back at the end of the day—perhaps: work consumes more waking hours, the boundaries between work and off-work dissolve in an online haze of nonstop digital connectedness, and even time spent truly away from the job is increasingly likely to be spent under the control of some sort of private enterprise. The result is a diminishing sense of time and space for free speech.

The principle of state action is a major culprit because of the fundamental line it draws between the actions of government, which is obligated to respect constitutional rights, and private parties, which are not. As we'll see in Chapters 4 and 5, your rights to expression on and off the job do vary a good bit depending on whether you work for a public- or a private-sector employer. Even so, neither kind of workplace brings much in the way of freedom of expression. To understand why, I turn next to a basic principle of labor law, one that is chiefly responsible for the inhospitable climate for free speech in the American workplace.

THREE

Unemployment at Will

LET'S START WITH A QUIZ. Which state has the most progressive, employee-oriented laws protecting workers from being fired for no good reason? Hint: it's not a state in the Northeast or on the West Coast. I'll reveal the answer later.

In this chapter I discuss the second foundation in law that defines the reach of free speech and other rights on the job: the fundamental principle in U.S. labor law known as the rule of *employment at will*. Employment at will is the default approach to employment arrangements between worker and employer. By "default" I mean that it sets the rules of employment—and specifically the rules about ending employment—in the absence of some sort of contract. And the rules are, well, that there are no rules. The essence of employment at will is that an employer can fire you at any time for any reason, and you have the right to leave a job at any time for any reason. It's almost as simple as that, although there are many variations and exceptions that make it not really as simple as that.

A sense of where the employment-at-will rule comes from and how it works is critical to understanding rights to—and limits to—freedom of expression at work and after work. The rule gives employers extraordinarily wide latitude to hire and fire "at will," which is why a worker's supposedly free speech can get her in trouble with her employer, even when that speech has little or nothing to do with work or workplace. But there are many job situations that fall outside the at-will rule because of legal exceptions, giving workers the ability to resist or challenge a dismissal. After a brief look at the origins of employment at will, I will discuss its all-important exceptions and will close the chapter with a snapshot of the arguments, legal and philosophical, for and against this long-standing but controversial approach to employment.

A BIT OF HISTORY

The precise origins of our employment-at-will system is a subject of disagreement among legal scholars and labor historians. This disagreement isn't terribly surprising, given that the history here is largely about the emergence of an influential piece of common law. The term "common law" as I use it here refers to law that comes from court decisions by judges, rather than from statutes enacted by legislatures.[1] The development of common law is inevitably scattered and haphazard until a reasonably coherent picture comes into focus. When the process works the way it's supposed to, with case decisions and legal analyses building upon one another over time, the law that results "can become intelligible and rational," writes law professor James Gordley. The principle of state action that occupied our attention in the last chapter is a form of common law, but of a more distinctive type: state action may be difficult to apply in some circumstances and is perpetually controversial, but it is a fairly simple principle and a *single* principle that affects only federal constitutional law. Employment at will, on the other hand, is a matter for the states rather than for the federal government, which means fifty separate legal arenas for the development of fifty different variations.[2]

The conventional version of the history of employment at will locates its origins in the second half of the nineteenth century, a time when courts were examining employment disputes on a case-by-case basis without consistent, codified rules to guide them. Sketching this history in their book *Employment and Employee Rights*, business ethicists Patricia Werhane and Tara Radin point to a "mishmash of decisions" that left courts "frustrated and confused" until the appearance in 1886 of a treatise, by New York lawyer Horace G. Wood, titled *A Treatise on the Law of Master and Servant*.[3] Before the development of U.S. employment law, a traditional "English rule" held that employment was presumed to be for one year if not otherwise specified. Wood wrote:

> In this country a general hiring, or any hiring indefinite as to time, is a mere hiring *at will*, and may be put an end to at any time by either party, unless from the language of the contract itself it is evident that the intent of the parties was that it should at all events, continue for a certain period, or until the happenings of a certain contingency.[4]

In 1884, two years before this appearance of what came to be known as "Wood's rule," a court case in Tennessee was decided that is frequently cited as the original judicial statement of employment at will. A store owner sued a nearby railroad that had told its employees they would be fired if they did business with the store. When the store owner raised the firing threat as evidence of the railroad's malicious intent to harm his business, the railroad responded by claiming the right to condition employment on anything it chose. This claim compelled the Tennessee Supreme Court to take up the question of what sorts of things people can legally be fired for. The short answer: anything at all. Siding with the railroad, the court made this now-famous pronouncement (in labor law circles, anyway) on the meaning of at-will employment:

> Railroad corporations have in this matter the same right enjoyed by
> manufacturers, merchants, lawyers and farmers. All may dismiss their
> employees *at will*, be they many or few, for good cause, for no cause
> or even for cause morally wrong, without being thereby guilty of legal
> wrong. . . . Trade is free; so is employment. The law leaves employer
> and employee to make their own contracts; and these, when made,
> it will enforce; beyond this it does not go. Either the employer or
> employee may terminate the relation *at will*, and the law will not inter-
> fere, except for contract broken. This secures to all civil and industrial
> liberty. A contrary rule would lead to a judicial tyranny.[5]

What sort of "judicial tyranny" the judges had in mind is hard to fathom, but we do know now that the United States stands virtually alone among advanced nations in perpetuating an at-will scheme of employment; other countries appear to have managed somehow to avoid said tyranny. A dissenting opinion in the 1884 Tennessee case foreshadowed the kind of free speech concerns about coercive practices raised by employment at will that motivate this book:

> The principle of the majority opinion will justify employers, at
> any rate allow them to require employees to trade where they may
> demand, to vote as they may require, or do anything not strictly
> criminal that employer may dictate, or feel the wrath of employer
> by dismissal from service.[6]

According to some legal and labor historians, this version of the history of employment at will tells only part of the story. The idea that employment at will was abruptly invented by Horace Wood and late-nineteenth-century courts glosses over earlier developments. An alternative reading of history is that at least eight states had adopted employment at will before 1880, three of them before the Civil War.[7] Another suggests that the origins in practice of employment at will go much further back, it having appeared "in colonial times due to the needs of an agricultural economy characterized by labor scarcity, and not in the late-nineteenth century in order to meet the needs of capital in an industrial society."[8] I'll leave that debate to the historians. Clearly the events of the late nineteenth century catalyzed the growing influence of employment at will as a formal legal rule. Early in the twentieth century the U.S. Supreme Court cemented the rule's power in a pair of cases establishing the employer's unfettered ability to control employee hiring and termination as a constitutionally protected property right.[9] By that time it had become the default employment arrangement in the United States.

EXCEPTIONS

Although the essence of employment at will—an employer can fire you for any reason or no reason, at any time—is stark and to the point, its actual meaning in the real world of jobs and employers is narrowed by exceptions that limit how and when it applies. These exceptions are important to understanding how the law treats employee speech because they erect limits to the circumstances in which an employer can fire someone for his expressive activity. Some of these limits take the form of common-law exceptions, which is to say exceptions crafted or carved out over time by judicial decisions. Other exceptions are statutory, written into the law by legislatures. When state legislatures get involved in these matters, however, the goal is not always to create exceptions or expand those that judges have carved out. Sometimes what the legislature has in mind is narrowing an exception—pulling the law back from the common-law places to which judges have already taken it.

A discussion of exceptions begs for a necessary clarification about the legal roots of employment at will. I mentioned earlier that the history of employment at will is largely a story of the development of an area of common (judge-made) law. True enough as history, but the fact that state legislatures have been willing to shape how it works in practice by writing exceptions into law (or, at times, narrowing those exceptions) means that employment at will isn't properly labeled a "common law doctrine" in the sense that lawyers use the term "doctrine" to describe a rule that arises from legal precedent. It's really more of an idea or a principle on which the employer-employee relationship is built. Patricia Werhane and Tara Radin in their book on rights at work call it "the philosophical underpinning of employment practices in the United States."[10]

In discussing exceptions, it bears repeating that employment at will does not apply where an explicit contract specifies terms and conditions of employment and dismissal. Most commonly, a contract could take the form of a written individual employment contract, or it could be a labor contract secured through collective bargaining. Beyond formal contracts, we can think of exceptions as being of three broad types: exceptions tied to *categories* (of people or behaviors), exceptions that result from *implicit understandings*, and exceptions based on *public policy*. Let's take them in turn.

CATEGORY-BASED EXCEPTIONS

By category-based exceptions, I mean limits to employment at will that are based on identifying specific categories of people or of behavior that are given legal protection from otherwise arbitrary actions by an employer to punish or dismiss. Although the regulation of employment-at-will rules has been largely a state-by-state enterprise, category-based exceptions represent the area where *federal* government involvement in creating exceptions has been greatest. We can point first to the 1930s and the creation of the National Labor Relations Act (NLRA), which barred employers from punishing or firing workers for participating in union activity.[11] With the NLRA in place, union organizing led to collective bargaining agreements protecting workers from being fired without good reason ("just cause" in labor legalese) and incorporating due-process mechanisms (such as grievance procedures) for when individuals challenge discipline or discharge.

A few decades later, the federal government enacted civil rights legislation, especially Title VII of the Civil Rights Act of 1964, which created category-based exceptions to employment at will based on individual characteristics (race, color, religion, sex, and national origin).[12] Congress later added protections related to age, illness, disability, and pregnancy status, among others.[13] Some states have put in place employment protections for individual attributes that aren't addressed in federal law. Roughly half the states, for instance, have laws that bar employment discrimination based on marital status. A smaller number of states (fewer than a dozen) and some municipalities have laws prohibiting discrimination based on sexual orientation, and some states bar discrimination based on an individual's arrest record.[14]

The wide latitude allowed by employment at will means employers can send you packing if they don't like your activity choices *after* work. To many this seems ludicrous, and an encouraging development in the states is the creation of laws that protect employees from being punished or fired for off-work behavior—activities engaged in on one's own time. This punishment has come to be known in civil liberties circles as "lifestyle discrimination," and we find in the states a hodgepodge of laws creating protections for specific activities. The most common laws are those protecting the consumption of certain legal products; tobacco and alcohol, with powerful lobbies behind them, have been the focus. Over two dozen states protect off-work tobacco use against employer discrimination (many of the laws the result of a visible industry-led "smokers rights" campaign during the 1990s);[15] several states protect alcohol consumption as well. These laws typically carry a qualification about the off-work product consumption not interfering with employee performance or with the operation of the business. Some laws exempt certain industries or employer types. For example, Missouri's law protecting off-work use of tobacco and alcohol doesn't apply to religious organizations or to "not-for-profit organizations whose principal business is health care promotion."[16] Taken at face value, and illustrating rather nicely the hodgepodge effect of these laws, it appears that a nonprofit hospital in Missouri can fire you for having a cocktail after work, but a for-profit hospital cannot.

Many states have laws protecting political activity by employees. Although the approach and emphasis vary, these laws are plainly relevant to the issue of employee speech. Some of these laws are designed to prevent employers from imposing their own political ideology on employees, some are intended to prevent employers from penalizing workers for their off-work political involvement, and some are designed to protect employees' ability to vote or seek elective office. For people with government jobs, there is the additional complication that seeking or holding elective office might create a conflict with their government service. A small number of states offer broad protections for just about any legal off-work activities. I'll have more to say about these kinds of laws in Chapters 4 and 5, where I discuss the legal status of employee expression in public- and private-sector workplaces.

In sum, category-based exceptions to employment at will are laws protecting a person from being fired because of some category of personal identity or behavior. An employer can still fire someone for no particular reason, or for an arbitrary reason, as long as there are no obvious indications that one of these categories of personal identity or protected behavior is the *real* reason for the termination.

IMPLICIT AGREEMENT EXCEPTIONS

An employer who fires someone can land in legal hot water, even when there is no written employment contract, if the (now ex-) employee can convince a court that her employer acted in violation of an enforceable obligation of some sort. States have recognized two key forms of these implicit exceptions: One is the more common *implied contract* (that's shorthand for the legalism "implied-in-fact contract") exception. The other is the less common, if verbally more cumbersome, *implied-covenant-of-good-faith-and-fair-dealing* exception.[17]

Implied contract exceptions to employment at will, recognized by courts in all but a dozen states, arise when employers give concrete indications to workers that certain policies and procedures will be followed in disciplinary or termination situations. These indications can be conveyed orally or in writing. For example, procedures spelled out in employee handbooks or policy manuals can give rise to an implied contract unless the handbook includes an explicit disclaimer that the document does not constitute a contract and does not alter the employee's at-will status. Not surprisingly, these disclaimers are very common.

In fact, it is remarkable how far employers—or perhaps more accurately their lawyers—feel they must go to ensure that no court down the line will infer any conceivable implied-contract exception to employment at will. Consider a case involving Wal-Mart in Arizona. A store pharmacist named Jerry Roberson got in trouble for having an argument with another store employee in front of customers; he was fired the next day following a "coaching" session with a superior when he refused to sign a performance improvement plan.[18] Two things are noteworthy about the case. First is the almost comically repetitious measures Wal-Mart used to make sure it was really clear that employment was indeed at-will. When Roberson applied for the job, he signed an application that included these statements:

> I understand that this is not a contract for employment and that, even if employed, I will remain terminable-at-will and free to resign at any time I wish.

> I . . . understand that if hired I will be a "terminable-at-will" employee, and that my employment and compensation can be terminated with or without cause and with or without notice, at any time.

> I further understand that no personnel recruiter or interviewer or other representative of the company other than the President of Wal-Mart Stores, Inc., or Vice President of Personnel has any authority to enter into any agreement for employment for any specified period of time.

Once hired, Roberson received an employee handbook, which he acknowledged reading, that included these passages:

> The Company reserves the right to terminate any associate's employment at Wal-Mart's discretion. Furthermore, nothing stated in this handbook or by any member of management is intended to create any guarantees of any certain disciplinary procedures.

> We do not work under contracts at Wal-Mart. Employment depends on performance and the Company's needs. . . . If management determines a working relationship should be dissolved, it may be done totally at Wal-Mart's discretion. Likewise, you are not under contract and may resign from the Company at any time.

> The Associate Handbook is not intended to create any contractual right in favor of you or the Company. The Company reserves the right to change any section of the Associate Handbook at any time.

Clear enough? With perhaps a hint of wry sarcasm, the judge who wrote the Arizona appeals court ruling in Roberson's lawsuit called Wal-Mart's employment-at-will disclaimers "clear and comprehensive to the point of redundancy."[19]

The second interesting thing about Roberson's case is that despite the redundancy about there being no contract, no way, no chance, not ever, there was one judge on the appeals court panel who saw here a possibly legitimate claim for breach of (an implied) contract! It turns out that the company's standard policy around disciplinary "coaching" included a right for the misbehaving employee to have a "decision-making day" to think about things before signing off on the action plan, and Roberson wasn't given that day. An employer is certainly free to say in an employee handbook that the job is at-will, said the dissenting judge, but once the employer creates a procedure "and by its language or actions encourages reliance thereon, he is no longer free to selectively abide by it."[20] That view didn't carry the day—the court sided with Wal-Mart—but the fact that even one appeals court judge detected a possible implied contract in this case goes a long way toward explaining why employers feel compelled to hit employees over the head with at-will disclaimers. For employers, protecting the power to fire workers "at will" means preserving the unmitigated right to punish employee speech without repercussions.

The *implied covenant of good faith and fair dealing* refers to an assumption that the parties in an employment relationship are dealing with each other fairly, in good faith, and without malice.[21] This exception to employment at will means that someone fired was not terminated in bad faith and that the employer was not driven by malice to do so. Or, to put it another way, people act in good faith when they live up to their obligations—not the ones set out in a specific contract but the obligations imposed *by law* regarding how contracts are generally supposed to be fulfilled. Viewed that way, this good-faith "covenant" is an implied aspect of every contract, no matter what the subject or context. However, only about a dozen states have recognized it as an exception to employment at will. One state is California, where a 1980 case involving airline worker Lawrence Cleary is often mentioned as the first to apply it to an employment situation. Fired after eighteen years on the job, Cleary sued American Airlines, charging he was wrongfully terminated for involvement in union organizing activities. A California appeals court said the length of Cleary's service combined with the airline's employment polices created an obligation not to terminate him without good cause or deprive him "of the benefits of the employment bargain . . . accrued during plaintiff's 18 years of employment."[22]

An important thing to keep in mind about the implied covenant of good faith is that it applies even where there is no contract, so it's not just another way to frame a contract violation. The California court in Lawrence Cleary's case said that the covenant can potentially apply in *any* employment situation, even where no contract, written or implied, exists. An example of bad faith dealing that violates the covenant would be firing a long-time at-will employee shortly before retirement in order to deny him access to an anticipated benefit, such as a pension.[23]

The covenant of good faith and fair dealing, if widely applied, has the potential to inflict serious damage on the reach of employment at will, which explains why state courts have been reluctant to recognize and enforce it in work-related situations. Widespread acceptance of the covenant, labor law experts Michael Kittner and Thomas Kohler caution, "would completely undermine the at-will rule and make every discharge potentially reviewable by a third party."[24] As a result, they point out, it is potentially the most powerful of employment-at-will exceptions, but it is also the least enforced.

PUBLIC-POLICY EXCEPTIONS

The most significant limitations on employment at will, and the most important for our purposes here, are known as "public-policy exceptions." We can say generally that public-policy exceptions come into play when people are fired for reasons that run counter to an explicit public policy of the state, as defined in statutes, administrative regulations, court decisions, or constitutional provisions.[25] The devil, as always, is in the details. As with the various exceptions already discussed, the precise meaning of public policy that qualifies varies from state to state and at times from case to case. The vast majority of states recognize public-policy exceptions in some form. The best way to get a handle on how these exceptions work is to look at some examples.[26]

The case that is generally credited with launching the public-policy exception came out of California (which seems frequently in the vanguard of common-law developments in employment) in the late 1950s. A fellow named Peter Petermann was employed by the Teamsters Union as a business agent—an at-will employee of the union itself, not someone falling under a collective bargaining agreement. Petermann said he was instructed by the union to give false testimony—to commit perjury—in an upcoming appearance before a California legislative committee. During that appearance Petermann testified truthfully, and the next day the union fired him. Petermann went to court claiming wrongful termination on the grounds that being compelled to perjure oneself to avoid being fired is contrary to public policy. He lost in a trial court but won on appeal.

Up until that point, courts in many states had invalidated contracts and transactions found to be contrary to public policy, whatever that meant. In a 1928 case about a financial transaction (not employment), a California appeals court wordsmithed a broad definition: a violation of public policy is an action "injurious to the public or against the public good," including actions that "undermine that sense of security for individual rights, whether of personal liberty or private property."[27] Intent is what matters, added the court, not necessarily the actual result. Using this 1928 definition as a logical stepping stone, the court in *Petermann* in 1959 connected the dots between employment at will and public policy. Making someone's job contingent on committing a felony at the employer's behest, the court said, encourages criminal conduct, contaminates honesty in public affairs, and is "patently contrary to the public welfare." The court concluded that "*the public policy of this state requires*" that actions by employers having these effects be struck down.[28]

Although it was in just one state and focused narrowly on situations where employees are pressured to break the law, the *Petermann* case hatched the public-policy exception to employment at will. The spread of the public-policy exception to other states began slowly—it was a decade after *Petermann* before another state recognized a public-policy exception—and it took more than two decades for half the states to follow suit.[29] In a 1981 decision that has since been frequently quoted for its pithy definition, the Illinois Supreme Court said that a matter of public policy "must strike at the heart of a citizen's social rights, duties, and responsibilities."[30] That definition sounds like an umbrella that would readily encompass free speech, but as we'll see shortly, that hasn't been the case.

Meanwhile, in an influential law review article published in 1967, Lawrence Blades launched a broadside against employment at will as a relic of a preindustrial age and a threat to liberty:

> Such a philosophy of the employer's dominion over his employee may
> have fit the rustic simplicity of the days when the farmer or small entre-

preneur, who may or may not have employed others, was the epitome of American individuals. But the philosophy is incompatible with these days of large, impersonal, corporate employers; it does not comport with the need to preserve individual freedom in today's job-oriented industrial society.[31]

Blades's article is credited with influencing the spread of public-policy exceptions to employment at will, although it was not so influential as to bring about the kind of broad employee rights with due-process protections he really had in mind. Blades wanted courts to correct the imbalance of power between employers and workers by creating an all-purpose "abusive discharge" cause of action that would be defined as "interference with the freedom or integrity of the employee in respects which bear no reasonable relationship to the employment," leaving courts to flesh out the details, the results of which would be "a detailed bill of rights for all employees."[32] Heady stuff, but states weren't ready to go that far.

The public-policy exception initially covered illegal activity—situations where someone is fired (as in the *Petermann* case) for refusing to violate the law. As the exception spread, it expanded in scope in many states to include situations where one is fired for doing something that involves exercising a job-related right or fulfilling a legal obligation. For example, in many states you can't be fired for filing a worker's compensation claim, for making yourself available for jury duty, or for objecting to illegal behavior or reporting it to authorities (whistleblowing).

Even though most states now recognize a public-policy exception, as a practical matter the scope of protection against unfair dismissal is irregular, and it isn't clear how much of a counterweight to employment at will it really provides. According to labor law expert Clyde Summers, public-policy exceptions are "grudgingly applied," with courts too eager to dismiss claims when the public policy involved isn't explicitly spelled out in a statute or constitutional provision. Summers points to disturbing outcomes that result from this approach; in one, an employee raising product safety issues was fired for being a troublemaker, and the individual's wrongful-discharge claim went nowhere because no statute explicitly required that products be safe.[33]

What is required to find that a firing offends public policy varies by state. Some states take a narrow approach, making it possible to challenge a dismissal only when the state's legislature has explicitly defined something *by statute* as contrary to public policy. (An even narrower approach is to recognize a cause of action for a public-policy violation only if the law says you can't be fired for doing the thing that got you fired.) Other states pursue a broader approach, allowing that a firing can offend public policy when a court says so, even though no legislative statute explicitly does. In other words, some states are willing to accept common-law (judge-made) public-policy exceptions, while other states recognize statutory exceptions only.

Public-policy exceptions are still not recognized at all in about a half-dozen states.[34] One is New York, where the state's highest court has repeatedly declined opportunities to create a common-law exception, insisting instead that "major alterations in employment relationships are best left to the Legislature."[35] New York does happen to be one of the few states with a broadly written law providing so-called "lifestyle discrimination" protection for off-work activities, but otherwise it remains a jurisdiction that is especially friendly to the concept of employment at will.

EMPLOYMENT AT WILL AND FREE SPEECH

Does employment at will mean that people forfeit their free speech rights when they enter the workplace door? The answer, as you may have guessed based on the legal twists and turns associated with employment at will, is an unqualified "it depends." This is an answer with unfortunate consequences, because rights that are hard to identify can become rights that are hard to exercise. A person's ability to speak freely, not just at work but also after work, without worrying that it could cost him his job depends on whether the at-will rule applies. Someone who isn't sure whether he can be fired for speech is more inclined to be circumspect in his expressive activities. The challenge to free speech posed by employment laws that are complex and sometimes ambiguous is compounded by an imbalance of power and information separating workers and employers. Individuals do not routinely hire attorneys to help them understand their everyday rights—but employers, of course, do precisely that, giving them a clear, informed picture of their power to regulate worker behavior.

For a private-sector worker who is employed unambiguously at-will, with no exceptions that apply, rights to expression (beyond whistleblowing, which I will come to shortly) are largely nonexistent. By some estimates this description applies to well over half of the private-sector workforce in the United States.[36] For many workers and situations, exceptions do potentially apply, and some of them have clear free speech implications. I mentioned, under the label of category-based exceptions, that some states have laws with specific protections against an employer's disapproval of individual political activity, and a small number of states offer broad protections for just about any legal off-work behavior, as long as it doesn't interfere with operation of the employer's enterprise.

For protecting expressive activity from the wrath of employment at will, the fertile ground lies in the public-policy exception. First Amendment devotees like to remind us how pivotal free speech is to a working democracy, and many states disallow arbitrary job terminations that threaten public policy as it exists in our laws and Constitution. So you'd think that employment at will might end where the First Amendment begins—that the public-policy exception would prevent employers from firing people for exercising (non-work-related) First Amendment rights. You'd be wrong. I will mention a couple of the many cases that illustrate the unwillingness of courts to let free speech protections in federal or state constitutions interfere with employer property rights to manage employment.

The first case involved Lawrence Korb, a corporate vice president for the defense contractor Raytheon who was responsible for the company's relations with Congress and various government agencies, including the Defense Department. With his employer's permission, Korb in his spare time served on the board of a nonprofit organization devoted to raising public interest in national security issues and preventing nuclear war. In 1986 Korb participated in a press conference held by this organization that drew news coverage, including a newspaper article that mentioned Korb and that named Raytheon. Some military officials complained to Raytheon, which decided to remove Korb from his job; the company offered him an alternative position that Korb said was inferior in salary, benefits, status, and responsibility. Korb sued in Massachusetts Superior Court alleging wrongful termination on the grounds that his firing violated the state's public policy supporting freedom of speech (a free speech clause in the Massachusetts Declaration of Rights). In *Korb v. Raytheon* the court sided with the company, holding that as a lobbyist (rather than just any employee), Korb's private speech ran counter to the firm's interests and that "there is no public policy prohibiting an employer from discharging an ineffective at-will employee."[37]

The second case occurred in Wyoming, where two employees at a newspaper were fired after refusing as a matter of conscience to comply with a management order to wear buttons urging a no vote on an upcoming unionization vote. The employees argued in a wrongful-discharge lawsuit in state court that the newspaper violated public policy when it fired them for exercising free speech rights found in the Wyoming constitution. The Wyoming Supreme Court disagreed, concluding in *Drake v. Cheyenne* that an at-will employee who refuses to comply with a directive like this at work during work hours doesn't violate public policy. The court wryly added, "The fact that irony exists in this case because the employer purports to be an advocate of free speech does not create a public policy exception to at-will employment."[38]

These cases are complicated by the fact that neither involved speech that was wholly private and unrelated to employment. But that's when people tend to get in trouble for their expressive activity—when it makes the employer take notice. In the *Raytheon* case, the court hid behind the assumption that an employee's expression of personal opinions at odds with the aims of the corporation made him ineffective. In the *Drake* case, the court hid behind the fact that the compelled speech was to occur on the employer's premises. In either of these cases the court could have used the occasion to assert that a free speech-based firing implicates public policy, but neither was willing to go there.

A much-noticed case in the early 1980s out of Pennsylvania brought a federal appeals court to the defense of an insurance company employee who refused to participate in his employer's lobbying effort for insurance reform. The outcome was one of the first and one of the few to say clearly that free speech by a private-sector employee can be a public-policy exception to employment at will: "The protection of an employee's freedom of political expression," said the court, "would appear to involve no less compelling a societal interest than the fulfillment of jury service or the filing of a workers' compensation claim."[39] But it turned out that this decision had no legs. Pennsylvania courts elected not to follow it, believing that you can't claim wrongful discharge under a provision of the Constitution unless you can show state action, which is almost impossible when the employer punishing the speech is a private corporation.[40] Free speech may be the heart of constitutional law, but it's apparently the appendix of employment law.

The one form of expressive activity that has gained widespread protection from employer punishment or termination is *whistleblowing*. The idea that workers deserve protection from retaliation for reporting on or participating in investigations into employer wrongdoing is a widely recognized exception to employment at will in common law, and it has been the basis for both state and federal statutes.[41] At the state level, whistleblowing statutes are common, but they vary substantially in their coverage of employers, employees, and circumstances. At the federal level, protection for whistleblowers has also advanced noticeably in recent years. In 1991, Congress created sentencing guidelines for corporate crime offenses, guidelines that added incentives for organizations to protect whistleblowers internally. In the wake of corporate scandals that were dominating headlines in the business press around the turn of the century, Congress wrote broader whistleblower protections into the Sarbanes-Oxley Act of 2002.[42] I will have more to say about whistleblowing in the next chapter.

THE FUTURE OF EMPLOYMENT AT WILL

Employment at will persists as the dominant employee relations policy in the United States. An often-cited but clearly dated estimate from the 1980s suggested that 2 million nonunion private-sector workers were dismissed annually without the right to a hearing, of whom 150,000 would have had legitimate wrongful-discharge claims if just cause were required for firing someone.[43] Updating those numbers in a quick-and-dirty way—using growth in nonagricultural payroll employment 1984–2004 as a multiplier—suggests that current numbers might be on the order of 2.7 million dismissed annually and over 200,000 dismissed without just cause.[44] Is this a significant number in an economy with an overall civilian labor force in the neighborhood of 150 million? One can argue about that in relative terms, but by itself it's certainly a big number—almost a quarter of a million people with lives disrupted by what may have been arbitrary employer action each year is hardly trivial. And let's not forget the inevitably hidden statistics behind these numbers: the uncountable many who are discouraged or even intimidated from engaging in legitimate behavior (like expressive behavior) because arbitrary discipline without due process is readily available to their employers.

The main story line of the past forty years in employment law is found in the exceptions written into law—and in the dramatic rise of litigation that came with them. Before 1980 there were few wrongful-discharge claims of any type, and by the early 1990s there were approximately 20,000 such cases on court dockets.[45] The volume of federal cases filed alleging employment discrimination rose by over 2100 percent between 1970 and 1990 (compared with just 125 percent growth in the overall federal civil caseload during that period).[46] But have changes in the law and a flood of litigation translated into an actual, meaningful weakening of employment at will? For the most part, exceptions don't reduce the overall number of workers whose employment is "at will," but increase the number of situations where an at-will employee can challenge a dismissal. There's no question that these exceptions create opportunities for people on the receiving end of the employment ax to have their day in court—depending, of course, on why you were fired and what state you happen to be in.

Experts differ, however, on whether exceptions amount to significant erosion of the employment-at-will rule. On one side are those, like labor lawyer Jürgen Skoppek, who fear that the exceptions are expanding to swallow the rule: "Prohibiting discharge for the exercise of a statutory or constitutional right can theoretically encompass the whole universe of social activity. Almost any activity can be linked to the exercise of such a right."[47] Others say the exceptions, though numerous, fail to tilt the balance of power away from employers to any significant degree because the courts that actually decide individual wrongful-discharge cases are reluctant to apply them. Clyde Summers describes judges as generally motivated by a belief that employers deserve "unfettered freedom to determine who should be employed and that workers are subordinate to the employer's decisions—however arbitrary they may be."[48] Legal exceptions to employment at will do not dilute its power if judges are unwilling to recognize and apply those exceptions.

One state where the rule has been swallowed, not by exceptions but by an act of the legislature, is (of all places) Montana, which has on the books a wrongful-discharge statute that goes a long way toward effectively killing employment at will. Montana's Wrongful Discharge from Employment

Act, adopted in 1987, is unique in allowing employees to sue for wrongful discharge if an employer does not have "good cause" for the termination.[49] "Good cause" means "reasonable job-related grounds for dismissal based on a failure to satisfactorily perform job duties, disruption of the employer's operation, or other legitimate business reason." The Montana law also provides for a wrongful-discharge claim if a person is fired for a refusal to violate public policy (or for reporting a violation), or if an employer violates its own personnel policies. Although the idea of requiring just cause for firing someone seems inherently friendly to workers, the Montana law was backed by Montana business interests hoping to do away with large jury awards in wrongful termination cases in favor of a more predictable and manageable legal environment.

Taken at face value, Montana would seem to have largely abandoned employment at will for workers who are on the job past a probationary period (which the law defines as six months if the employer doesn't say differently). After all, a just-cause requirement is essentially the opposite of employment at will. In practice, though, the test of the law's reach lies in how courts interpret an employer's "legitimate business reason." In one important case, the Montana Supreme Court said a legitimate business reason is "neither false, whimsical, arbitrary or capricious, and it must have some logical relationship to the needs of the business."[50] It's better than nothing but hardly a high standard; courts appear willing to give Montana's employers quite a bit of latitude to staff and run their business as they see fit. Nevertheless, this unusual (in the United States) law does give workers a genuine just-cause environment in which horribly arbitrary dismissals under employment at will can become a thing of the past. (And, yes, for those playing along at home, "Montana" is the answer to the quiz at the start of this chapter.)

Unjust dismissal laws similar to Montana's have been proposed in several states. Economist Alan Krueger shows that such laws are more likely to be offered in states that have already departed significantly from employment at will. We tend to assume that employers prefer minimal interference with their "property right" to manage employment so would oppose a just-cause requirement like Montana's. Krueger suggests, however, that the uncertainty that employers face with what he calls "employment-sometimes-at-will" leads business interests to consider a just-cause requirement as a plausible alternative to the inherent risks of legal costs and damage awards that are part of the unpredictable system they have now.[51] That's basically how it went in Montana, which twenty years after the passage of its wrongful-discharge law remains the only state to have put in place such a requirement.

In the early 1990s, the Uniform Law Commissioners, a national body promoting uniform state laws in areas where that might be a good idea, proposed a Model Employment Termination Act (META) that would mandate a just-cause standard for termination in place of employment at will. The idea was to create a balanced measure that would guarantee to workers certain material rights to due process and job security while giving employers relief from the unpredictable risks of current wrongful-discharge law. The emphasis in resolving disputes would be on arbitration before court action. One law professor involved in drafting META points to its "cheaper, faster, and more informal enforcement procedures," allowing employers to maintain efficient operations while freeing employees from arbitrary treatment.[52] META, like the Montana law, hasn't caught on. At all.

With the alternatives languishing, the system of employment at will remains both powerful and controversial. Defenders argue that employment at will makes sense on grounds of fairness, liberty, and efficiency in a competitive marketplace for labor.[53] Critics reject these market assumptions as flawed given the imbalance of power in the workplace, and they assail employment at will as a uniquely oppressive system (unique among industrialized nations) that exploits employee vulnerabilities and treats employer prerogative as boundless.[54] In theory it's a way to reconcile competing interests—with employers and employees both able to exit the arrangement "at will"—but in practice it's a system well suited to a society that wants to privilege the interests of capital over labor.[55] For those with the good fortune to be working in occupations for which demand for labor exceeds supply, there is potentially a balance of interests that dilutes the force of employment at will. For everyone else, employment at will is an instrument of dominion, giving employers nearly limitless autonomy and flexibility to manage labor and its costs without fussing over such niceties as due process in the workplace or just cause for employee firings.

Even with employment at will, employers are often advised by attorneys and consultants to maintain policies of "progressive discipline"—communicating expectations, giving workers opportunities to improve perform-ance, documenting disciplinary steps, and establishing grievance systems.[56] Progressive discipline has some of the look and feel of due process, but it doesn't replace employment at will. The Wyoming Supreme Court made this point explicit in the case mentioned earlier where two newspaper employees were fired for refusing to wear antiunion buttons. As part of their lawsuit, the two claimed that the newspaper's practice of progressive discipline amounted to a kind of oral contract guaranteeing them some degree of due process. The court rebuffed that argument with dispatch, deciding that "subjective understandings and expectations do not establish an employment contract provision."[57] Looking progressive and fair is all well and good, but that need not get in the way once the ax starts its down-ward trajectory. Or as one lawyer giving advice to managers in a human resources trade magazine put it, "Employers should fight to maintain the right to be arbitrary, capricious, whimsical, mean, cruel, etc. They just shouldn't act that way."[58]

My aim in Chapter 2 and this chapter was to lay the groundwork for the discussion that comes next on the specific legal status of expression in and around the workplace. The two key principles of law I have discussed, state action and employment at will, are quite different from each other. State action is an aspect of federal constitutional law that speaks to whether a private party is legally responsible for the rights-based consequences of an action. Employment at will, a concept in state law, is about absolving em-ployers from responsibility for the rights-oriented consequences of their actions. But while different in emphasis, these principles are alike in impor-tance and controversy. Both are core principles of their respective areas of law. Both are perpetually debated as falling somewhere between the essence of freedom and the antithesis of it. Both sides of debates around both doc-trines cling to liberty interests as their touchstone and see constraints on liberty as the weakness in the other side's point of view.

Finally, both principles have outlasted experts writing premature obitu-aries. Four decades ago, law professor Jerre Williams wrote an influential article asserting that "the sun is setting on the concept of state action as a test for determining the constitutional protections of individuals."[59] More recently, business law professor Deborah Ballam insisted that employment at will "has no future."[60] Yet both of these critical principles remain alive and well, together forming the legal basis for employer hostility to freedom of expression in the American workplace. How hostile? How much freedom? That's where we turn next.

FOUR

Public Employee Speech

A MAN IN WILLIAMSON COUNTY, TENNESSEE, published a letter to the editor in a local newspaper giving his views on welfare policy. A man in Will County, Illinois, published a letter to the editor in a local newspaper giving his views on education policy. The man in Tennessee was fired from his job.[1] The man in Illinois first lost his job, then went to court and fought successfully to get it back.[2] The difference? The Tennessee letter writer on welfare policy worked as a computer consultant for a *private* firm. The Illinois letter writer worked as a high school teacher for the local *public* school system.

Placed side by side, these two situations point to concrete differences in employee free speech rights, differences that depend on whether a job is in the public or the private sector. Because of the rule of state action (as discussed in Chapter 2, the Constitution applies only to "state actors," not to the actions of private parties), people holding government jobs generally do have more legal rights to free expression than people in private-sector positions. Government employees have more legal avenues to challenge infringements on free speech, as the Illinois school teacher discovered. But by recognizing fewer types of public-employee speech as "protected" and by giving more weight to the desire by government employers to limit speech in the name of workplace efficiency, courts are making it harder to win these challenges.

The divide between public and private is basic, not just to understanding employee rights but to a political and philosophical understanding of life and the law writ large in a modern democratic society. "Nothing is more central to our experience in American culture than the split between public and private," write law professors Alan Freeman and Elizabeth Mensch. "It is the premise which lies at the foundation of American legal thought, and it shapes the way in which we relate to each other in our daily lives."[3] The origins of the divide trace back at least to classical liberal political philoso-

phers such as John Stuart Mill and John Locke, who discussed the importance of the divide for theorizing about the limits of governmental power
and the relationship between religion and society.[4]

The boundary between public and private is a natural and appropriate
place to explore the ways in which free expression is permitted (or is stifled)
in employment. This chapter looks at how the law treats expression by
public-sector employees, and Chapter 5 examines the private sector. The
state of free speech in the public-sector workplace is important not merely
because it differs from that in the private sector but because a large number
of people are involved. Even though the vast majority of jobs in the United
States are found in the private sector, the 16.3 percent of jobs in the public
sector amounts to almost 22 million people living and working among us as
teachers, police officers, social workers, public works employees, and, yes,
bureaucrats.[5] The ability of these people to speak freely and publicly about
the agencies where they work is an important way of keeping tabs on the
effectiveness of the critical services they provide, and by extension the
effectiveness of open government in a democratic society.

In public-sector employment, one works for the government (federal,
state, or local), so one's employer is unambiguously a state actor. Accordingly, public-sector employers can be held responsible for abusing the constitutional rights of workers, although the operative phrase here is "can be"
(as opposed to "will be"). A government employer is theoretically accountable for constitutional violations, but in the real world of legal practice that
accountability has meaning only when courts (or legislatures) have recognized that some particular action—like firing someone because of his expressive activity—amounts to a distinct constitutional wrong that can be
remedied.

Free speech has been a core constitutional value in the United States for
well over 200 years, but recognition that government employees deserve
some protection for expressive activity on the job goes back only to the
middle of the twentieth century. Since then, the speech rights of public
employees have evolved mainly through an ebb and flow of court decisions,
some of which expanded rights and some of which deflated them. As with
the principles discussed in Chapters 2 and 3, in this history we find a haphazard blend of court decisions (common law) and actions by legislatures

(statutory law). The inescapable result is a legal landscape for public employee speech that features moving targets, imprecise outcomes, and inconsistencies across cases and jurisdictions. Where this history leads is to the conclusion that public-sector employees have some definite, but distinctly limited, free speech rights. Where it starts is in a small town in Massachusetts in the late nineteenth century.

IT CAME FROM MASSACHUSETTS

The history of public employee speech begins, in one of the few free speech cases prior to World War I, with John McAuliffe, a police officer in New Bedford, Massachusetts. In February 1891, McAuliffe was fired by the mayor for breaking a police department rule prohibiting officers from campaigning for candidates or soliciting aid for any political purpose. He sued in state court, charging (among other things) that the rule violated his right to express political opinions. The Massachusetts Supreme Judicial Court ruled against McAuliffe's right to private political speech in an opinion written, somewhat ironically, by Oliver Wendell Holmes, who thirty years later as a U.S. Supreme Court justice would author key opinions in landmark political speech cases. Holmes famously wrote that McAuliffe "may have a constitutional right to talk politics, but he has no constitutional right to be a policeman" and added, in an interesting juxtaposition, that employees when they take a job agree to suspend their "right of free speech, as well as of idleness."[6]

Although the decision involved one employee in one isolated case in a single state, *McAullife v. Mayor of New Bedford* was a proxy of sorts for all of constitutional law regarding public employee rights for the next half century. The U.S. Supreme Court many years later acknowledged the importance of what Holmes had said, noting that from the time he wrote his famous sentence in the early 1890s until the Court began to recognize public employee rights in the 1950s, "Holmes' epigram expressed this Court's law."[7] During those sixty years, much like the preceding century, the free speech and free association rights of public employees were scarcely different from the rights of private employees, which is to say they scarcely had any at all.

THE 1950S: LOYALTY, SUBVERSION, AND ASSOCIATION

With rising anxiety about Communism and the Soviet threat in the early 1950s, the federal courts started to see what would become a string of cases in which suspicions about membership in "subversive" groups cost people their jobs. As has so often been the case in the history of constitutional law, the Supreme Court got it wrong before getting it right.

The Court got it wrong in a case brought by group of teachers who were challenging a New York law that disqualified from employment in public schools anyone who advocated, or joined a group advocating, the forceful overthrow of the government. The law also required state education officials to work up a list of such organizations and to treat membership in them as evidence of guilt. Sixty years had passed since the Massachusetts police officer's case, but the Supreme Court's majority in *Adler v. Board of Education* in 1952 was clinging to the same minimalist view of public employees' rights—if you don't like the rules, too bad: "They may work for the school system upon the reasonable terms laid down by the proper authorities of New York. If they do not choose to work on such terms, they are at liberty to retain their beliefs and associations and go elsewhere."[8] In treating schools and classrooms as places requiring vigilance for potentially subversive activities, the Court seemed unconcerned with guilt by association:

> From time immemorial, one's reputation has been determined in part by the company he keeps. In the employment of officials and teachers of the school system, the state may very properly inquire into the company they keep, and we know of no rule, constitutional or otherwise, that prevents the state, when determining the fitness and loyalty of such persons, from considering the organizations and persons with whom they associate.[9]

In a brief but spirited dissent, Justice William O. Douglas raised a core issue about rights that the Court's majority was willing to overlook: "I cannot . . . find in our constitutional scheme the power of a state to place its employees in the category of second-class citizens by denying them freedom of thought and expression."[10] As long as a teacher is law abiding and meets professional standards, Douglas wrote, "her private life, her political philosophy, her social creed should not be the cause of reprisals against her."[11]

The Court had another opportunity just months later in a case about an Oklahoma law that required state employees to sign a loyalty oath promising not to advocate revolution or forceful overthrow of the government and to pledge to avoid (and to have avoided for the previous five years) membership in Communist or subversive groups.[12] State officials in Oklahoma thought the law was constitutionally dubious and apparently weren't enforcing it. The case that reached the Supreme Court started as a lawsuit by a citizen-taxpayer trying to force state officials to stop paying state employees who hadn't signed the oath. The Court threw out the law as arbitrary and unfair because it didn't distinguish between people who attached themselves to subversive groups and causes innocently versus those who did so knowingly. Although in this case, *Weiman v. Updegraff*, the Court wasn't yet ready to kill the notion that public employees should follow the rules or go elsewhere, it did assert that freedom of association matters, both for personal dignity and for larger principles of free speech:

> There can be no dispute about the consequences visited upon a person
> excluded from public employment on disloyalty grounds. In the view
> of the community, the stain is a deep one; indeed, it has become a badge
> of infamy. . . . Yet under the Oklahoma Act, the fact of association alone
> determines disloyalty and disqualification; it matters not whether asso-
> ciation existed innocently or knowingly.[13]

The Court went on to link freedom of association with the "flow of democratic expression" in society, a compelling example of how two principles— freedom of expression related to the workplace and free speech in society at large—are interlaced.

The Supreme Court faced an interesting twist on freedom of association eight years later (in 1960) in a dispute over an Arkansas law requiring all teachers at public schools, including those at universities, to declare group memberships or lose their jobs. Unlike in the earlier cases, this law didn't merely seek disclosure of ties to "subversive" groups; it required teachers to list *all* groups of any type to which the teacher belonged or contributed, going back five years. The Court struck down the law. Although still willing to tolerate some interference with the associational rights of public employees, the Court said the state of Arkansas had overreached by going "far beyond what might be justified in the exercise of the State's legitimate inquiry into the fitness and competency of its teachers."[14] As a historical footnote, this case, *Shelton v. Tucker*, is one of a few that emerged from efforts in Southern states, as the civil rights movement gained steam, to hamper the NAACP by forcing disclosure of the group's membership lists.[15]

In 1967, in the important case *Keyishian v. Board of Regents*, the Supreme Court parted ways for good with the view that public employees surrender their constitutional rights when they go to work. Harry Keyishian and some faculty colleagues at the University of Buffalo (which had just become a public university) refused to sign statements, required by state law, certifying that they were not then or had previously been associated with Communists or linked to any group advocating government overthrow. In going to court, Keyishian and his fellow professors were challenging the same set of laws (slightly modified in the interim) that the Court had found acceptable in the *Adler* case fifteen years earlier.

Although it believed that a state can try to protect its educational system from subversion, the Court now felt that the New York laws were unacceptably vague, punishing employees for association that is entitled to First Amendment protection. It was, however, a tight 5–4 decision, an indication that the Court was still struggling with the reach of expressive rights and other rights in public workplaces, especially schools. The four dissenters viewed subversive speech and association as legitimate threats to educational institutions and by extension as threats to democracy. The issue was not freedom of speech, assembly, or association, they said, but whether someone who deliberately advocates or teaches that government "should be overthrown by force or violence" ought to be disqualified from teaching in its university.[16]

Although close, the *Keyishian* decision signaled the Court's broader willingness to start a death watch for the long-standing principle that employer prerogative almost always trumps employee rights. The Court's majority wrote: "The theory that public employment which may be denied altogether may be subjected to any conditions, regardless of how unreasonable, has been uniformly rejected."[17] With the run of cases that began after the unfortunate outcome in *Adler* in 1952 and culminated with this one in 1967, the Court had expanded public employee rights to free expression and association and breathed life into the idea that employment ought not be conditioned on a wholesale denial of constitutional liberties.[18] But, as we will see, the life turned out to be not such a long and happy one.

MR. PICKERING GOES TO WASHINGTON

The First Amendment dustups during the 1950s and 1960s were mainly about association—the rights of public employees to participate in supposedly "subversive" causes without fearing for their jobs. Next came a more direct test of the willingness of courts to tolerate not just association but actual speech. It began with a science teacher at Lockport East High School in Illinois who in September 1964 wrote a letter to the editor of his local newspaper. It ended almost four years later with a landmark U.S. Supreme Court decision on speech by public employees.

Marvin Pickering's letter in the *Lockport Herald* criticized the school board and administrators for their handling of a series of funding issues going back three years (when funding for two new high schools was approved) and addressed current events (a recent defeat by voters of a tax hike that would have further funded these schools).[19] Pickering, who taught at one of the new schools, complained about the balance in funding between athletics and academics and charged that officials were misleading people about how money would be used. His letter rambled somewhat over a variety of concerns but was pointedly critical, with passages that included the following (excerpted here to illustrate the letter's tone rather than its arguments):

> I am not saying the school shouldn't have these facilities, because I think they should, but promises are promises, or are they?

> The superintendent told the teachers, and I quote, "Any teacher that opposes the referendum should be prepared for the consequences." I think this gets at the reason we have problems passing bond issues. Threats take something away; these are insults to voters in a free society.

> That's the kind of totalitarianism teachers live in at the high school, and your children go to school in.

> The bond issue is a fight between the Board of Education that is trying to push tax-supported athletics down our throats with education, and a public that has mixed emotions about both of these items because they feel they are already paying enough taxes, and simply don't know whom to trust with any more tax money.[20]

Pickering closed by saying that he wrote the letter "as a citizen, taxpayer and voter, not as a teacher, since that freedom has been taken from the teachers by the administration." His offhand distinction between speaking as a citizen versus as an employee turned out to be prophetic: it was the mainspring of a key Supreme Court ruling on speech by public employees thirty-eight years later—but that's a story for later.

Before sending his letter to the paper, Pickering showed a draft to his wife, who told him, "You're probably going to get fired."[21] After it appeared, and after a hearing, the board of education did indeed fire Pickering on the grounds that he had breached an obligation of loyalty to his superiors; the letter, they concluded, contained factual errors and was "detrimental to the efficient operation and administration of the schools of the district."[22] Pickering challenged his firing as a violation of First Amendment rights in state court, losing first in circuit court and then in the Illinois Supreme Court, which found that "a teacher who displays disrespect toward the Board of Education, incites misunderstanding and distrust of its policies, and makes unsupported accusations against the officials is not promoting the best interests of his school, and the Board of Education does not abuse its discretion in dismissing him."[23]

The U.S. Supreme Court took the case, and in a near-unanimous ruling (one justice dissented in part), it handed Pickering a resounding victory. Referring to some of the earlier cases I discussed above involving freedom of association, the Court made it clear again that public employees cannot be compelled to relinquish constitutional rights that they would otherwise enjoy as citizens. But Thurgood Marshall, writing for the Court, did allow that speaking out as a citizen and speaking out as a public employee are not quite the same thing:

> The problem in any case is to arrive at a balance between the interests of the teacher, as a citizen, in commenting upon *matters of public concern* and the interest of the State, as an employer, in promoting the efficiency of the public services it performs through its employees.[24]

The key phrase is the one italicized—*matters of public concern*—because it implies that Pickering's speech would not have been protected had it not been on such matters. The Court said school funding qualifies as a legitimate public concern on which "free and open debate is vital to informed decision-making by the electorate" and added that teachers are uniquely positioned to have informed opinions about it: "It is essential that they be able to speak out freely on such questions without fear of retaliatory dismissal."[25] This goes to the heart of why free expression in the public-sector workplace is crucial: Government employees are uniquely positioned to understand and form opinions about the often vital public services to community and society they help to deliver. Silencing their views about how the government is working is no way to run a democracy.

As an aside, the notion of "public concern" as a basis for First Amendment protection was not new, just new to the context of employee speech. Its origins lie in an important 1940 case on the rights of labor unions to peacefully picket, a case in which the Supreme Court said speech on matters of public concern illuminates "issues about which information is needed or appropriate to enable the members of society to cope with the exigencies of their period."[26] The importance of speech on public issues has been an essential idea in the development of law during the twentieth century in such diverse areas as libel and defamation, protest speech, and corporate speech, among others.[27] The court cases on symbolic expression (especially flag desecration) that I mentioned in Chapter 1 breathed life into the idea that speech on matters of public concern deserves special attention and protection.

By the way, the Court wasn't particularly concerned that some things said in Pickering's letter were factually incorrect. A few years earlier in the historic free speech case *New York Times Co. v. Sullivan*, the Court had established the principle that false statements against public officials are legally defamatory only if it can be demonstrated that the speaker knew they were false or acted with "reckless disregard" for the truth.[28] In Pickering's situation, said the Court, the mistakes were made in good faith—more careless than reckless. Marvin Pickering returned to his job at Lockport East High School in 1969 and taught there for twenty-eight more years until his retirement.

CONCERN ABOUT PUBLIC CONCERN

Pickering is among the most important cases on workplace expression because it was the first where the Supreme Court made it clear that public employees can't (necessarily) be fired for exercising First Amendment rights to speak out on matters of public interest. Some decisions of the

Supreme Court qualify as landmarks, however, not because they settle a critical matter of law but because they launch one. *Pickering* turned out to be one of those cases that did far more launching than settling. It marked a significant expansion of public employee speech rights, but in doing so it left a couple of critical questions unanswered:

- In *Pickering*, the Court said that speech merits protection when it addresses matters of "public concern." The Court asserted that the school funding issue in that case qualified, but it didn't provide a detailed analysis of how or where that line should be drawn in other situations. So what's included and what's not?

- In *Pickering*, the Court said that the employee's right to expression should be balanced against the employer's interest in promoting the efficiency of its public services. The Court mentioned such factors as maintaining discipline, ensuring harmony among co-workers, and preserving close working relationships, but it declined to draw general standards for assessing this balance. How much discretion does a public employer have to sacrifice individual rights in the name of efficiency?

By establishing the broad principle that public employees have free speech rights worth protecting, *Pickering* spawned many court cases in which individuals sought to assert First Amendment rights in the government workplace. Over the next decade, three of these reached the U.S. Supreme Court. Although none of them were as momentous as *Pickering*, each shed additional light on the Court's view of the speech rights of public employees. All three cases again involved teachers. It is worth saying a few words about each.

First, *Sindermann* (1972): This case involved a Texas junior college professor named Robert Sindermann, who was employed under a series of one-year renewable contracts. As a leader of a statewide junior college teachers association, Sindermann testified on several occasions before state legislative committees and was involved in public disagreements with college administrators. When after four years the college declined to renew his contract with no explanation, he filed a federal lawsuit claiming that he was being punished for his public criticism of administrators—a violation of his free speech rights. He also charged that the lack of explanation or opportunity for a hearing violated his due-process rights. Sindermann lost initially in a lower court, but he won on appeal and prevailed in the U.S. Supreme Court.[29]

What made this case important is that Sindermann (unlike Pickering in *Pickering*) wasn't fired; he was simply not rehired to a new contract when the old one expired. The Court was recognizing here that even though a person has no inherent right to a government benefit (like a contractual teaching job with no tenure), the government cannot withdraw a benefit for reasons that infringe on that person's constitutional rights. To put it another way, there's no need for a hearing or due process when someone's contract is not being renewed unless the decision not to rehire is rooted in a denial of a liberty interest (such as free speech). And you don't have to have tenure to defend yourself against such a denial.

Second, *Mt. Healthy* (1977): Fred Doyle was an untenured public school teacher in Ohio whose contract was not renewed after he had verbal altercations with school employees and directed an obscene gesture toward two students. Separately, the teacher conveyed information about a proposed dress code policy to a local radio station, which reported the policy as a news item. In deciding to let him go, the school system's administration grouped all these actions together as "a lack of tact in handling professional matters." Doyle sued in federal court claiming a violation of First Amendment rights. He initially won reinstatement and back pay, but on appeal the Supreme Court disagreed, finding that although Doyle's communication to the radio station was protected speech, his other behavior wasn't, and might have cost him his job anyway.[30] (A lower court later concluded that it indeed would have.)[31]

The Supreme Court in this case was retreating from its deference to employee free speech rights: a public employee fired for exercising free speech has to prove that it was *the* motivating factor; an employer can fight back by showing that even without the protected speech, the employee would have been fired anyway. This principle seems reasonable at first glance, especially given the facts of this particular case: a free speech claim ought not be able to cover for truly bad behavior. It does, however, open the door for employers to engage in a form of bad behavior of their own—contriving other grounds to discipline or terminate as a way to mask objections to employee speech. An employee speaking out now has to worry that the boss might have another reason to fire him, or in any event might be able to persuade a jury that another reason exists.[32]

Third, *Givhan* (1979): Mississippi school teacher Bessie Givhan lost her job because of (among other things) an "antagonistic and hostile attitude" toward school administrators.[33] That phrase was shorthand for a series of private encounters between Givhan and the school principal during which she expressed concerns about possible discriminatory employment practices. Administrators thought she was making "petty and unreasonable demands," but in the lawsuit that Givhan brought, a federal court found that the demands were neither petty nor unreasonable. The judge ruled in her favor, but she lost in an appellate court, which found that her complaints to the principal did not amount to protected speech because they were conveyed *in private*:

> Neither a teacher nor a citizen has a constitutional right to single
> out a public employee to serve as the audience for his or her privately
> expressed views, at least in the absence of evidence that the public
> employee was given that task by law, custom, or school Board decision.
> There is no evidence here that Givhan sought to disseminate her views
> publicly, to anyone willing to listen. Rather, she brought her complaints
> to [Principal] Leach alone.[34]

But Givhan ultimately prevailed at the U.S. Supreme Court, which rejected the notion that free speech on matters of public concern has to be aimed at the public to deserve protection. Speaking for a unanimous Court, Justice William Rehnquist wrote that "neither the [First] Amendment itself nor our decisions indicate that this freedom is lost to the public employee who arranges to communicate privately with his employer rather than to spread his views before the public."[35]

So in the twelve years following the crucial Pickering case, the Supreme Court had pushed the public employee's right to free speech forward in a couple of constructive ways: First, public employees can challenge not just being fired for their protected speech but also for not being rehired after a contract expires. Second, public employees' protected workplace speech doesn't lose its protection when delivered in private rather than directed at a public audience. But the Court had also pulled back somewhat when it said that an employee dismissed because of protected speech has to show that speech was the deciding factor—that she would not have been fired but for the expressive activity. In fact, given the basic rule of employment at will—the ability to fire for any reason or no reason—a fired worker's need to show that he lost his job for one particular reason (like speech) can be difficult indeed.

At this point in the early 1980s, protection of public employees' expressive rights was probably at its highest point. We still didn't have clear answers, however, to those two questions raised twelve years earlier in the wake of the Pickering case: First, what does speech on "matters of public concern" really mean? And, second, how do we balance an employee's free speech interest against a government employer's efficiency interest? Then came Connick.

LAWYERS NOT IN LOVE

Sheila Myers worked for Harry Connick. She was an assistant district attorney (ADA) in New Orleans. He was the district attorney (DA) for Orleans Parish (and still is the father of musician and actor Harry Connick Jr.). In October 1980, Myers learned that she was being transferred to a different section of the criminal court. Unhappy with this news and with other things going on in the district attorney's office, Myers prepared and distributed to several ADA colleagues a questionnaire seeking their views on various issues concerning transfer policies, staff morale, grievance procedures, and pressures to work in political campaigns. After learning about this, Connick fired Myers, telling her that it was because she wouldn't accept the transfer and because her questionnaire amounted to an act of insubordination.[36]

Myers sued in federal court, saying she'd been fired for exercising her First Amendment rights. She argued that the questionnaire was a form of protected speech and that it was the real reason for her dismissal. Connick maintained, then and long after, that Myers's refusal to accept the transfer was the reason he fired her.[37] Lower courts agreed with Myers, ordering her reinstated with back pay and damages. A divided (5–4) U.S. Supreme Court overturned the outcome, siding with Connick and concluding that Myers did not have a valid First Amendment claim.[38] The ruling in *Connick v. Myers* is significant—*Connick* and *Pickering* are the "big two" on public employee speech—because it took on directly the two key unresolved issues from *Pickering*: the meaning of "public concern" and the nature of the balance between speech rights and employer interests.

In denying relief for Sheila Myers, the Court said her questionnaire amounted to speech on a matter of public concern only to a very limited extent: one item (out of fourteen) asked if ADAs felt pressured to help out with certain favored political campaigns. The rest of it, said Justice Byron White for the Court's majority, looked more like a workplace grievance about internal office matters. Unless the employee's speech relates to "any matter of political, social, or other concern to the community," White wrote, government employers should be able to manage their agencies without interference from judges in the name of the First Amendment.[39]

The ruling went on to lay out a mechanism for determining whether speech qualifies as a matter of public concern: it must be determined "*by the content, form, and context of a given statement, as revealed by the whole record.*"[40] Applying this test, the Court said that Myers's concerns about office morale, trust, and grievances were mere extensions of her own dispute over being transferred and not efforts to inform the public about the perform-ance of the district attorney or the ability of his office to fulfill its responsi-bilities. Although it might be good practice for public officials to be recep-tive to constructive criticism, said the Court, "the First Amendment does not require a public office to be run as a roundtable for employee concerns over internal office affairs."[41]

The Court also spoke to the tricky issue of how to balance employee and employer rights. (Because Myers's one questionnaire item about political campaign activity did touch on a matter of public concern, the Court couldn't sidestep this.) The Court conceded that the questionnaire did nothing to impair Myers's ability to perform her job, but it accepted Connick's view that as an act of insubordination, Myers's actions jeopard-ized working relationships. Most important, White's opinion included a couple of general statements that had the alarming effect of clearly tilting the balance toward employers: "When close working relationships are essential to fulfilling public responsibilities, a wide degree of deference to the employer's judgment is appropriate." And this: "The fact that Myers . . . exercised her rights to speech at the office supports Connick's fears that the functioning of the office was endangered."[42]

Writing for the four justices who dissented in *Connick*, William Brennan disagreed sharply with the idea that the internal workings of a public agency like a district attorney's office are not a public concern: "Unconstrained discussion concerning the manner in which the government performs its duties is an essential element of the public discourse necessary to informed self-government."[43] The dissenters were saying, quite reasonably, that we can't know if the public will care to learn that morale is poor at some public agency; the First Amendment protects the spread of that information so that the people, and not the courts, can decide if it's useful. The dissenters also were justifiably alarmed at what they called the Court's "extreme deference" toward employer judgments.

Rejecting the notion that speech should be suppressed simply because an employer is apprehensive about possible disruption, Brennan predicted that the *Connick* outcome would "inevitably deter public employees from making critical statements" about how government agencies work for fear of being fired.[44] The *Connick* decision, with its test for speech that qualifies as a matter of public concern and its fealty to employer judgments, put a halt to the expansion of public employee speech rights that had been occurring since the 1960s. It didn't, however, do much if anything to reduce the volume of employee free speech cases.

The Supreme Court in *Connick* seemed to want to draw some lines that would limit the number of disputes around employee speech that reached the courts. The *Pickering* outcome fifteen years earlier had spawned a lot of litigation that cynics (including some on the Court) regarded as "glorified workplace gripes."[45] The majority in *Connick* worried that "government offices could not function if every employment decision became a constitutional matter," and their solution was to exclude speech about the internal operations of an office from the province of public concern.[46] But it didn't really work; since *Connick*, dockets have been replete with employee speech cases. Attorney Tom Goldstein, a prominent Supreme Court practitioner, calls the state of the law in this area "very confused in the lower courts" in large measure because of *Connick*'s "very flexible standard."[47]

AFTER CONNICK: MORE CONCERN ABOUT PUBLIC CONCERN

For all its attention to the public-concern test, the *Connick* decision did little to clarify the question of when employee speech addresses a matter of public concern and is therefore deserving of protection. A number of courts and law review articles have grappled with this issue in the years following the decision. As one writer, in an article published seven years after *Connick*, puts it: "No one knows what 'public concern' is. . . . [The Court's] descriptions of public concern provided just enough guidance to confuse everyone."[48] Another writer complains that the public-concern test is too broad because it doesn't require employers to define any policies for the kind of speech they will tolerate or punish. As a result, the Court is letting employers make "ad hoc and standardless terminations" in response to speech they don't like.[49]

The next employee speech case to reach the Supreme Court, *Rankin v. McPherson* in 1987, involved a very different (some might say disturbing) sort of expression but provides a good illustration of the confusion over the principle of public concern. Ardith McPherson was a data-entry clerk in the constable's office in Harris County, Texas (Houston). After hearing a radio report on March 31, 1981, about the attempt to assassinate President Ronald Reagan, McPherson remarked to a co-worker, "If they go for him again, I hope they get him." Someone who overheard the remark mentioned it to Constable Walter Rankin, who promptly summoned McPherson to his office. When she confirmed that she had said it, he fired her.[50] She sued.

Does expressing hope for a successful presidential assassination attempt amount to speech on a matter of public concern? The case largely turned on this question. McPherson lost initially in a district court, where a judge found her remark to be "more than political hyperbole," and in fact "violent words, in context."[51] A federal appeals court disagreed, finding that although her comment was distasteful, "the life and death of the President are obviously matters of public concern."[52] The Supreme Court agreed: "The inappropriate or controversial character of a statement is irrelevant to the question whether it deals with a matter of public concern."[53]

The decision in the Supreme Court was close (5–4) again, with another spirited dissent, this one penned by Antonin Scalia. Scalia seemed incredulous at the notion that criticizing a president and wishing for his assassination ("expressing approval of a serious and violent crime") could both fall within the province of public concern. "The public would be 'concerned' about a statement threatening to blow up the local federal building or demanding a $1 million extortion payment," wrote Scalia, "yet that kind of 'public concern' does not entitle such a statement to any First Amendment protection at all."[54] But if McPherson's remark was not something that could be prosecuted as a criminal threat—and all sides apparently agreed that it wasn't—then perhaps it is Scalia who succumbed to hyperbole.

The *Rankin* case also shed light on the balancing issue—the weighing of employer interests against employee rights that had been a key aspect of employee speech law for almost twenty years (since *Pickering*). Constable Rankin pointed to issues of workplace mission, efficiency, and disruption, insisting he shouldn't have to employ someone who "rides with the cops and cheers for the robbers."[55] Although a district court judge agreed with this viewpoint, an appeals court and the Supreme Court didn't find it persuasive: as a back-office clerical worker, McPherson had no law-enforcement duties, no access to sensitive information, and no contact with the public. Justice Lewis Powell, in a concurring Supreme Court opinion, put the overreach of the constable's argument in helpful perspective: "The risk that a single, off-hand comment directed to only one other worker will lower morale, disrupt the work force, or otherwise undermine the mission of the office borders on the fanciful."[56]

The balance tilted back toward employers as a result of an employee speech case that reached the Supreme Court in 1994. A nurse at a public hospital in Illinois was fired for critical statements about supervisors and hospital policies that she made to a co-worker.[57] An investigation by the hospital *at the time* led it to conclude that the nurse's comments should not be treated as protected free speech because they were potentially disruptive. After the nurse sued the hospital, the court proceedings revealed that there was a dispute about the content of her speech after the fact and that perhaps her speech was protected and nondisruptive.

What's important here is the Court's conclusion that if the hospital had conducted an adequate inquiry at the time and relied on it when it fired the nurse, then that was good enough. In other words, the Court was saying, an employer is off the hook when it makes a sensible prediction based on a reasonable inquiry that speech will be disruptive; it need not be held accountable for information that comes out later in litigation. The Court also helped the cause of future employers inclined to punish employee speech by making it clear that *actual* disruption is not the test; an *expectation* of disruption is sufficient.[58]

A win of some significance for speech over repression came in one final 1990s case that reached the high court. A Kansas county's board of commissioners cancelled a private firm's contract to haul waste, supposedly because the hauler was an outspoken critic of the board. When the hauler's lawsuit challenging this action reached the Supreme Court, justices used the opportunity to provide government contractors with essentially the same First Amendment protections that public employees enjoy.[59] The ruling signaled that a government agency generally cannot terminate a contract, or halt an automatic contract renewal, solely in retaliation for the contractor's speech on a matter of public concern. Given a rise in outsourcing of government services in recent years, this was an important step in protecting the expressive rights of people who work with, rather than for, government.

PUBLIC CONCERN WITH SEX

The Supreme Court has twice taken up employee speech in this decade, first in a case that was entertaining, if ultimately not all that significant, and second in a case that was far more significant if perhaps not all that entertaining. Although the first case didn't reshape the law on employee speech, it is worth recapping here because it did inspire the Court to get a bit more specific about the meaning of "public concern." It began when a San Diego police officer was fired after his supervisors discovered that he was selling videotapes (on eBay) of himself stripping out of a police uniform and masturbating. The officer, whose username on eBay was Code3stud@aol.com (a detail I mention here mainly to buttress the claim that the case is entertaining), failed to remove the items for sale when asked by superiors to do so and was fired.

In the officer's lawsuit charging that his First Amendment rights were violated, the Supreme Court rejected his claim out of hand, calling it "not a close case." The Court said that to be on a matter of public concern, speech has to address "something that is a subject of legitimate news interest . . . of value and concern to the public at the time of publication."[60] The San Diego officer's speech didn't qualify, said the Court, nor was it aimed at helping citizens understand the functioning of the police department. Accordingly, it failed the public-concern test and deserved no protection, a finding that freed the city to fire the officer on the grounds that his actions were detrimental to the department's mission or in violation of department rules about off-duty conduct or both.

A remarkable thing about this case is that the officer actually *won* his case in the Court of Appeals for the Ninth Circuit before it went to the Supreme Court.[61] Conceding that the videos were "crude and sexually explicit, but . . . not obscene," the appeals court said the officer's expression "was not about private personnel matters, was directed to a segment of the general public, occurred outside the workplace and was not motivated by an employment-related grievance."[62] The point of the public-concern test, the court reasoned, is to weed out claims in which the punished speech relates to an employee's personal job situation, not to filter out a vast range of non-job-related speech. Interpreting public concern to mean "speech that does not relate to internal office affairs or the employee's status as an employee," the two (of three) judges on the Ninth Circuit panel essentially concluded that the officer's strip-and-masturbate videos were in fact speech on a matter of public concern! The Supreme Court obviously didn't think so, nor did the dissenting judge in the Ninth Circuit, who called it an "absurd result."[63] But the very fact that two of three federal appeals court judges (even in the reputationally challenged Ninth Circuit) would adopt this view makes for a compelling illustration of how capricious the public-concern doctrine can be.

The whimsy deepens when one delves further into the casebooks for related examples. I mentioned in Chapter 1, for instance, a Baltimore police officer who spent his off-duty time giving musical performances in blackface makeup. A court found his performances to be speech on a matter of public concern because it was artistic expression of interest to people who paid to attend.[64] On the other hand, a Little Rock police officer's costume featuring blackface makeup at a Halloween party was not speech on a matter of public concern because the setting was a private party rather than public entertainment.[65] These examples, drawn from what one hopes is a limited body of police-in-racist-garb jurisprudence, illustrate the kind of enigmatic issues that the public-concern test compels courts to wrestle with. Is the stripper cop's video more like a public "artistic" performance? Or a private act meant to convey no particular message? The majority and dissenting opinions in the San Diego case in the Ninth Circuit took up these weighty issues at some length. One is tempted to speculate that over-worked judges with busy dockets have better things to do with their time.

Although having nothing to do with sex, race, or videos, possibly the most significant employee speech ruling since *Connick* occurred in 2006 when the Supreme Court ruled against a prosecutor who got in trouble for bring-ing concerns about the integrity of a pending case to his boss's attention. Richard Ceballos, a deputy district attorney in Los Angeles, had reason to believe that sheriff's deputies had falsified an affidavit to get a search war-rant in an auto-parts-theft case. After looking into it, Ceballos shared his suspicions with his supervisors in a memo and in conversations and urged them to drop the case. They declined, and Ceballos ended up being sub-poenaed by defense lawyers to testify in a hearing on a motion to dismiss the case. According to Ceballos, his supervisors punished him for his actions by removing him from the prosecution team, demoting him, and transferring him to a less desirable branch of the district attorney's office. He sued in federal court charging retaliation for speech protected by the First Amendment and won in a federal appeals court, but he ultimately lost in the Supreme Court.

The Supreme Court in *Garcetti v. Ceballos* concluded that Ceballos's comments amounted to "job-related speech," not speech on a matter of public concern. Writing an internal memo about an upcoming case is what a deputy district attorney is supposed to be doing, the Court reasoned, so the commentary contained within cannot be protected speech. Writing for the Court's majority in (another) tight 5–4 decision, Justice Anthony Kennedy said that limiting job-related speech "does not infringe any liber-ties the employee might have enjoyed as a private citizen."[66] But this doesn't seem right. Drawing a line between speech that is part of the job and speech that is "enjoyed as a private citizen" denies the possibility that speech can be both at the same time. Justice David Souter made this point in dissent: "A citizen may well place a very high value on a right to speak on the public issues he decides to make the subject of his work day after day."[67]

The distinction between speech-as-employee and speech-as-citizen raises the odd possibility that the same message can be protected or unpro-tected speech, depending on how the speaker casts himself and how he elects to convey the message. It's conceivable, for example, that a job-related remark to the boss can get you fired, but the same remark made to a journalist (to whom one speaks as a "citizen") could bring First Amendment protection. The Court assumed that this distinction wouldn't pose a problem because the test isn't where or to whom a message is delivered; it's whether delivering the message is part of the employee's official duties. The Court's logic here isn't terribly persuasive because it's not that hard to imagine circumstances in which the line is blurred. What if a school teacher criticizes the curriculum both to the principal and at a public school board meeting?

Government employers may take from this case an incentive to write very broad job descriptions that would bring more expressive behavior under the umbrella of "job related." Souter's dissent raised the possibility of a school that now writes a teacher's job description to include an obligation to contribute to the sound administration of the school. In that hypothetical example (which Souter transparently calibrated to the 1968 *Pickering* case's outspoken teacher), the simple expedient of writing a more expansive job description would undermine the important speech protections that *Pickering* created almost forty years before.[68] The Court's majority tried to minimize this concern, insisting that future courts will evaluate what a person in a job actually does, not what a job description says. This declaration isn't wholly reassuring. In Souter's teacher example, how do we know if a nonspecific, immeasurable contribution to the soundness of the school is something the teacher actually does? And what happens when the employer and the employee disagree about that? After more than twenty years of marked judicial deference to employer judgments in workplace speech cases, it is hardly a stretch to surmise that courts will be more inclined to look at job-related speech through an employer's eyes than through an employee's.

Notwithstanding the ongoing confusion over what speech on "public concern" actually means, the whole idea that public concern should be the benchmark for speech by public employees that is or isn't protected has a philosophical dark side. Superficially, the idea of a public-concern test makes some sense: speech on public affairs has, after all, been regarded as essential to the health of deliberative democracy at least since James Madison and his compatriots were drafting the Bill of Rights. But critics point to several troubling aspects of the public-concern test in practice.

First, we may not want to give judges the discretion to decide in each case whether speech is or is not on an issue of public concern. Cynthia Estlund worries that giving this power creates "a judicially approved catalogue of legitimate subjects of public discussion"—an alarming development given that "the Constitution empowers the people, not any branch of the government, to define the public agenda."[69] Judges are generally fine people, and we grant to them the authority to make important calls on serious matters, but that doesn't mean they should determine which issues are and are not worthy of public attention.

Second, the public-concern requirement affects the choices individual government workers make about their speech, a result that can give rise to a potentially serious class bias in how those choices play out. Again Cynthia Estlund: the public concern formula "favors those who have the resources to publicize their concerns through the mass media or to 'petition the government,' through lobbying, for official intervention . . . [and] favors those who can afford to consult counsel, and who can tailor the form of their complaints and choose their forum accordingly."[70] In other words, giving priority to speech on matters of public concern creates an inherent bias toward speakers who are educated, organized, and know how to get their issues aired in the broader sphere of political discourse.

Third, the public-concern standard favors those with points of view that an employer happens to like. The First Amendment generally forbids government actors from discriminating against disfavored ideas or views. It's this principle, known as "viewpoint discrimination," that prevents a city from, say, allowing Democrats but not Republicans to rally in a public park or from allowing Christians but not Muslims from airing a program on a public-access television station. Chicago municipal attorney Lawrence Rosenthal argues that the public-concern standard has the undesirable effect of making viewpoint discrimination by a public employer perfectly acceptable. Because expression that is not on a matter of public concern is left unprotected by the First Amendment, Rosenthal writes, when such speech occurs the employer is free to take punitive action "motivated by hostility to the ideas or viewpoints expressed rather than by any reasonable fear of workplace disruption."[71]

The public-concern test is a convenient vehicle that courts can use to rebuff free speech claims when employees are punished for speaking out about workplace practices, and it is one they are not shy about using. Constitutional law professor Stanley Ingber describes the courts post-*Connick* as "notably solicitous toward public employers" when they weigh workplace speech claims.[72] Some would say this inclination is a good thing—discouraging employees from making a federal case (so to speak) out of their petty personal complaints about working conditions. But at what cost? In the name of reducing the volume of employee speech lawsuits, we make it harder to inject new issues into the public discourse, which means some worthwhile speech is inevitably suppressed, which in turn distorts the larger climate for public discussion on important issues. And many would say that's a bad thing.

WHISTLING IN THE DARK

When people think of employee speech that ought to be legally protected from an employer's retribution, one of the first things that comes to mind is whistleblowing—reporting on illegal, unethical, dangerous, or otherwise inappropriate behavior. Whistleblowing can target a number of types of behavior, including a violation of the law, a regulatory infraction, a danger to public health or safety, an abuse of authority, financial malfeasance, a violation of corporate policy, or gross mismanagement.[73] The employee who speaks out as a whistleblower can do so internally (reporting to higher-ups within the organization where he works) or externally (reporting to law enforcement or regulatory authorities, or perhaps to the press). In her book *Whistleblowing—When It Works and Why*, Roberta Ann Johnson describes whistleblowing as "a common means of dissent in a bureaucracy" that in the United States is not just a growing phenomenon in workplaces but an expanding part of our cultural landscape, with whistleblowers portrayed as heroes and experts in films and news broadcasts.[74]

The legal origins of employee whistleblowing go all the way back to the Civil War, and a law called the False Claims Act, which was enacted in 1863 (and strengthened in 1986) in an effort to curb fraud by government suppliers.[75] Courts in many states began accepting whistleblowing as an exception to employment at will during the second half of the twentieth century, shielding employees from employer discipline or termination for blowing the whistle on illegal behavior. By the turn of the twenty-first century, most states had enacted statutes protecting whistleblowers.

At the federal level, the law is not now as accommodating to whistleblowers as it was a decade ago. A number of federal laws are in place that protect whistleblowers in specific regulatory areas, such as banking, occupational health and safety, and the handling of toxic materials.[76] But ongoing controversy around a federal law known as the Whistleblower Protection Act (WPA) has called the protection of whistleblower speech by federal employees into serious question. Congress first passed the WPA in 1978 and strengthened it in 1989 and again in 1994.[77] But then, in 1999, a provocative ruling by a federal court seriously weakened it.

The case involved a civilian employee of the air force, John White, who went public with allegations of gross mismanagement of an educational program by air force officials. A government review board found that White's disclosure deserved whistleblower protection under the terms of WPA, but an appeals court disagreed, finding that White did not have a sufficient basis to believe that mismanagement occurred. In doing so, the court wrote these crucial words redefining the standard that whistleblowers need to meet:

> The proper test is this: could a disinterested observer with knowledge of the essential facts known to and readily ascertainable by the employee reasonably conclude that the actions of the government evidence gross mismanagement? A purely subjective perspective of an employee is not sufficient even if shared by other employees. . . . This review would start out with a "presumption that public officers perform their duties correctly, fairly, in good faith, and in accordance with the law and governing regulations. . . . And this presumption stands unless there is '*irrefragable* proof to the contrary.'"[78]

Employee rights groups and whistleblower advocacy groups were justifiably outraged. Pointing to the definition of "irrefragable"—"incontestable, undeniable, incontrovertible"—the Washington-based nonprofit Government Accountability Project said the ruling in *LaChance v. White* "makes it virtually impossible for a government employee to be legally protected as a whistleblower. It creates a higher standard of proof than securing a criminal conviction, simply to be eligible for protection from retaliation."[79] Since the ruling (which the Supreme Court declined to hear on appeal), federal employees have prevailed before the board that hears claims for whistleblower protection less than 10 percent of the time.[80] A sizable coalition of groups came together to back legislation in Congress to restore WPA protections (essentially undoing the appeals court ruling).[81] By late 2005 committees in both houses of Congress had approved versions of the bill, but neither chamber had held a floor vote on the matter before the 109th Congress adjourned at the end of 2006.

The bottom line on public employee whistleblowing is that it is a form of expression that is widely protected—except when it's not. Stephen Kohn, board chair of the National Whistleblower Center and author of *Concepts and Procedures in Whistleblower Law*, starts his book with the observation that during the last half century, "a growing consensus has recognized that whistleblowers positively contribute to society and need protection against retaliation."[82] He also reminds us that whistleblowing cases are costly and difficult and often leave the individual emotionally bruised and wishing he or she hadn't bothered to come forward. There may be a consensus about the personal virtues of whistleblowers, but the role of courts as interpreters of whistleblowing law means, as the *LaChance* case amply illustrated, that threats to public employee speech rights are rarely more than a courtroom away.

HATCHING POLITICAL PARTICIPATION

Public employees who choose to become involved in politics in their spare time confront a paradox. On the one hand, many public employees enjoy a form of legal protection for political speech through laws that prevent employers from connecting job rewards or punishments to political activity. On the other hand, a long tradition of legal restrictions governs public employee participation in partisan activities. These restrictions, however, are not as stringent as they once were, leaving many public-sector workers with considerable latitude for political involvement and activism off the job (except, of course, in those jurisdictions where the law restricts latitude).

The protection comes from laws that say that employment outcomes cannot be tied to or made conditional upon an employee's involvement in (or avoidance of) some political activity. Federal workforce rules prohibit coercing another employee into participating in political activity, and it is also against the rules to take action as a reprisal for someone's refusal to engage in political activity.[83] Separately, it's a criminal offense to condition any sort of offer or promise of federal employment on "political activity or for the support of or opposition to any candidate or any political party."[84] In other words, a government job cannot be linked to political support or a political kickback.

Those rules are examples of efforts to purge the government workplace of political patronage and cronyism—which are essentially forms of compelled political speech—through legislation. The courts have also played a role here through cases in which public employees have challenged dismissals connected to the practice of party-based patronage. In two cases that reached the Supreme Court just a few years apart during the late 1970s, the justices made it clear that the First Amendment is not friendly to the kind of compelled association that patronage firing entails.

The first case grew out of the election of a new sheriff of Cook County, Illinois, a Democrat who was replacing a Republican. Following past practice, non-civil-service employees were expected to either affiliate with the Democratic party, obtain the party's sponsorship, or forfeit their job to party loyalists. This kind of patronage pressure may have been age-old, but a few employees who were losing their jobs because of it decided enough was enough and challenged the system as a violation of their First Amendment rights.

Ultimately, the Supreme Court in 1976 agreed with them, finding in *Elrod v. Burns* that patronage firings don't just compromise freedoms of belief and association; they also impair the electoral process as a whole.[85] The Court reasoned that as government employment expands, patronage gives the party in power more opportunities to starve the political opposition, tilting the political process toward incumbency in unhealthy ways. Patronage firings are allowable, the Court said, only for employees whose jobs involve confidential, policymaking roles. Interestingly, the Court rejected an argument by the sheriff that patronage firings serve the constructive aim of enhancing efficiency and accountability in delivery of public services. It had only been a few years since the Court took government efficiency into account in creating the balancing test in the landmark *Pickering* case on employee speech. Here, though, the Court believed that the affront to free expression was compelling and saw no need to weigh it against the notion that government services somehow benefit from firing employees simply because they won't join the boss's political party.

The question of what specific job roles can be subject to patronage firings was at the heart of a second case four years later, in 1980. A newly appointed public defender in Rockland County, New York, a Democrat, gave two assistant public defenders (who were otherwise satisfactory performers) their walking papers because they were Republicans. It sounds like a rerun of the earlier *Elrod* case, but here the official doing the firing tried to argue that lawyers in a public defender's office need mutual confidence and trust to be effective, making them the kind of employees who are subject to patronage firings. The Supreme Court demurred: The fired assistant public defenders may have had broad authority for their individual assigned cases, but they had little or no operational involvement in management or planning of the office as a whole. The test, said the Court, is "whether the hiring authority can demonstrate that party affiliation is an appropriate requirement for the effective performance of the public office involved."[86] In this situation the answer was no.

The Supreme Court in 1990 extended the rule against patronage firing to include not just terminations but also hiring, promotions, transfers, and recalls after layoffs.[87] In taking this long overdue step, the Court rejected the dubious argument that job-related encroachments on free association offend the First Amendment only if they are punitive (firings) but are perfectly okay otherwise. With no small amount of understatement, Justice William Brennan, writing for the Court, called this argument "not credible," pointing to people who would like to be hired or promoted as clearly harmed by patronage rules when they do not share a party affiliation with the boss.

Political patronage took another hit in 1996 when the Supreme Court extended protection to independent contractors.[88] The city of Northlake, Illinois, kept a list of private companies that on a rotating basis would tow vehicles for the police department. One company, which had been on the list for almost thirty years, was removed after its owner refused to con-

tribute to the mayor's reelection campaign and in fact supported his oppo-
nent's campaign. The towing company owner's lawsuit charged that
removal from the list was retaliation for political speech and invited the
Court to extend the prohibition on patronage "firing" to private contractors who perform municipal services. The Court accepted this invitation,
finding no reason to deny contractors the same First Amendment protection against compelled speech and association that employees receive.

Although antipatronage laws do provide public employees with some freedom of political speech, other laws constrain their rights to expression by
setting limits on partisan political activity. The best known of these is the
federal Hatch Act, enacted in 1939 and named for its author, Senator Carl
Hatch of New Mexico. The history of restrictions on government employees' political activity, however, goes a lot further back than that.[89] As early
as 1801, Thomas Jefferson noted with disapproval the idea of government
officials "taking on various occasions active parts in the elections of public
functionaries." Although Jefferson conceded that officials have the right to
vote, he warned that they should not try "to influence the votes of others
nor take any part in the business of electioneering, that being deemed
inconsistent with the spirit of the Constitution and [their] duties to it."[90]

After the Civil War, lawmakers dabbled on several occasions in the creation of rules about financial contributions for political activity. Acts of
Congress in 1867, 1868, 1870, and 1876, among others, placed restrictions
on the kinds of payments that could be solicited or received by government
officials for political purposes.[91] A constitutional challenge to the 1876
measure—which made it a crime for a government employee to give to or
receive from any other employee money, property, or anything else of value
for political purposes—caught the Supreme Court's attention. In an 1882
ruling the Court found these kinds of restrictions perfectly constitutional as
a way to foster "efficiency and integrity in the discharge of official duties"
and to protect "those in the public service against unjust exactions."[92] At
that time (and indeed until well into the twentieth century) the Court
wasn't much concerned with First Amendment issues. However, a prescient
Justice Joseph Bradley offered a spirited dissent that foreshadowed some of
the major legal battles over money and political speech that would grab the
Court's attention almost a century later. Bradley wrote that laws designed

to limit the corrupt use of money in elections were fine, but this one went too far:

> To take an interest in public affairs, and to further and promote those principles which are believed to be vital or important to the general welfare, is every citizen's duty. . . . To deny to a man the privilege of associating and making joint contributions with such other citizens as he may choose, is an unjust restraint of his right to propagate and promote his views on public affairs.[93]

The passage of the Hatch Act in 1939 took restrictions on political activities by public employees to a new level. It prohibited most government employees from taking "any active part in political management or in political campaigns." A year later the law was extended to include state and local government employees who worked in conjunction with federally funded programs.[94] Under the Hatch Act, federal employees could still contribute money to parties but not collect any funds on behalf of a candidate. They could still attend rallies but not organize one. They could sign nominating petitions but not circulate them.[95]

The Hatch Act in its original form was a draconian measure that seriously impaired rights to engage in political speech for a very large number of people. The act's constitutionality was challenged on multiple occasions, but to no avail. In cases that reached the Supreme Court in 1947 and in 1973, the Court applied the same basic logic it had used back in 1882: the government's interest in delivering public services with efficiency and integrity outweighs any constitutional concerns.[96] In the 1973 case, Justice William O. Douglas picked up the mantle of dissent that Justice Bradley had held ninety years earlier. Like Bradley, Douglas thought that the harmful effects of the law swamped its good intentions: "It is of no concern of Government what an employee does in his spare time, whether religion, recreation, social work, or politics is his hobby—unless what he does impairs efficiency or other facets of the merits of his job."[97]

In 1993 the Hatch Act was amended—gutted, you might say—to remove most restrictions on involvement in political activity that takes place off the job. As a result, federal employees can now actively manage political campaigns, as long as they do it after work and don't handle the money (the prohibitions on fundraising were not just kept but strengthened).[98] The changes refocused the act on policing abuses and strengthened provisions aimed at discouraging political coercion of employees. The restrictions that remain are mainly geared to keeping partisanship in the operation of government bureaucracy in check by barring political activity while on the job. Many state and local governments, by the way, have written their own statutes addressing limits on political activity by their public employees. These are typically modeled after the federal Hatch Act, and are often referred to as "Little Hatch Acts."

The laws and court decisions I've been discussing tinker with public employee speech rights as a way to limit corruption in government. One clever (or sinister, depending on your point of view) alternative to an outright ban on speech is to stop people from making money on their expression. This issue of money-for-speech was at the heart of a 1989 ethics-in-government law that barred many federal workers from accepting an honorarium for making a speech or writing an article—on any subject, related to work or not.

Soon after the ban was put in place, a group of federal employees who in the past had received honoraria for expressive activity on such diverse subjects as religion, history, dance, and the environment (in almost all cases wholly unrelated to their jobs) challenged the law as unconstitutional. The Supreme Court agreed, finding the ban to be an unacceptable burden on free speech rights under the First Amendment.[99] The Court used the occasion to impress us all with its bookish erudition by mentioning past luminaries who had held day jobs as federal employees while on the side making significant literary contributions—Nathaniel Hawthorne, Herman Melville, and Walt Whitman, among others. (The Court in citing these examples was perhaps taking a bit of literary license of its own, given that the ban on honoraria exempted books, including works of fiction and poetry, from its coverage.)

How can we synthesize and sum up the state of the law on free expression in the public-sector workplace? The short answer is, not easily: The relevant legal developments over the past fifty years have come at the subject from various angles. Like so much of the law on free speech and other civil liberties, the outcomes of cases involving workplace expression often turn on interpretations of vague and shifting standards, balancing tests designed to weigh competing interests that are inherently subjective, and the ever-changing happenstance of a court's ideological composition at a given time. But I will give it a try nonetheless.

If you are a public employee, you can generally speak your mind away from work on issues that have nothing to do with your job or your workplace without risking reprisal. Assuming your message is wholly unrelated to work, you can publish an article, make a speech, call a radio talk show, or write the great American novel without fearing for your job. And you can even accept payment for your efforts. It doesn't mean that anything goes, however, as the stripper cop from San Diego discovered a few years ago.[100] In fact, courts generally are more sympathetic to employer interests when the employer is a police department, on the theory that law enforcement organizations depend more than most public agencies on maintaining order, discipline, and close working relationships.[101]

If your speech is on a subject that is in some way related to your job or workplace, your speech *might* be protected if it addresses some social, political, or community issue that a court would say qualifies as a matter of public concern. Then the balancing test kicks in: If the agency you work for can convince a court that your remarks are nontrivially detrimental to its efficiency, discipline, or workplace harmony, then your speech, even though it's on an issue of public interest, loses its protection. If your boss can persuade a court that what looks like a public concern is really just a workplace grievance, then your speech loses its protection. If your boss can persuade a court that your speech, whether on a public concern or not, is a legitimate, required part of the job you were hired to do, then your speech loses its protection.

If the purpose of your speech about work is made for the specific purpose of alerting authorities to illegal activity, unethical behavior, or serious mismanagement, then you are likely to be protected as a whistleblower from retaliation (with the caveat that laws vary from state to state). This protection will be available regardless of the disruption it might cause. Your protection for whistleblowing at the federal level may evaporate, however, if your boss can convince a court that your belief about the wrongdoing falls somewhere short of irrefragable.

If you are at work but speaking about something not related to work (say, the merits of a presidential assassination), the same basic rules apply. If it's on a matter of public concern and nondisruptive, you can't be fired for it even if the message is provocative or even disturbing. If it's on a trivial matter and nondisruptive (say, a critique of last night's ball game), you should be okay because due-process protections should shield you from a termination for arbitrary or trivial reasons.

If your speech is about something that *is* clearly about your workplace, and even occurs at work but is not a required part of your job, it can be protected from retaliation if it bears on a matter of broader public concern and isn't disruptive. Your speech can be conveyed either in private or in public and still retain its protection. It can contain false or incorrect statements, as long as no malice or reckless disregard for the truth is involved. Courts often (not always, but often) defer to employer judgments about what qualifies as a threat to the agency's mission or a disruption to the workplace, so your battle for the right to make provocative workplace-related remarks may well be an uphill one.

If your speech is, over the boss's objections, protected by the First Amendment (on a public concern, not disruptive, not part of your job), you can still lose your job if the boss can convince a judge that you were saying or doing some other things that aren't protected and you would have been fired for those anyway.

Outside of work you may join any groups you like for political or other purposes, and you cannot be compelled to disclose your memberships as long as they involve no conflicts of interest with your work. Rules governing your political activity vary somewhat from state to state, but as a federal employee, unless you work in a few select agencies, you may be involved in politics in many ways. You can run for office (but only in a nonpartisan contest), manage or participate in a campaign (but not engage in fund-raising or receive contributions), organize an interest group, circulate petitions, and so on—as long as it all happens off duty. A government employer cannot fire you, or refuse to hire or promote you, because of your political activity or party affiliation, unless you are a confidential, policy-making employee, in which case it can.

To sum it up in one sentence: as a public employee you have rights to free expression except when you don't. To say that there is ambiguity and inconsistency in the law, however, is not necessarily to blame the lawyers. The subject lends itself to inherent difficulties in drawing lines. Take this example: The law says that if a public employee speaks about internal workplace matters—say, about how bad office morale is—then the speech is probably not protected because office morale is the stuff of internal politics, not a matter of public concern, and airing it may have a disruptive effect. But what if, hypothetically, that employee speech about office morale is directed to the state legislature, which summoned the employee to ask the question about it? Disruptive speech about an internal workplace problem? Or a matter of public concern?

Okay, it's not hypothetical: a Wisconsin legislative oversight panel in 1991 summoned Cyneth Dahm, the personnel director of the state lottery, to question her about morale problems in the lottery office. Soon after, her boss (the lottery's director) altered Dahm's job responsibilities in ways that she didn't appreciate, so she filed a lawsuit charging retaliation for protected speech. The federal court that reviewed this case said her speech "on its face clearly appears to be on a matter of public concern."[102] Maybe so, but had Dahm spoken about office morale to a reporter, a court might have called it just airing an internal workplace matter. Discussing it internally with fellow employees would likely not be protected. But her speech was to a legislative panel at their request, and if concern about a public agency's internal affairs by the legislature isn't "public concern," then it's hard to imagine what is. But wait a minute: The Supreme Court in 2006 said speech isn't protected if it's a required part of your job. By that logic, it's possible that Dahm's remarks about morale to the legislature now merit *no* protection.

As I said, you have rights to free speech except when you don't.

FIVE

A Chill in the Private Sector

THIS CHAPTER WILL BE SHORTER than the last one, and for a good reason: there is less to say about legal protections for free expression in private-sector employment than there is about the public sector. I ended the last chapter a bit sardonically by saying that as a public-sector employee, you have rights to free speech except when you don't. In the private-sector workplace, I can say, perhaps no less glibly but also no less appropriately, that you have *no* right to free speech except when you do.

For most of the nation's history, expressive rights for both public- and private-sector workers were virtually (and equivalently) nonexistent. By the last third of the twentieth century, however, the courts had settled on the principle that government employees do not relinquish First Amendment rights just because they hold public-sector jobs. From that point forward, as we saw in Chapter 4, a succession of court rulings, punctuated here and there with actions by legislatures or regulatory bodies, established the opportunities and limits of public employee speech, sometimes expanding rights and sometimes restricting them.

But if expressive rights in public-sector employment are rooted in the development of an area of First Amendment Law, rights in private employment enjoy no First Amendment protection to speak of. That doesn't mean, as we'll see in this chapter, that there are no protections at all—private-sector speech rights are tenuous but not nonexistent. But those protections that do exist are more diffuse, coming from a variety of disconnected sources of law rather than emerging from the reasonably coherent development of a legal doctrine. The safeguards for expression in the private-sector workplace, as one expert on labor law poetically puts it, "are like islands of protection in a sea of employer discretion."[1] (This chapter, accordingly, will feel perhaps more like an inventory than a history.)

Although I focus in the book on free expression at work in the United States, at the end of the chapter I will look briefly at the status of workplace expression in other countries. The system of employment at will, as I mentioned in Chapter 3, is uniquely American. The American system of employer-worker relations differs in crucial ways from the approach taken by other free societies with advanced economies, and we will look at the distinct approaches from country to country in how expressive activity at work is accommodated and regulated. Americans, as we will see, enjoy markedly less protection of free speech rights at work than their overseas counterparts.

WHEN PRIVATE IS REALLY PUBLIC

The meagerness of private employee speech rights is an inescapable result of the two key legal principles discussed in Chapters 2 and 3. The first, *state action*, speaks in the language of constitutional law to the conditions under which someone can use the courts to remedy a violation of First Amendment rights. Filing a lawsuit because someone infringed upon your right to free speech is generally possible only when "the state" is the one doing the infringing. The second principle, *employment at will*, speaks in the patois of labor law to an employer's leeway to create such an infringement in the first place—to hire and fire without dwelling over niceties like due process and other constitutional rights. I risk artifice only slightly to say that in the private sector, employment at will is what gets you fired for your speech, and state action is what makes it almost impossible for you to do anything about it.

But in some situations where the paycheck is signed by a private employer, the law treats that private employer much like a public employer—as a state actor—when it comes to the obligation to honor constitutional rights. This treatment is most apt to happen when the links between government and a private firm are so extensive that the two are largely inseparable. An important example of this—not related to work but establishing a principle that does apply to workplaces—came in a 1974 case involving a customer who sued a privately owned utility for shutting off her electric service. The customer charged that her rights to due process were violated, a constitutional claim that would have legs only if the utility was treated as a state actor. The U.S. Supreme Court decided that merely being regulated (even heavily regulated) by government isn't sufficient and ruled against the customer. In doing so it formulated a rule: state action is present when government and a private firm are sufficiently intertwined that the acts of the firm "may be fairly treated as that of the State itself."[2]

This rule went out for a free-speech spin in a case brought by Michael Holodnak, who lost his job at the Avco Corporation after publishing an article in a labor movement newsletter discussing Avco's labor-management climate as well as some broader issues of union effectiveness. The company said Holodnak was fired for violating a policy against "making false, vicious and malicious statements concerning any employee or which affect the employee's relationship to his job, his supervisors or the company's products, property, reputation or goodwill in the community."[3] Holodnak's situation is precisely the kind in which the fired employee suing for relief might have a case were he a government worker but probably is out of luck as an employee of a typical private firm.

In this case, however, Avco wasn't your average private employer; it manufactured helicopter engines at a facility whose land and buildings were owned by the government, with most of the production coming under contract with the Department of Defense. On that basis, an appeals court sided with Holodnak, finding that there was state action involved even though it was a private employer who punished him for his speech. The court notably rejected an argument that government involvement should be measured against the full range of activities of the larger corporate conglomerate of which this facility was a part (rather than just in relation to this division). The government's entanglement with the private company here, said the court, is not diminished just because the parent corporation happens to engage in other, separate commercial activities.[4]

This example makes clear that some employees in the private sector can take advantage of First Amendment protections available to public employees. It is difficult to know how many Americans work for private employers that are similarly situated. In any event, although the Avco outcome might seem straightforward, the application of the law to similar circumstances— claims that a private employer should be treated as a state actor—turns out to be difficult and inconsistent. Or as one court put it, "muddled."[5] Perhaps this predicament shouldn't be surprising, given that the standards for deciding if a private employer is really a state actor are extraordinarily subjective, inviting courts to see what they wish to see in a given situation.

A compelling illustration is the case of an employee of a private correctional firm under contract to operate a prison in Southern California. The employee, Jon George, spoke up about concerns regarding safety and security during a corrections officer training class, and later mentioned them to management. The company fired him for making false allegations, and he sued, charging violations of free speech rights under the First Amendment and the California constitution. To have even a hope of winning, George first had to show that a private firm operating a public prison should be treated as a state actor.

A federal appeals court considered this possibility, refracting the circumstances of the case through four different analytical lenses that courts have used to weigh state action.[6] First, was the private firm performing a traditionally exclusive governmental function? The court interpreted that to mean the company's role as an *employer* (as opposed to its role as a jailer) and said the answer is no. Second, was there close state involvement in the decision to fire George? Although the county's contract with the firm allowed the county to be involved in employment decisions, it hadn't been, so no. Third, was there joint action or a symbiotic relationship between the state and the private firm? In one of the historically important cases on this question, a restaurant became a state actor merely because it leased its space in a government building.[7] But not here: incarcerating citizens under contract with the government doesn't qualify. Fourth, a private entity can become a state actor when its behavior is compelled by some state law or custom. That was clearly not the case here.

So the outcome was a ruling that the firm's personnel actions involved no state action, and the prison employee, George, was out of luck. This seems like an illogical result, or at the very least a flawed argument. Sure, the test for state action is untidy, but the Supreme Court has said with clarity (the public function test) that a private firm engages in state action when its conduct involves something that is traditionally government's exclusive responsibility.[8] Legal scholars writing about private prisons draw the nearly inescapable conclusion that the conduct of private corrections firms amounts to state action.[9] The appeals court in George's case said, well, yes, it might be a public function to incarcerate criminals, but a private firm can be state actor in one respect (incarceration) but not in another (employment). By this logic the privatization of any government function would never result in the rights of employees being preserved. Some might say that's a good thing, but mostly it's a highly arbitrary thing. Put this prison case alongside the Avco case I discussed earlier. In one situation, the government and a corporation are in a contractual bed together building military aircraft, so an employee's speech is protected. In the other situation, the government contracts with a corporation to incarcerate criminals, and employee speech is not protected.

The vagueness and subjectivity of the tests used to find state action in the behavior of a private employer make it difficult, as I said earlier, to know how far speech rights for private-sector workers really extend. More important, this vagueness means that for employees in these kinds of situations—working for private firms with close contractual or other ties to government—the availability of enforceable rights is unpredictable. Given the extreme potential costs of exercising your rights only to later discover you don't have them (say, after you've been fired), a chilling of expression by private-sector employees who work in and around the public-private divide is likely. Few workers will be inclined to gamble a job on the prospect that a court will come down on their side of a subjective, complicated argument about the kind of employer they work for. And few workers, of course, will want to incur the personal and financial costs involved in pressing the issue legally. The more public services governments privatize, the more workers there will be who lose the (already limited) free speech protection found in public-sector jobs and end up in the rights-free no-man's-land of the private-sector workplace.

WHEN PRIVATE IS PRIVATE, BUT PROTECTED

We've been discussing situations where private-sector employees are entitled to free-expression protections because of the quasi-public status of their employer. Given the right set of circumstances connecting an employer's aims and activities with those of government, not to mention the right court willing to view that connection in a particular light, a private employee becomes akin to a government employee in terms of the application of the First Amendment to his speech. But there are several grounds for protection of expression by workers in the private sector that don't rely on convincing a court that the doctrine of state action has kicked in. These are protections created mainly by statutes, with some common law tossed in, and we can think of them as falling into four general areas: (1) speech in connection with labor organizing, (2) speech related to whistleblowing, (3) speech related to political activity, and (4) speech receiving legal protection even though it is related to no subject in particular.

SPEECH AND LABOR

Protection for expression by private-sector employees (and public employees as well) comes out of labor laws governing collective bargaining and union activity. It's fair to say that this is protection with limited reach, given the small and shrinking size of the unionized segment of the American workforce. The proportion of the civilian, nonfarm workforce that is unionized (a measure known as "union density") has dropped from a high of over 35 percent in the 1950s to under 8 percent today.[10] This "extraordinary decline" in the labor movement, to use the words of labor law professor James Brudney, can be explained by a variety of factors, including globalized markets, aggressive corporate antiunionism, laws that inadequately protect rights to organize, and an ossified and less than imaginative labor movement itself.[11]

But speech protections need not necessarily be as limited as the retrenchment of unionism would tend to imply. One reason is that protections for expression found in labor law are potentially quite broad in scope. The extent to which freedom of speech is actually created and protected by these laws is as much a function of how they are interpreted and enforced as what they say, and some experts argue that labor laws potentially protect a range of speech that is impressively broad. The starting point—the seminal text for speech rights in labor law—is Section 7 of the 1935 National Labor Relations Act (NLRA). It reads in part:

> Employees shall have the right to self-organization, to form, join, or assist labor organizations, to bargain collectively through representatives of their own choosing, and *to engage in other concerted activities for the purpose of collective bargaining or other mutual aid or protection.*[12]

The italicized passage is the part of the act from which expressive rights flow. How much speech is protected by the vague language of "concerted activities for the purpose of . . . mutual aid or protection"? A later section of the act calls it an unfair labor practice for either an employer or a union to coerce or interfere with employees who are exercising their rights guaranteed under Section 7.[13] But how far do those rights really go?

To judge by what lawmakers backing it in Congress in the 1930s were saying at the time, the idea behind NLRA Section 7 was to ensure legally protected rights to association, which would help equalize bargaining power between employer and employees, which in turn would make for cooperative relations between management and labor.[14] And we do find in the history of labor law evidence that courts were willing to view Section 7 protections liberally.

To cite one example, a case that reached the U.S. Supreme Court in 1962 involved a group of workers who were fired after they walked off the job at a machine shop to protest unacceptable workplace conditions (it was a bitterly cold day and the shop furnace wasn't working). The employees challenged their termination, arguing that even though there was no union and no attempt under way to organize one, their actions under the NLRA's Section 7 were a form of "concerted activity." The National Labor Relations Board agreed and ordered them reinstated with back pay. A federal appeals court refused to enforce the order, however, finding that the workers had not made a clear demand (presumably, for some heat) to which the company could have responded and thereby averted the walkout. The Supreme Court begged to differ, and in siding with the heatless workers articulated an expansive view of Section 7:

> We cannot agree that employees necessarily lose their right to engage
> in concerted activities under § 7 merely because they do not present a
> specific demand upon their employer to remedy a condition they find
> objectionable. The language of § 7 is broad enough to protect concerted
> activities whether they take place before, after, or at the same time such
> a demand is made. . . . The seven employees here were part of a small
> group of employees who were wholly unorganized. They had no bar-
> gaining representative and, in fact, no representative of any kind to pres-
> ent their grievances to their employer. Under these circumstances, they
> had to speak for themselves as best they could.[15]

Concerted activities are not protected, said the Court, when they involve behavior that is illegal, involves violence, creates a breach of contract, or shows unnecessary disloyalty to an employer.

On another occasion, the Supreme Court interpreted Section 7 as applying to political expression that is relevant to the workplace. A union's newsletter (distributed during nonworking hours, in a nonworking part of the workplace) included criticism of a presidential veto of a minimum-wage bill and urged members to register to vote against those who would oppose a rise in the minimum wage. The employer argued that the minimum wage is a political issue and that Section 7 is not a protection for a union's political opinions. The Supreme Court rejected that argument, reasoning that almost any issue can be viewed in political terms by someone; allowing that sort of judgment to dissolve protection for speech would render Section 7 almost meaningless. "There may well be types of conduct or speech that are so purely political or so remotely connected to the concerns of employees as employees as to be beyond the protection of the clause," said the Court, adding that this determination must be made on a case-by-case basis.[16]

Cases like these would appear to leave a lot of room for expressive activity aimed at improving working conditions, and indeed some employment law experts see in Section 7 a kind of workplace microcosm of the First Amendment. One labor law scholar pondering the NLRA's history says that its aim was to ensure that "the protected process of concerted activity in the workplace would be comparable to the rights of freedom of speech and association the first amendment guaranteed to workers in their political lives."[17] Another argues that although we generally think of the NLRA as protecting union activity and collective bargaining, Section 7 can be construed as protecting employee expression and advocacy that is unrelated to traditional union organizing, making it "a potentially significant source of free speech rights in the workplace on issues of concern to workers."[18] A third finds germinating seeds of self-government: "NLRA policies set out steps to make workplaces more democratic and to empower workers by giving them the skills to be citizens of a democracy."[19]

These buoyant takes on how labor law can create a safe space for workplace expression turn out to be tinged with more than a little optimism. Yes, the language of the NLRA has an expansive feel. Yes, its architects were motivated by noble intentions about rights and democracy and truth and justice for all. And, yes, courts have at times interpreted Section 7 broadly.

But the reality is that the act hasn't really protected all that broad a range of workplace expression, and today its power to protect speech is very limited. One key reason is that labor laws give as much or more protection to employer speech as they do to employee speech. A major aim of the 1947 Taft-Hartley Act, adopted twelve years after NLRA, was to codify employers' rights to campaign against unionization, through this passage in particular:

> The expressing of any views, argument, or opinion, or the dissemination thereof, whether in written, printed, graphic, or visual form, shall not constitute or be evidence of an unfair labor practice . . . if such expression contains no threat of reprisal or force or promise of benefit.[20]

That might read like a neutral application of a free speech principle to both sides of the labor-management divide, but both its intended and practical effect was to assert management power and prerogative. Senator Robert Wagner (namesake of the original NLRA, also known as the Wagner Act) put it this way in 1947 when Taft-Hartley was being considered:

> The talk of restoring free speech to the employer is a polite way of re-introducing employer interference, economic retaliation, and other insidious means of discouraging union membership and union activity, thereby greatly diminishing and restricting the exercise of free speech and free choice by the working men and women of America. No constitutional principle can support this.[21]

Wagner's fears turned out to be well-founded. Labor law gives employers significant latitude to oppose concerted employee activity, to shower workers with antiunion messages, and to chill employee dissent. The protections for speech available to workers are *statutory*, coming as they do from NLRA Section 7. In contrast, the protections available for speech by corporations are *constitutional*, giving rise to an imbalance that disfavors employees, because firms enjoy a constitutional right to speak while workers in private-sector jobs do not.[22]

A firm's right to speak on union-related matters isn't unlimited; labor law does force employers to be careful not to threaten workers for union activity. But there is nonetheless an imbalance, one that results not from differences in the status of the speakers (employer versus employee) but from differences in the status of those who act in the role of "regulators" of speech. There is no private entity with the power and incentive to closely regulate corporate speech; corporations, after all, derive their right to speak freely from the Constitution, given that courts have carved out a corporate right to free speech. But there is a private entity—the corporation—with the power and the incentive to regulate employee expression. So although we like to think of the First Amendment as granting individuals free speech protection against the tyranny of large institutions, the reality is that corporations enjoy, in a sense, freer speech than the individuals they employ.

The underwhelming ability of labor law to protect much employee speech can also be explained by the highly politicized nature of the National Labor Relations Board (NLRB). The Wagner Act in 1935 created the NLRB as an independent federal agency to oversee union certification elections and to hear, decide, and remedy complaints about unfair labor practices. The board has five members, each appointed by the president (with Senate consent) to five-year terms. The NLRB was conceived as a nonpartisan and impartial entity, and it managed to stay that way through the early 1950s, with Presidents Roosevelt and Truman appointing board members drawn mainly from government service and academia—not from the ranks of management lawyers or labor activists.[23]

Things changed when President Dwight Eisenhower appointed a couple of management partisans to the board, beginning a trend in this direction by Republican presidents. Democratic presidents Kennedy and Johnson continued to name essentially independent board members. Richard Nixon and Gerald Ford picked up on the Eisenhower approach, appointing management lawyers to some (but not all) open seats on the board. Ronald Reagan abandoned all pretext of nonpartisanship, naming to the board "apostles for union avoidance" (in the words of one law professor), including as board chair a consultant whose specialty was helping firms defeat union organizing drives.[24] President George H. W. Bush named two management-side lawyers but also tried (unsuccessfully) to appoint a board member with a union background.

By the end of the Clinton administration, the appointment of management- and union-side attorneys to the board had become routine. Clinton named two of each, plus a neutral attorney as board chair. By this point, the original notion of a nonpartisan NLRB had become a quaint and distant memory. In an article dissecting this history, former NLRB staff counsel

Joan Flynn (now a law professor) frets that the board has "come 180 degrees from its origins."[25] With a mix of members who can be regarded, essentially, as representatives of employers and representatives of employees, the NLRB has become, Flynn says, precisely the sort of body that Congress over seventy years ago specifically tried *not* to create.

President George W. Bush, showing little interest in sustaining Bill Clinton's effort to strike ideological balance on the board, has named mostly management partisans. By the middle of the current decade, the NLRB had initiated through its decisions what two union attorneys call an "extraordinary attack on employee rights."[26] It remains to be seen whether this is merely another pendulum swing in the management-labor balance of the NLRB that will shift again with future changes in White House occupancy. It's important to add that the national board sees only those cases that come up through its regional offices, whose staff members are not political appointments and presumably are less motivated by partisan concerns. It does seem, however, that the apparently permanent politicization of the NLRB has made it harder for employees to assert rights, including expressive rights. The board's partisan stance, writes labor law expert James Brudney, has "undermined the rights and protections sought by those invoking the Board's jurisdiction in the first place" and threatens to accelerate the NLRB's "downward spin into irrelevancy."[27]

The bottom line on rights to workplace expression arising from labor law is a thinly drawn one. Section 7 of the NLRA laid a theoretical foundation for the protection of expressive rights on issues related to the private-sector workplace, and for a time the NLRB and the courts were willing to get behind it. But the shifting winds of a business and political climate that has grown increasingly hostile to worker rights to organize have had an unmistakably corrosive effect on free speech. It is also plausible, as Suffolk University employment law professor David Yamada argues, that the ability of Section 7 to protect employee speech rights is compromised by a simple lack of knowledge that this protection even exists. Although most people have some awareness of their First Amendment rights, Yamada contends, few realize that the protection of "concerted activity" in the workplace can extend to workplace expression in situations that are outside the union-management setting.[28] In any event, the NLRA excludes the millions of workers—managers, supervisors, independent contractors, and agricultural workers—who do not legally fall under its jurisdiction. As the eminent labor historian David Brody sums it up, "Section 7 rights are weak rights, trumped every step of the way by property rights, by employer free speech, by liberty of contract."[29]

WHISTLEBLOWING

As in the public sector, laws at various levels of government protect workers in the private-sector who report on behavior that is illegal, immoral, unethical, or otherwise contrary to the public interest. These protections are a relatively recent phenomenon. As I mentioned in Chapter 4, legal safeguards for whistleblowing by *public*-sector employees go back as far as the nineteenth century. In the private sector, however, employees privy to wrongdoing until the past few decades had few options other than to raise the matter internally within the firm. The employee ultimately had no choice but to either accept the outcome of the inquiry, whatever it might be, or resign.[30]

Now many private-sector employees enjoy legal protections for whistleblowing speech. Whistleblower protections originally emerged from common law, typically from court decisions in some states carving out exceptions to employment at will. These courts understood employee reporting on illegal or unethical behavior to be a matter relevant to public policy, so they regarded retaliation by an employer against a whistleblower as a violation of public policy. Exceptions to employment at will based on public policy are accepted by courts in many states.

Whistleblowing, though, has come to be seen as a sufficiently concrete and serious affair that most states have moved beyond reliance on common law to enacting statutes that explicitly protect whistleblowers. In many states, however, these protections cover only government employees. In about half the states, protection is extended to both public- and private-sector workers.[31] Whistleblowing speech by employees, by the way, receives only limited protection from the "concerted activities" feature of labor law that I discussed in the last section. The NLRA (Section 7) protects speech intended to cultivate "mutual aid or protection" in the workplace. Accordingly, whistleblowing on an issue related to the interests of employees (for example, a workplace safety concern) might earn Section 7 protection, but whistleblowing intended to protect others, such as consumers or the general public, probably would not.[32]

State whistleblowing laws typically bar an employer from punishing or terminating an employee who blows the whistle in the "right" way—in a way that conforms to the requirements of the specific state law in place. These laws vary quite a bit in their coverage of employers and actions.[33] Several are comprehensive, covering many types of employers and a wide variety of potential wrongdoing, while others specify particular kinds of complaints that are eligible for whistleblower protection. Some statutes are limited to situations where an employee has specific knowledge of *actual* wrongdoing, while others protect workers who participate in an investigation or inquiry into their employer's *possible* wrongdoing. Some require that the bad behavior has already occurred, while others will protect an employee who believes that the employer will engage in wrongdoing in the future. Some laws protect whistleblowers who have a *strong belief* that there is wrongdoing, while others protect those with a *mere suspicion* of bad behavior. Some laws limit their reach to whistleblowing by actual employees of the firm, while others are drawn more broadly to include whistleblowing by independent contractors. Typically the wrongdoing has to be committed by the *employer*, although a few courts have protected whistleblowers who are reporting on the behavior of *other employees*. Most whistleblower statutes require that external reporting of bad behavior be directed to an appropriate government body or agency, not to the press or to a public-interest group.

Most whistleblowing statutes are limited to situations where the inappropriate behavior involved is concretely illegal, as opposed to behavior that is unethical or managerially incompetent. The definition of "illegal" can be broad, however, and can include violations of state and federal civil and criminal codes as well as violations of regulations addressing matters of public safety or public health. However, illegality is not always sufficient; the bad act must in some states rise to the level of a felony or in other states must be an illegal act that poses a specific threat of harm to public health or safety. This leaves a lot of speech that might blow the whistle on illegal behavior unprotected.

Consider the example of Lance Schultz, a regional manager for a tax services firm in Fairport, New York, who was fired in 1997. Schultz filed a wrongful-discharge lawsuit, charging that he was fired to prevent him from disclosing that the firm had engaged in overbilling of clients and other irregular business practices. Unfortunately for Schultz, New York's whistle-blower statute is one of those requiring illegality plus broader harm. The statute bars retaliation against a worker who discloses an employer's viola-tion of a law or regulation, but only if that violation "creates and presents a substantial and specific danger to the public health."[34] A federal judge dis-missed Schultz's complaint, finding that "fraudulent economic practices do not constitute a danger to public health or safety."[35] There is, in sum, an awful lot of speech that looks like protected whistleblowing but really isn't.

THINKING OUTSIDE THE SOX

A whistleblower protection law (such as New York's) that applies only if offending behavior poses a substantial danger to public safety leaves un-protected the person who blows the whistle on the kind of financial wrong-doing that has led to so many corporate scandals in recent years. But it was these very scandals that inspired Congress to enact the Sarbanes-Oxley Act of 2002 (often described in shorthand as "SOX"), which provides federal whistleblower protection to employees who disclose information about fraudulent activities by their private-sector employer. Sarbanes-Oxley ap-plies directly to publicly held companies only, although some legal experts note that it also covers the actions of privately held firms when they act as contractors or agents of public companies.[36]

The protection afforded by Sarbanes-Oxley to private employee whistle-blower speech is significant. Section 806 of the act says that a company may not "discharge, demote, suspend, threaten, harass, or in any other manner discriminate against an employee" who provides information or assists in an investigation, not just of new financial accountability rules contained in the act but of *any* rule or regulation of the Securities and Exchange Commis-sion, or *any* provision of federal law that has to do with fraud against share-holders.[37] A Sarbanes-Oxley whistleblower who encounters employer retal-iation can file a complaint with the U.S. Department of Labor and can then sue in federal court if there is no resolution from the Labor Department within six months.

Sarbanes-Oxley has run into a maelstrom of criticism, mainly from champions of free markets who find its audit and reporting requirements for firms to be excessively burdensome.[38] Most critics don't fuss about the whistleblower provisions of the act, presumably because they find it reasonable to expand protections for individuals who bring corporate fraud to the light of day. One who does fuss, though, is Larry Ribstein, a professor of corporate and securities law, who sees the new whistleblower protections as a threat to trust and communication within the firm, and as a temptation for employee mischief:

> Workers who have been demoted or terminated for any reason now have an incentive to "cause information to be provided" concerning a securities violation . . . and those who are concerned about a potential demotion or termination have an incentive to threaten such action. . . . The new law obviously can give significant leverage to employees, including in cases in which the firm has good reason to take action against the employee. It is an open question whether the benefits of exposing fraud will outweigh the disruptive effects of this new form of job protection.[39]

Those who look at corporate misbehavior and see market opportunities might bemoan new whistleblower protections as regulatory intrusions, but those who put their effort into expanding employee rights are delighted. "We view the law as whistleblowing reaching the promised land," says Tom Devine of the Government Accountability Project, a nonprofit organization that advocates for public- and private-sector whistleblowers. Devine calls Sarbanes-Oxley "a legal revolution in corporate freedom of speech."[40]

Whistleblowing is one area where the law has constructively advanced free speech rights for employees by giving that speech legal protection. But we must keep in mind that these are limited rights, applicable only to the narrow domain of speech about wrongdoing and often available only under rather restrictive circumstances. And even though whistleblowing laws typically are designed to protect workers from suffering retaliation for speaking out, the reality is that workers who work up the courage to blow the whistle on managerial bad behavior put workplace relationships, and their careers, in serious jeopardy. William K. Black, a lawyer and professor who has written extensively about white-collar crime (and who himself was a whistleblower during the savings and loan scandal of the 1980s), notes that "once you blow the whistle on the powerful you are never fully trusted again by powerful people. They always fear that you may blow the whistle on them next." Retaliation, he adds, "is inevitable."[41]

POLITICAL ACTIVITY

Richard Shovelin was an energy conservation adviser during the mid-1980s for Central New Mexico Electric Cooperative. In 1986, Shovelin mentioned to his supervisor at work that he was thinking of running for the office of mayor of Mountainair, New Mexico, where he lived. His boss expressed concern that the responsibilities of the (part-time) office would interfere unreasonably with Shovelin's duties at the cooperative, and told Shovelin that if he ran for mayor and won, he'd be fired. Shovelin ran, was elected, and was fired. He sued the cooperative, claiming (among other things) that he was a victim of retaliatory discharge for exercising a civic right to seek political office.

New Mexico was at the time a state that recognized a public-policy exception to employment at will, meaning that one could sue for wrongful termination if the firing violated some element of public policy. Shovelin argued that an individual's right to hold office and the public's right to vote for candidates of their choice were public policies grounded in the New Mexico state constitution and in federal and state law, and that these policies were offended by the cooperative's actions. The New Mexico Supreme Court disagreed, finding no basis for a public-policy exception that would enable Shovelin to make a case that his employer engaged in retaliatory discharge.[42] Interestingly, New Mexico had on the books a law making it a felony to punish employees for their political beliefs or for their intentions to vote or refrain from voting in elections.[43] The court determined, however, that in Shovelin's case there was no attempt to interfere with voting, only with office-seeking.

This result was not all that startling given where it occurred. Yes, New Mexico at the time recognized public-policy exceptions to employment at will, but very narrowly, and the court could not locate the exception sought by Shovelin—for seeking political office—in any existing statute or constitutional provision or in any past judicial decision made in the New Mexico courts. Fair enough, but this is the kind of case that draws dramatic attention to the woeful lack of rights to workplace expression that many

Americans are forced to endure. The court in this case did not find that the employer had a legitimate complaint that occupying the position of mayor in his spare time would interfere with Shovelin's job responsibilities or otherwise disrupt the cooperative's operations. It simply found that the law gives a private-sector employer the right to decide that an employee cannot both keep his job and hold public office in his community in his spare time. If it feels as though this outcome offends common-sense principles of a citizen-based democracy, it's only because it does.

There are protections in federal law against interference with one's right to vote or campaign for elective office, and these protections do apply in both public- and private-sector settings. Specifically, it is a federal crime to intimidate or interfere with voting or campaigning "by force or threat of force" in any primary, special, or general election.[44] This didn't help Richard Shovelin, presumably because there was no suggestion of violence in the employer's restraint of Shovelin's desire to be elected mayor. In fact, as an analysis of this issue in the legal compendium *American Law Reports* concludes, "Courts have consistently ruled that no liability attaches to an employer who has discharged an employee because of the employee's political views or conduct where such a discharge is not expressly or impliedly proscribed by statute or by the contract of employment."[45]

The question, then, is, to what extent are there laws in place that protect political speech and conduct from (nonviolent) interference by employers in the private sector? Federal law makes it illegal to intimidate, threaten or coerce someone for the purpose of interfering with their voting behavior in federal elections or to use financial inducements to get someone to vote or not vote a certain way, and most states have laws that create similar prohibitions.[46] Federal law also bars promises or threats related to employment in the private sector that is connected to federal funding (such as a private-sector job created by a federal grant). So it is more or less clear that employers cannot use promises of jobs, promotions, or financial rewards (or threats of adverse action) to induce specific voting behavior on the part of employees.

Everyday threats to employee political expression, however, are about more than naked intimidation intended to influence actual voting behavior. The salient issue for far more American workers is the extent to which employers can encourage or frown upon political activity that doesn't involve running for office and casting a ballot but instead involves run-of-the-mill political speech—sporting a political button, working for a campaign, writing a letter to the editor, expressing an opinion to a colleague, that sort of thing. Recall the example that opened the book: a woman fired for the political bumper sticker on her car in the employer's parking lot. Protections here are harder to come by. Although many states have broad assertions of rights to free expression in their state constitutions—in many cases more expansively phrased than in the First Amendment to the U.S. Constitution—relatively few states have written into their laws specific protection for nonspecific political speech in the realm of private employment. One that has is California, which includes this clause in its Labor Code:

> No employer shall coerce or influence or attempt to coerce or influence
> his employees through or by means of threat of discharge or loss of
> employment to adopt or follow or refrain from adopting or following
> any particular course or line of political action or political activity.[47]

The California Supreme Court has described this piece of labor law as protecting "the fundamental right of employees in general to engage in political activity without interference by employers."[48]

One state with exceptionally broad statutory protection of employee political speech is Louisiana, where it is illegal to prevent employees from participating in politics or becoming a candidate for office. Under the expansive language of Louisiana's law, an employer may not

> control or direct the political activities or affiliations of his employees,
> nor coerce or influence . . . employees by means of threats of discharge
> or of loss of employment in case such employees should *support or become*
> *affiliated with any particular political faction or organization, or participate in*
> *political activities of any nature or character.*"[49]

This copious protection came in handy for one James Davis of Kenner, Louisiana, who was fired by his employer when he decided to run for the city council. The firm he worked for did a substantial amount of business with the local school board and other governmental bodies. Executives at the company told Davis, who was running against a candidate who had support from some key local officials, that the firm would benefit if he withdrew from the race; when he did not, the firm fired him. In Davis's lawsuit challenging the dismissal, his employer played the business necessity card, arguing that the candidacy would have jeopardized profits by antagonizing people in a position to withdraw business from the firm. As we have seen in previous chapters, courts tend to give significant, even excessive, weight to claims that speech is disruptive or threatening to employers' interests. But in this case the plain language of the law carried the day: "The policy of the statute is unmistakable," wrote a Louisiana appeals court, "the employer may not control political candidacy of his employees. We see no exemption from the legislative purpose because of the nature of the employer's business."[50]

The contrast between Richard Shovelin, the mayoral candidate in New Mexico, and James Davis, who ran for city council in Louisiana, paints a compelling picture of how variable legal protections for private employee political speech can be. Shovelin, with no clear statutory or common-law protection to help him out, lost his job and could do nothing about it. Davis, aided by a comprehensively written law that left little room for error, taught his employer the hard way that political activism and free enterprise can cheerfully coexist. In other states we find a hodgepodge of laws protecting specific political activities, including a law mandating time off for someone who is part of a political party's governing machinery to attend party meetings (Minnesota), a law requiring employers to grant leaves of absence to employees who win election or appointment to public office (Delaware, Montana), and a law prohibiting discrimination against employees who run for or serve in the state legislature (Connecticut).[51]

Seeking public office is an unmistakably expressive undertaking, but no act of political expression in a representative democracy is more fundamental than casting a vote. As we will see in Chapter 9, many employers encourage workers to participate in community and society through the political process. This is what executives at retail behemoth Wal-Mart claimed to have in mind in the fall of 2006 when they launched an internal voter registration drive directed at the company's 1.3 million employees. CEO Lee Scott called it an effort to "strengthen the communities we serve by encouraging our associates to register to vote and empowering them to participate in America's democracy."[52] At the same time that Wal-Mart was registering employee-voters, however, it was steering large amounts of money through its political action committees (PACs) to campaigns, most of them Republican, leading some to speculate that the voter-registration initiative might be less about communities and democracy than about partisan politics.[53] You don't have to be an overindulgent cynic or a conspiracy theorist to look askance at a politically energetic corporation with partisan interests seeking to stimulate political activity among its workforce.

Employers cannot coerce employee votes or try to forcibly prevent someone from voting, but they are nonetheless entitled in much of the country to make it difficult for employees to vote, and in any event they incur no obligation to make it easy. According to the advocacy group Time to Vote, thirty states have so-called voter leave laws requiring employers to accommodate employees seeking time off to vote.[54] A typical example is Oklahoma's statute requiring employers to grant workers two hours of time off on election day to vote, without loss of pay or other penalty.[55] Many of these laws allow employers to require advance notification of an employee's intention to vote, and they let the employer select the time interval for voting. Roughly two-thirds of these laws, including Oklahoma's, grant paid leave, and some permit the employer to require proof that voting occurred. In twenty or so states, including the populous states of Pennsylvania, New Jersey, Michigan, and Florida, there is little to stop an employer from firing someone for taking time off to vote.

Given that in the United States most elections are held on weekdays, with polls typically open no more than twelve to fourteen hours, finding time to vote can be an inconvenience for the many people who combine the roles of parent, commuter, and employee, especially those whose workplace is located far from home and voting precinct. According to the Census Bureau, one in five registered voters who didn't vote in the 1996 presidential election (nearly 5 million people) failed to do so "because they couldn't take time off from work or were too busy"—a proportion that had tripled since 1980 and remained at one-in-five in the 2004 election.[56] It would be overreaching to lay most of the blame for America's low voter turnout compared to other representative democracies at the feet of employers. But it is clear our system of polling is another element of law where employee expressive rights are nontrivially constrained.

SPEECH RELATED TO NOTHING IN PARTICULAR

"Nothing in particular" is a bit of an unwieldy label for a category of speech protection, but it is an apt one. What I mean is that we find a small number of state laws that by their language appear to protect a wide range of expressive activity from the wrath of a private-sector employer. Unlike laws that prevent employers from interfering with certain specified political activities by employees, these laws do not address a particular form of expressive activity. I say that these laws by their language "appear to" provide broad protection because, as with so much of employment law that carves out exceptions to employment at will, there is almost always a balancing test that invites courts to weigh an employee's expressive rights against an employer's discretion to conduct business as it sees fit without interference or disruption.

The kind of protection I have in mind here comes in legal safeguards against so-called lifestyle discrimination—laws that bar employers from penalizing workers for off-work behavior that is otherwise legal. As I indicated in Chapter 3, many states have laws in this general realm, but most are aimed narrowly at protecting the off-work use of lawful products (typically tobacco and alcohol).[57] Only a handful of states have sweeping protections that extend to a wide range of legal, off-work activity. Although these laws tend not to single out expressive behavior for protection, they are written in a way that clearly would cover at least some forms of expressive off-work behavior.

To experience the legal protection of a wide variety of off-the-job behavior, you'll want to work in North Dakota, Colorado, New York, or California. Statutes in North Dakota and Colorado offer protection that is broadly worded while balancing employee rights against employer interests. North Dakota's statute outlaws discrimination based on a person's "participation in lawful activity off the employer's premises during non-working hours."[58] It accommodates employer interests in two ways. First, the off-work behavior must be "not in direct conflict with the essential business-related interests of the employer." Second, the off-work behavior loses protection if it is "contrary to a bona fide occupational qualification that reasonably and rationally relates to employment activities and the responsibilities of a particular employee." Colorado's law is essentially identical.[59] New York's law is a more verbose one, explicitly naming four categories of protected behavior, including "recreational activities" (defined as "any lawful, leisure-time activity, for which the employee receives no compensation"), political activities, use of consumable products, and union membership.[60]

California's law is the most recent (it became effective in 2000) and potentially the most sweeping. It allows an employee to seek remedies when demoted or fired because of "lawful conduct occurring during nonworking hours away from the employer's premises."[61] What makes it unique is that unlike the other states' provisions, California specifies no exceptions or counterbalancing factors (such as employer interests). The bill was pushed by California firefighters after a couple of incidents involving retaliation for participation in local politics. At the time the measure took effect, some attorneys worried that its broad language might call into question the validity of employer efforts to regulate off-duty conduct that threatens business interests, such as "moonlighting" for a competitor or supervisor-subordinate dating.[62] San Francisco employment lawyer Michelle Barrett says she was initially concerned that the state "would take a pretty draconian approach" to enforcing the law on the side of workers; in the short time it has been on the books, however, courts have taken employer interests into account.[63]

In the states that have lifestyle discrimination protection, the key question is, to what extent are courts willing to accommodate or dismiss employer concerns that off-duty speech threatens business interests? The answer is elusive. In one case in Colorado, a Delta Airlines baggage handler was fired after he wrote a letter to the editor of a Denver newspaper criticizing the airline's cost-cutting employment practices. He lost a legal challenge in federal court, where a judge ruled that the sharp criticism in his letter was inconsistent with a "bona fide occupational duty to be loyal to Delta in his public communications" and did not deserve protection under Colorado's lifestyle discrimination statute.[64] In a case in North Dakota, a man was fired from his job as a staff chaplain at a nursing home after he was caught masturbating in a bathroom stall at a local Sears. In his lawsuit he sought protection under North Dakota's prohibition on discrimination for legal off-work activity. There was disagreement about whether his act was legal or not (a disorderly conduct charge against him was dismissed), but the North Dakota Supreme Court rejected the nursing home's argument that the employee's behavior, in light of his pastoral counseling role in his job, was in direct conflict with its essential business-related interests.[65] Clearly, making judgments about when off-work behavior does and does not threaten the firm's interests is a highly subjective enterprise—one that the language of these lifestyle discrimination statutes does little to clarify.

Protection for off-work speech may exist in other states if one is willing to put a generous spin on laws regarding use of legal products off-work. Among the many states with laws protecting off-work product consumption, most limit coverage explicitly to tobacco and alcohol. A few, however, have laws that contain a nonspecific provision; Wisconsin's, for example, makes it illegal to discriminate based on "use or nonuse of lawful products off the employer's premises during nonworking hours."[66] Constitutional law specialist Eugene Volokh speculates that courts could conceivably locate expressive activity (off-work blogging was the subject of his analysis) within the realm of "use of a 'lawful product.'"[67] Are not a computer and the Internet "lawful products"? There are not yet any test cases on this, but if courts did find that use of lawful products includes use of tools of expression, then protection for extracurricular employee speech would expand beyond those very few states with broad protections against lifestyle discrimination. Even then, we're talking about perhaps six additional states, so protections for off-work expression arising from lifestyle discrimination laws would exist in fewer than a dozen states.

In general, laws protecting off-work expression can significantly curtail employment at will as a threat to expressive behavior, at least with respect to expression that occurs off the job and is unrelated to the business. But interpreting these laws can also pose thorny challenges, as in the case of New Jersey convenience store clerk whose employer discovered in newspaper articles that his after-work hobby was running a "mail order neo-Nazi skinhead music company."[68] (The clerk was fired and lost in court when a judge ruled that commercial hate speech does not qualify as a public-policy exception to employment at will.) Lifestyle discrimination laws, if sensibly interpreted and applied by courts, can strike a constructive note in favor of employee expression. On the other hand, these laws may encourage unscrupulous employers to give no reason for termination, as employment at will strictly observed permits, when the actual catalyst is off-work behavior. In the final analysis, since these laws usually include a serious nod to employer interests as a counterweight to employee speech, the true measure of speech rights inevitably plays out in a courtroom, where a judge gets to decide how slender the threads of employer discontent with employee speech can be.

Finally, there are just a couple of states with laws on the books that appear by their language to grasp the holy grail of workplace speech protection: extending broad First Amendment protection to the private-sector workplace. One is a unique Connecticut law enacted in the 1980s that bars employers from disciplining or firing employees

> on account of the exercise by such employee *of rights guaranteed by the first amendment to the United States Constitution* . . . provided such activity does not substantially or materially interfere with the employee's bona fide job performance or the working relationship between the employee and the employer.[69]

On its face this is a remarkable statute, appearing as it does to compel private employers to extend the capacious rights to free expression found in the First Amendment to their employees. One legal scholar described it as "the most sweeping recognition to date of 'First Amendment' values in the private sector workplace."[70] (It was under this law that the factory worker refusing to participate in a Gulf War celebration, mentioned in the Introduction, filed suit.) But has the reality of interpretations by Connecticut courts matched the law's promise?

Well . . . no. In an analysis of this question after the law had been around for about a decade, law professor Martin Margulies said the Connecticut trial courts had developed two alternative views on the law's protections.[71] One approach is to see the law as extending to workers in the private sector the employee speech rights available to public-sector workers (rights described at length Chapter 4). This means protecting speech only when it's on a matter of "public concern" and only if it is not excessively disruptive to workplace efficiency, authority, or harmony. The other approach begins with recognition that the First Amendment rarely protects unwanted speech on private property and so concludes that this law protects no speech on the employer's premises.

The first approach—giving private employees essentially the same rights as public employees—would be promising, except that Connecticut courts have shown great deference to employer interests in weighing the inevitable balance.[72] And as Margulies points out, the second approach is almost useless as a source of rights. Although it might seem like a protection of off-work speech (away from the employer's premises), the fact is that the First Amendment protects private speech only from *government* interference, not from discipline or termination by one's private employer. This way of thinking, says Margulies, reduces the statute "to a silly and empty tautology."[73] He urges courts to read the law as protecting all nondisruptive speech that would ordinarily enjoy First Amendment protection, regardless of where it occurs or whether it is on matters of public concern. Alas, the reasonableness of this strategy is matched by the remoteness of probability that courts will actually adopt it.

A similar law in South Carolina makes it illegal to "discharge a citizen from employment or occupation . . . because of political opinions or the exercise of political rights and privileges guaranteed . . . by the Constitution and laws of the United States or by the Constitution and laws of [South Carolina]."[74] Here, like in Connecticut, we have sweeping language that on its face appears to pull the First Amendment into the private-sector workplace wholesale. Once again, though, the courts are reticent. The South Carolina Supreme Court has made it clear that the law does create a public-policy exception to employment at will for some political speech. For example, the court said that an employee fired because he refused to contribute money to his employer's political action committee has a cause of action for wrongful discharge.[75]

A more difficult scenario presented itself in the high-profile case of Matthew Dixon, a mechanic at Coburg Dairy in Charleston, South Carolina. In 2000, at a time when South Carolinians were considering whether to remove the Confederate battle flag from their state capitol dome, Dixon (an active member of the Sons of Confederate Veterans) put two Confederate flag stickers on his personal tool box that he used at work. A co-worker told Dixon that he found the stickers racially offensive and a violation of the firm's harassment policy. After efforts to mediate a solution failed, the company offered to buy Dixon a new tool box so that he could keep his flag-adorned one for use at home. He resisted both that offer and Coburg Dairy's eventual insistence that he just remove the stickers and was fired.

Dixon's wrongful-discharge lawsuit invoked the South Carolina law as a major element. The firm said it fired him for violating its antiharassment policy. Dixon said he was fired for exercising his constitutional rights, and it is true that in the general realm of First Amendment law, display of a Confederate flag is clearly protected speech. As it happens, there has been no concrete legal outcome in this case because of a jurisdiction problem: the case was heard and decided in federal court, only to have the outcome erased when a federal appeals court decided that it really belonged in state court.[76] We can, however, look at the court's reasoning in the decision that was tossed out as an indication of how courts might interpret the South Carolina law.

The court decided against Dixon, concluding that although the First Amendment gives him the right to display the flag at home, on his vehicle, or in a public place, it does not give him the right to bring his political speech into Coburg's privately owned workplace. Finding otherwise, said the court, "would lead to the absurd result of making every private workplace a constitutionally protected forum for political discourse."[77] Some might say that was part of the purpose of the South Carolina law. Nonetheless, the court thought it reasonable that the employer, in the name of maintaining a harmonious workplace and avoiding liability for racial harassment or discrimination, wanted Dixon to engage in his political speech off the job. The judicial reasoning here on the meaning of South Carolina's statute echoes how some courts in Connecticut have viewed that state's similar law. By starting with the principle that the First Amendment doesn't protect your speech on someone else's private property, these courts are surgically removing all meaning from statutes that otherwise would extend a lot of protection for expressive activity to the private-sector workplace.

But *Dixon v. Coburg* does revisit a difficult issue related to the regulation of workplace expression: what happens when an impulse to tolerate expressive rights collides with an equally legitimate desire to limit behavior that might be construed as racial, sexual, or religious harassment? This question has over the past fifteen years consumed the attention of some legal scholars who argue that the climate for workplace expression is constrained by the effects of harassment law regulating a "hostile work environment." The argument, simplified, is that vague legal standards addressing what is or isn't harassment chill expression because employers facing potential liability for employee speech have little choice but to overregulate.[78] Others respond that the collision between free speech and harassment is overstated because the test for a hostile environment is not as vague as critics believe; also, harassment by definition involves behavior that is directed at a captive audience and that incites tangible harm and therefore deserves a lower degree of free speech protection.[79] No court to my knowledge has accepted the idea that the First Amendment or other free speech protections can dilute the liability involved when expressive behavior at work creates a hostile work environment. I will have more to say about this in the discussion of employee speech and civil rights laws in Chapter 7.

State laws, such as those on the books in Connecticut and South Carolina, that appear through their language to extend broad First Amendment protections to the private-sector workplace offer a promising way to expand employee free speech rights. But as with other legal measures I've described in this chapter (and in Chapter 4 on the public sector), the true implications for free expression are found not in the language of statutes but in the decisions of judges when difficult cases arise. Unfortunately, the promise of these seemingly speech-friendly sweeping state laws has been overcome by the reality that state courts weighing worker speech against employer interests tend to side with employers.

BEYOND OUR BORDERS

I close this chapter with a few words about how protections for employee speech under U.S. law differs from those in countries with which we like to compare ourselves. Given systems of constitutional law and justice that are unique to each country, the task of synthesizing the legal status of workplace speech in other nations is impossible here. The constitutions of most nations with political systems that qualify as similar to ours—popular democracies with developed market economies—include a free speech provision. (So do many that don't qualify.) Some constitutions include language suggesting a broader reach of free speech principles, such as application to private-sector institutions, than is the case in the United States, although as with American law, the meaning of a given constitutional provision may well be elusive until a large body of case law is closely examined.

One aspect of labor relations bearing on expression that does represent a demonstrable difference between the U.S. economy and other economies is the balance between at-will arrangements and just-cause (due-process) protections. The system of employment at will that underpins U.S. labor law, which for most workers allows dismissal without cause, notice, or severance, is uniquely American; almost every other industrialized nation, and many developing countries, have through statute or common law created protections against dismissal without just cause or notice. The United States is unique in assuming no property right in employment for workers and in placing no obligation on employers to engage in systems of procedural due process before dismissing someone. As the author of an academic study of employment law in five countries wryly concluded, "this does not mean that American employers lack any sense of moral obligation to be fair to their employees, but the great majority insist on the right to be unfair."[80] For those who worship free markets, the employer's "right to be unfair" is a virtue of employment at will, and there is certainly the risk that governments dominated by free-market conservatives will try to replace just-cause protections with at-will arrangements. A recent case in point is Australia, where Prime Minister John Howard in 2005 announced plans to make unfair dismissal remedies no longer available to workers at firms with fewer than 100 employees.[81]

The conventions of the International Labour Organization (ILO) offer another window on comparative employment rights across borders. Among the ILO's 185 conventions are two in particular that address workplace expression. One is Convention 158, which says that an employee should not be discharged "unless there is a valid reason for such termination connected with the capacity or conduct of the worker or based on the operational requirements of the undertaking, establishment or service"; "political opinion" is included in a list of invalid reasons for termination.[82] The other is Convention 111, which cites "political opinion" as an unacceptable basis for employment discrimination, along with race, sex, religion, nationality, and other individual characteristics.[83] Convention 158 has been ratified by only 34 nations, but as of late 2006, Convention 111 has been ratified by 165 nations. The United States has ratified neither.

Some nations have codified protections against employment discipline for political opinions in their employment laws. For example, Australia's Workplace Relations Act cites "political opinion" as one among many bases for which termination is unacceptable.[84] New Zealand's Human Rights Act prohibits discrimination on the grounds of having or lacking a particular political opinion.[85] Canada does not prohibit employment discrimination based on political opinion at the federal level, but that protection does exist in the employment laws of seven of its provinces.[86] Employment rights in the United Kingdom, given in its Human Rights Act of 1998, are drawn in part from the European Convention on Human Rights (ECHR), which specifies a right to "hold opinions and to receive and impart information and ideas without interference by public authority and regardless of frontiers."[87] However, political opinions as a basis for unlawful discrimination or dismissal are not included in British law, so personal opinions and political dissent are left unprotected in the U.K. workplace.[88]

This modest comparison paints, admittedly, a limited global picture of rights to workplace expression. Most democratic countries include free speech protections of some sort in their national constitutions, and some countries include specific forms of expression—such as political opinion or speech related to union organizing and collective bargaining—in laws identifying rights for workers. These narrow protections of specific rights to hold opinions without negative job consequences are important, and the lack of protection for political views in the American workplace is alarming. But the critical difference between the United States and other nations lies in the presence (for them, not us) of due-process rights for all workers and the enforcement of prohibitions on unjust dismissal. A rule of due process means that a dismissal requires a legitimate reason, effectively protecting any speech that doesn't impair job performance or firm efficiency. Due-process guarantees have the added benefit of shifting the burden of proof from worker to employer, creating an obligation to justify expression-related discipline. Through the First Amendment, Americans enjoy a constitutional system of free speech protection that is unique and exceptional. Our approach to safeguarding expressive rights at work, however, is rooted in the unforgiving system of employment at will and is uniquely defective.

SIX

Why Free Speech Works

AMERICANS SEEM TO LIKE THE IDEA of free speech, but it's not clear that they understand it. A couple of recent national surveys show that when asked if the First Amendment goes too far in its protections of free expression, about three in four Americans say it doesn't.[1] This opinion is consistent across political party lines: roughly equal majorities of Democrats and Republicans find the reach of First Amendment protections acceptable.[2]

But if a comfortably large majority say they are satisfied with what the First Amendment does, few are able to say what that is, at least when quizzed by a pollster. A national survey in early 2006 asked people to name First Amendment rights (speech, press, religion, assembly, petition). Only 8 percent could name at least three of them, while 21 percent thought the First Amendment included the right to own and raise pets.[3] For those who could identify a piece or two of the First Amendment, speech is the familiar one. In the Nashville-based First Amendment Center's most recent annual "State of the First Amendment" survey, 63 percent mentioned free speech; the next highest mention, freedom of religion, came in at just 20 percent.

Relatively few Americans may know what the First Amendment really is, but a surprising number harbor alarming opinions about what it ought to be. The State of the First Amendment survey in 2005 found that 38 percent disagree with the idea that newspapers should be able to freely criticize the military, 38 percent disagree with allowing musicians to sing lyrics that others might find offensive, and 50 percent disagree with allowing people to say things in public that might be offensive to religious groups.[4] In a *Chicago Tribune* poll in 2004, 52 percent said the government should impose restrictions on information and content that appears on the Internet, 20 percent said the press should not be allowed to publish stories suggesting that the war is not going well, and 13 percent said groups opposed to a war should not be allowed to demonstrate and protest against it.[5] These are sizable minorities of people who apparently would prefer to prohibit expressive activities that are (at least for now) unambiguously protected speech.

Even those who are relatively well-informed about the First Amendment may not have given much thought to *why* free speech is a good thing. This is where free speech theorists come in. By "free speech theorists" I mean philosophers, legal scholars, political scientists, and other intellectuals who put aside (at least for a time) everyday questions about whether this or that speech should or shouldn't be protected and pose more fundamental questions about how free expression matters—when, to whom, and why.

Theories of free speech address a few basic questions: What forms of human activity represent "speech" or "expression"? (I discussed this in Chapter 1.) What are the values that underlie constitutional free speech protection? How should a society draw lines, if any be drawn, dividing expression that deserves legal protection from expression that doesn't? I am interested in these questions because they bring to the surface the reasons why freedom of expression is highly valued as one of the foundations of a modern, progressive social order. Understanding these reasons in turn helps us make sense of situations where rights to expression are limited, sometimes severely so—in and around workplaces, for example.

Let me offer three caveats at the outset. First, my aim here is not to offer my own personal theory of free speech or the First Amendment, nor is it my goal to survey existing theories comprehensively. The former would be gratuitous, and the latter would be tedious. What I am after is a basic understanding of the key issues of value, and the key points of contention, among those who think deeply about why free speech matters. These free speech "values" will be useful later as yardsticks against which legal and managerial approaches to workplace expression can be measured.

Second, free speech theories are generally directed at regulation of speech by *government*—the most significant "regulator" of speech because its rules affect more or less everyone. Even so, we can easily apply the logic of regulation of speech to a workplace context. Public employers, of course, *are* government. Private employers have the right to define themselves through the speech that occurs on their property or within their organization. And as we saw in Chapter 2, the actions of private employers are not always so easily separated from those of government. Employers—public and private—have many options available to them regarding the kind of expressive climate they'd like to cultivate inside their workplace. In this sense, employers, too, are "regulators" of speech. A sense of the underlying values and limits of free speech in civil society, as explored by free speech theorists, is therefore a helpful ingredient for understanding how free expression in the workplace does work and should work.

Third, the idea of "free speech theory" is a twentieth-century intellectual enterprise driven by the thinking and writing of a set of people with whom most readers are probably unfamiliar. Just as the U.S. Supreme Court didn't spend much time on free speech until a series of wartime protest cases during World War I, neither did legal theorists. As the Court moved forward from there, into issues of free association and compelled speech during the McCarthy era and on through the civil rights movement and the Vietnam War, an intellectual growth industry on the meaning of the First Amendment flourished. Many of the big players, however, remain somewhat obscure even to those who pay attention to constitutional law. Asked toidentify seminal figures in modern First Amendment history, many would summon the names of Supreme Court justices: Holmes, Brandeis, Douglas, Marshall, Brennan, and Black. Few outside the legal academy, though, would think of the academics Chafee, Meiklejohn, Emerson, Baker, Greenawalt, Schauer, Fiss, and Sunstein.[6] The names of Supreme Court justices in that first set surfaced frequently in earlier chapters as I discussed the history of free speech. Here we turn to ideas developed by the second set—theorists trying to figure out why free speech matters.

Theoretical arguments about free speech can be challenging to summarize. For one thing, they are numerous, coming from diverse intellectual and philosophical perspectives. Also, these theories fall into categories that are multifaceted and overlapping, with different labels at times describing similar ideas. I find it useful here to capitalize on one basic division that separates theorists who focus on the collective purposes of free speech from theorists who focus on individual objectives. In loose terms, a *collectivist* theory locates the value of free speech in its consequences for the collective enterprise of which we're all a part, which at a societal level means the health and welfare of democracy itself. By contrast, an *individualist* approach centers on the value of free expression for the individual citizen, as both speaker and listener. In an article published in 1919 in the *Harvard Law Review*, well before the arrival of most modern free speech theory, Zechariah Chafee (who is often described as the earliest First Amendment scholar) anticipates this theoretical divide:

> The First Amendment protects two kinds of interests in free speech. There is an individual interest, the need of many men to express their opinions on matters vital to them if life is worth living, and a social interest in the attainment of truth, so that the country may not only adopt the wisest course of action but carry it out in the wisest way.[7]

This split between collectivist and individualist approaches, with variations in jargon and nuance, has become a recurring theme among those who traffic in free speech theory. Cass Sunstein, for instance, invokes this divide in his 1993 book, *Democracy and the Problem of Free Speech*, though with different terminology. Sunstein favors a "Madisonian" approach to free speech rooted in the goal of creating and sustaining a deliberative democracy, and he contrasts it with an "autonomy" perspective that sees expression as how individuals maintain dignity and become "the authors of the narratives of their own lives."[8] Another venerable legal theorist, Owen Fiss, offers a "democratic" theory focused on how speech enhances collective determination. For Fiss, the alternative is a "libertarian" view of the First Amendment as protection for self-expression rather than as a vehicle to enhance collective freedom.[9]

Using the labels "collectivist" and "individualist," I will discuss each of these strands of free speech thought in turn and then seek to reconcile them. These theories matter because a sense of what free speech means for individuals and for society sheds light on the consequences of spending large amounts of time in places—workplaces—where freedom of expression is more likely to be stifled rather than encouraged.

COLLECTIVISTS

The basic collectivist idea is that free speech is important because of the contribution it makes to the effectiveness of liberal democracy. In practice this means that free speech supports political processes that make democratic institutions work the way that they should. When this happens, the result is a society where government usefully represents the interests of citizens, and through the give and take of politics, delivers on its promise to be an instrument of liberty, order, and prosperity. What makes a liberal democracy work, writes philosophy of law specialist Kent Greenawalt, is the ability of citizens to make informed choices. Free speech is the touchstone, enabling us to identify and develop our interests, grasp truths that are politically important, and act as a check on official misconduct or abuse of office. By this logic, free speech makes for a well-informed citizenry, which in turn produces better political outcomes and effective government.[10]

One way to approach free speech as a means to good collective decision making is through the metaphor of a "market" for speech. We sometimes hear a viewpoint described as one that may or may not flourish in the "marketplace for ideas." This way of thinking has its origin in the nineteenth-century writing of John Stuart Mill, who in *On Liberty* sees an uninhibited flow of ideas as the best way to cultivate truth as an aid to freedom and democracy. Popular opinions on important issues, says Mill, "are often true, but seldom or never the whole truth," and require nonconforming viewpoints to challenge them.[11] Mill does not speak explicitly of a "market" for speech, but we see in his writing a clear sense of the tension between competing forces—conflicting viewpoints—that is the underlying principle behind a free market for just about anything. Truth on issues that matter, writes Mill,

> is so much a question of the reconciling and combining of opposites
> that very few have minds sufficiently capacious or impartial to make
> the adjustment with an approach to correctness, and it has to be made
> by the rough process of a struggle between combatants fighting under
> hostile banners. . . . When there are persons to be found who form an
> exception to the apparent unanimity of the world on any subject, even
> if the world is in the right, it is always probable that dissentients have
> something worth hearing to say for themselves, and that truth would
> lose something by their silence.[12]

Without freedom to challenge opinions, says Mill, how can anyone assume that the conventional wisdom is accurate and appropriate as a basis for political action?

Mill didn't use the specific language of a market, but Supreme Court Justice Oliver Wendell Holmes did, in a famous dissenting opinion in a

1919 case about seditious speech. A group of Russian immigrants who distributed leaflets calling for a general strike were convicted and imprisoned for violating provisions of the Espionage Act of 1917. The act made it illegal to incite or encourage "resistance to the United States" and to engage in actions intended to "hinder the United States in the prosecution of the war." In *Abrams v. United States*, the Supreme Court affirmed these convictions. In dissent, Holmes wrote that persecuting people for their opinions is "perfectly logical"—if you are certain of your premises or your power and you want to erase all opposition and guarantee a certain result. But when people understand the fallibility of their own convictions, Holmes continued,

> they may come to believe even more than they believe the very foundations of their own conduct that the ultimate good desired is better reached by free trade in ideas—that *the best test of truth is the power of the thought to get itself accepted in the competition of the market*, and that truth is the only ground upon which their wishes safely can be carried out. That at any rate is the theory of our Constitution.[13]

Although Holmes made those famous remarks on the losing side of the *Abrams* case, the so-called marketplace model had staying power, becoming over the course of the twentieth century a dominant influence on the free speech decisions of the modern Supreme Court.

The marketplace approach to free speech is hardly an absolutist one that would protect all expression that conveys an idea of some sort. The market metaphor may conjure up a mental image of a forum for unrestrained speech, in much the same way that those who worship free markets imagine a forum for unrestrained trade. But the point of the speech marketplace is limited to a certain kind of market—the search for "truth" on subjects that help us understand the world around us. This means, as law professor Robert Post puts it, situations where speech is "embedded in the kinds of social practices that produce truth."[14] It won't always be obvious what those social practices are, or whether some given form of speech qualifies. But it isn't hard to find examples of expression where the "truth-seeking function of the marketplace of ideas" (a phrase used by Justice William Rehnquist in an important 1988 free speech ruling)[15] *isn't* really in play—commercial advertising, private communications between individuals, and certain forms of artistic expression, to name a few.

The notion that free speech feeds a marketplace for ideas fits with the (collectivist) view that the purpose of the First Amendment is to promote democratic processes. But the two viewpoints are not equivalent. For a time collectivists saw the First Amendment as applying only to expression on political matters, with no protection for other kinds of speech. Alexander Meiklejohn, an early and influential free speech theorist, argued in a celebrated essay in 1948 that the First Amendment protects only speech that has some relation to "issues with which voters have to deal—only, therefore to matters of public interest."[16] The test is whether listeners have opportunities to hear ideas that aid collective decision making, not whether speakers have opportunities to express themselves. As Meiklejohn famously writes, "What is essential is not that everyone shall speak, but that everything worth saying shall be said."[17]

Some collectivists find the marketplace-of-ideas approach to free speech troubling on grounds of fairness and neutrality. In economic markets, there are persistent concerns that the playing field for free trade is not always level. In classical economic theory, markets are theoretically free and fair when participants are rational decision makers and parties have equal access to information. Regulation, to the extent it exists, should be neutral, not favoring one set of interests over another. In practice, though, markets are easily manipulated by the powerful to their advantage. This occurs, for instance, when powerful actors have better control of information, or a greater ability to influence (supposedly neutral) regulators to tilt market rules and mechanisms in their favor.

Similar forms of distortion threaten a free market for speech-based ideas. Government as a regulator of the market for speech is presumably neutral; the First Amendment seems to read that way. But fairness is threatened if chances to speak and to be heard depend on wealth, entitlements, or other imbalances in the availability of expressive outlets. For collectivists, a system of free expression functions well when it generates a healthy system of political deliberation. This "Madisonian" approach, writes Cass Sunstein, requires broad public attention to key issues, exposure to diverse points of view, and political equality.[18] How realistic are these lofty objectives if markets for ideas are products of the existing economic and political order, where property rights and imperfect competition skew access to the resources that allow one's voice to be heard? Given these realities of social and economic opportunism, says Sunstein, markets for speech are "in many ways a Madisonian failure."[19]

The modern Supreme Court, a fan of marketplace thinking, has been reluctant to "regulate" markets for speech in a way that might amplify less powerful political interests or voices. The Court made this clear in the famous 1976 campaign finance case *Buckley v. Valeo*. Throwing out a law that limited campaign spending, the Court said the idea "that government may restrict the speech of some elements of our society in order to enhance the relative voice of others is wholly foreign to the First Amendment."[20] Collectivists are more willing than the Court to tolerate rules that would prevent diverse voices from being drowned out by inequalities of wealth, power, or access. Otherwise, writes Owen Fiss in his book *Liberalism Divided*, "we as a people will never truly be free."[21]

Contemporary collectivists would protect more speech than just the explicitly political, even if they do put a higher value on political expression. This intention leads to what are sometimes called *two-tier* theories: the idea that there are different classes of speech—high-value and low-value speech—deserving higher or lower levels of protection.[22] The Supreme Court first embraced the two-tier concept in the 1942 case of a man who called a city official a "damned fascist" and was convicted under a law banning offensive comments about another person in a public place. The name caller's attempt to challenge the law as an unconstitutional infringement on free speech failed; the Supreme Court declared that not all speech gets the same level of protection. Punishing people for obscene, profane, insulting, and libelous speech poses no constitutional problem, the Court said, especially when the speech involves words that "by their very utterance inflict injury or tend to incite an immediate breach of the peace."[23] Defining the boundary between these tiers of speech is where the hard work begins and where the hard cases come into play, on such issues as obscenity, hate speech, commercial speech, telecommunications policy, funding for the arts, and political campaign regulation.

INDIVIDUALISTS

"Individualist" is a bit clumsy as a label for this side of the free speech theory divide, but it creates a workable contrast with "collectivists." The basic idea, captured in a sentence by the eminent theorist C. Edwin Baker, is that speech "is protected not as a means to achieve a collective good but because of its value to the individual."[24] That value takes various forms, and goes by various labels, in different versions of individualist theory: autonomy, self-fulfillment, self-realization, individual liberty, and moral independence.[25] In pondering the value of freedom of speech, individualists elevate these principles above the pursuit of collective goals. Individual freedom is what makes free speech important as a constitutional principle; expressive rights both emerge from and reinforce that freedom. As we will see shortly, however, this emphasis on individualism doesn't lead these theorists to deny that free expression has important societal value and is a key constituent of effective democracy. I will highlight here the two most important individualist approaches to free speech theory.

EMERSON'S SYSTEM OF FREEDOM OF EXPRESSION

Among the most influential of free speech thinkers in the twentieth century was law professor Thomas Emerson, whose 1970 book, *The System of Freedom of Expression*, is a seminal text in First Amendment theory. Emerson, whose thinking about the First Amendment has had a profound influence on legal writing and court decisions, articulates four main premises, or values, associated with free expression in a democratic society.[26]

First, Emerson argues that the essential purpose of free expression is to assure individual self-fulfillment. Suppression of belief or speech, he writes, is "an affront to the dignity of man" and runs counter to basic human nature. Curbs on individual expression elevate society and its institutions to a position of tyrannical control over individual freedom.

Second, Emerson describes freedom of expression as essential for an individual's quest for knowledge and the discovery of truth. Echoing Mill, he argues that conventional wisdom often turns out to be wrong, so expression and discussion must be kept fully open to allow widely accepted ideas to be challenged.

Third, Emerson points to participation in decision making as a critical way to bring about social change through healthy, consensual government. "Governed men," he writes, "in order to exercise their right of consent, [must] have full freedom of expression both in forming individual judgments and in forming the common judgment." We can see that he veers here toward a collectivist mind-set in examining how expression feeds effective democratic self-government. But he pulls up short by emphasizing not how free speech directly improves democratic institutions but how it expands the ability of *individuals* to participate in that improvement.

Fourth, Emerson contends that free expression is how society uses reason to create a community that has the twin virtues of being both stable and adaptable. Suppressing speech makes it difficult to confront the real problems society faces and to cultivate new ideas for solving them. In such situations, rational judgments are impossible, increasing the chances that force rather than reason will prevail.

With a focus on the individual as beneficiary of a system of free expression, Emerson rejects the notion that the only speech worth protecting is speech that contributes to the development of democratic institutions:

> It is not a general measure of the individual's right to freedom of expression that any particular exercise of that right may be thought to promote or retard other goals of the society. . . . Freedom of expression, while not the sole or sufficient end of society, is a good in itself, or at least an essential element in a good society.[27]

A society may pursue other worthy goals, such as virtue, justice, or equality, but these are not the automatic result of free speech, and "society may not seek them by suppressing the beliefs or opinions of individual members." Emerson further departs from the collectivist position by pursuing a much broader approach to expressive content that deserves full First Amendment protection. Dismissing the idea that the contribution of free speech to effective democracy is mainly a matter of *political* expression, Emerson argues for a "right to participate in the building of the whole culture," a concept that includes freedom to express oneself in art, religion, literature, science, and all other areas of human knowledge.

BAKER'S LIBERTY THEORY

C. Edwin Baker's liberty theory, spelled out in detail in his 1989 book *Human Liberty and Freedom of Speech*, is among the most comprehensive of individualist theories. Baker adopts two of Emerson's four free speech values—individual fulfillment and participation in social change—as the core purposes of the First Amendment. These two are the crucial ones for Baker because they imply the existence of freedom to pursue self-actualization and self-determination. He sees Emerson's other two values—truth discovery and stable community—as important but "derivative," following logically from the two core ones. Stable community, for example, is something that results when you have social conditions that foster individual self-fulfillment and participation.[28]

Baker builds his individualist approach to free speech on top of a harsh critique of the marketplace-of-ideas approach. Recall that the marketplace model sees free speech as a good thing because it aids the discovery of truth that feeds constructive political processes. It also sees speech that doesn't contribute to that marketplace as less deserving of First Amendment protection. This way of thinking about free speech is built on key "market" assumptions that truth is objective and discoverable through a free and fair exchange of ideas and that people are able to weigh truth claims as rational decision makers.

But as Baker points out, truth is often subjective—chosen or created, not discovered. And, I hasten to add, chosen or created by those with an agenda or an ax to grind. People who gain advantage from some version of the "truth," Baker argues, and who have the means to package and promote it, will tilt the "marketplace" in their favor. On the receiving end as listeners and decision makers, individuals are constrained by their perceptions of the world around them. These perceptions are vulnerable to distortions owing to the social circumstances in which we find ourselves and to the power differences between groups of people who are competing for attention in the "marketplace." Liberty as a guiding legal idea, according to constitutional theorist Rebecca Brown, means that "the Constitution entitles all citizens to have their interests valued equally with those of all other citizens."[29]

Instead, says Baker, a marketplace-of-ideas approach gives us merely an illusion of open discussion leading to truth, one that overlooks the realities of unequal access to speak:

> Incredible inequalities of opportunity to use the marketplace also
> undermine claims that the robust debate provides a "fair" or otherwise
> justifiable process for regulating the struggle between opposing groups.
> Reliance on the marketplace of ideas appears improperly biased in favor
> of presently dominant groups. These groups have greater access to the

marketplace. In addition, these dominant groups can legally restrict opportunities for subordinate groups to develop patterns of conduct in which new ideas would appear plausible.[30]

According to Baker, this inequality fosters an unhealthy bias for status quo ideas in society. Influential groups tend to want to reinforce existing attitudes and seldom advocate significant change. They are apt to perceive the marketplace for ideas as working just fine, thank you, given that it responds well to those who participate most (them!) and tends to validate the viewpoints that influential groups are bringing to the table.

For Baker, the remedy is to cast a far wider net around expressive activity that deserves legal protection. Standing Meiklejohn's axiom that what is essential is that "everything worth saying shall be said" on its head, Baker asserts that the important thing is that "society deny no one the right to speak."[31] He would protect virtually all expression consistent with values respecting individual autonomy, as long as it doesn't involve harm or coercion. Baker would allow government restraint on just three types of expression: (1) speech involved in the taking of or injury to another's person or property; (2) coercive speech that disrespects and distorts the integrity of someone else's mental processes or autonomy; and (3) speech "not chosen by the speaker," meaning compelled expression that does not reflect the speaker's own legitimate values.[32]

The wider net of Baker's liberty theory avoids arbitrary, subjective distinctions about what kinds of communication are or are not important. Baker refrains from putting higher value on political speech, not because it isn't important but because of the impossibility of drawing clear lines between political and nonpolitical speech. He doesn't care if the information communicated meets someone's subjective estimate of whether or not it's useful or crucial. Speakers and listeners both have constitutional claims, says Baker, and listeners "have a right to demand that government not prohibit the listener from receiving or using otherwise available information."[33]

If the collectivist view is a product of John Stuart Mill's philosophical emphasis on the critical discovery of truth, the individualist perspective is grounded more in a Kantian argument about the paramount importance of personal autonomy and the risk that deceptive or manipulative communication will violate that autonomy.[34] For collectivists, the point of the First

Amendment is to create the conditions through which effective democracy through deliberative self-government can reach its full potential. For individualists, the point of free speech is not to make popular sovereignty work but to honor individual rights and prerogatives that might (but, emphatically, might not) enhance the collective enterprise. In this sense, individualists begin with what Kent Greenawalt calls a "minimal principle of liberty": government should not stop people from doing what they want unless it has a positive reason, and it "should not inhibit communications that pose no legitimate threat of harm."[35] Even so, individualist free speech theorists, no less than collectivists, have to wrestle with different kinds of expression and with hard questions about government limits on speech when potential harm to individuals, cherished institutions, or collective welfare is involved.

RECONCILIATION

Having spent much of this chapter erecting a divide between collectivist and individualist views of free expression, I now backpedal from it a bit, because these two approaches are far from mutually exclusive. It's difficult to imagine that a successful free society can exist without a healthy respect for both individual self-determination and for the collective process of deliberative government. Collectivist and individualist approaches to free speech, therefore, are really two sides of the same coin. I see three ways to reconcile them.

First, think about the notion of *autonomy* as a free speech value. Collectivists reject autonomy as an overly permissive guiding principle, one that fails to account sufficiently for the balance of interests between a speaker's autonomy to be heard and a listener's interest in avoiding harm.[36] The argument on the other side is that collectivists put too little emphasis on the importance of individual expressive interests; as political theorist Joshua Cohen puts it, they "miss the parallels between expressive liberty and liberty of conscience."[37] The result is a narrower view of protected speech than individualists would endorse. Yet these perspectives can be reconciled because neither actually rejects the other's premises. Those who privilege individual autonomy do, nonetheless, accept limits to it when violent or coercive expression comes into play. Those who emphasize the value of speech as an ingredient for effective democracy are sensitive to an individual rights perspective; they also seem to accept that regulation of speech can enhance rather than inevitably restrict autonomy. Indeed, as Robert Post points out, the "competing" values of individual autonomy and democratic self government are actually "inseparable."[38]

Second, the two perspectives are compatible in the sense that both are wary of government regulation of speech. Susan Brison, a philosopher writing about autonomy and free speech, observes that any free speech principle "generates a presumption against restricting speech, even harmful speech."[39] My reading of free speech theory is that this is an accurate account of both the individualist and collectivist perspectives. Although they may differ in the values that drive hard calls on such issues as obscenity and hate speech, they share a bias toward protection. Both favor protecting not just political speech but also artistic and literary expression, as well as private conversation.[40] On the whole, they share a sense that autonomy and democracy are often compatible, occasionally in tension, but rarely in complete opposition to one another.

A final reconciliation comes from the idea that individual autonomy and collective democracy can each be seen as a means to the other. In other words, the tension between free speech's individual value and collective value may be less about whether one is "more important" than the other than about which *precedes* the other. From an individualist perspective, Thomas Emerson describes freedom of expression as an individual's "private right" and as an end in itself. But it's not the only end; Emerson sees free speech also as a "method" for achieving broader social and political goals that shape democratic society.[41] The collectivist reply is that it works the other way around. Individuals fulfill their destiny—reach a state of self-realization—though a system of self-government that the First Amendment is first and foremost designed to encourage and preserve. Autonomy as a first principle is a problem from the collectivist perspective because it makes it hard to distinguish between high- and low-value forms of speech that deserve greater or lesser protection.[42]

I find the individualist argument more persuasive. The problem of inequalities in economic and political strength, which creates inequalities in access to the marketplace of ideas, leaves collectivist values for free speech appealing in theory but troublesome in practice. To be satisfied with a system of free expression based on the collectivist idea is to ignore the inconvenient realities of a power-driven social structure. It also denies the possibility that individuals, rather than institutions, are in the best position to decide what kinds of ideas and expressive acts best serve First Amendment values. The larger point is that a single, general theory of free speech is elusive and unrealistic, given that the many different, complicated ways that expression intersects with the rest of human existence.[43] Neither perspective—individualist or collectivist—offers much of an explanation (or justification) for the very narrow view of rights to expression that we find in the American workplace. In fact, both argue for expanding those rights.

The individualist view argues for freer expression in the workplace through its emphasis on the value of free speech as measured by the pursuit of individual self-fulfillment and self-actualization. Having said this, I hasten to admit that the importance that individualists attach to maintaining autonomy presents some complications. A right to autonomy would, of course, protect a person's right to enter into an employment contract where speech is restricted (for instance, an agreement not to criticize management). Autonomy also applies to listeners, so it might justify corporate prohibitions on religious proselytizing or political propaganda at work, where listeners may be a captive audience.

The collectivist approach to free speech also seems to compel expanded expressive rights in the workplace. One could argue that limits on workplace speech are harmful to effective self-government and therefore degrade the quality of democratic civil society. This is a position that some legal scholars have taken and is one that I will develop later in the Conclusion.[44] Tolerance for free speech on the job has beneficial consequences both for the individual citizen and for the health of the democratic processes that citizenship constructs. Accordingly, both ways of looking at how and why free speech works—the individual and the collective perspective—argue for a more tolerant legal and managerial climate for free speech on and around the job.

SEVEN

Civil Rights and Wrongs

IN DECEMBER 2004, J. Matt Barber of Villa Park, Illinois, a manager at the insurance company Allstate, published an online opinion essay critical of homosexuality. His supervisors later confronted him with the article, told him he was being suspended, escorted him from the building, and fired him a few days later.[1] Barber's piece, "'Intolerance' Will Not Be Tolerated! The Gay Agenda vs. Family Values," appeared on several Web sites, including one called *The Conservative Voice*, which in a tagline described Barber as a contributing editor.[2] Barber's essay critiqued the "destructive nature" of the "homosexual lifestyle," attacked same-sex unions, mocked "adulterous homosexual men," and praised "homosexual recovery organizations" as having helped thousands of people "addicted to homosexual behaviors." The essay concluded with a broadside against gay activists seeking to "quell all criticism of their behavior, force society to accept that behavior, and . . . alter the fabric of society by changing it to correspond with their own morally relative, androgynous notion of marriage."

Claiming he was fired for his own opinion expressed on his own time, Barber filed a lawsuit in federal court charging discrimination based on religion. Allstate's defense was that he was not fired for his opinions but for using company resources on company time for "personal journalism activities" that incidentally identified him as an Allstate employee. The company insisted that it "would not terminate an employee for expressing personal religious or lifestyle views on his or her own time."[3] Barber responded that he did his writing at home but admitted that he sent some personal emails related to it from his company laptop—a policy he said Allstate allowed—and added that he made personal use of his laptop no more than his coworkers did.[4]

Additional details about what happened showed up in a story that appeared in mid-2005 on the conservative news site WorldNetDaily.[5] First,

Barber insisted that he did not intend for his status as an Allstate employee to appear in the biographical description that accompanied some of his online articles; this information, he said, was added without his consent. Second, Barber surmised that his firing was motivated in part by the fact that he had previously filed a sexual harassment retaliation compliant with the Allstate human resources department. Barber believed that an executive had been treating him badly as a result of his earlier report of inappropriate behavior by that executive on an overseas trip. Third, Barber charged that Allstate had a pro-homosexual philosophy featuring mandatory diversity training that really amounted to "indoctrination hostile toward thousands of employees' Christian beliefs." His attorney added that "Allstate aggressively pushes and promotes the homosexual agenda in the name of tolerance, but the minute someone speaks up with what would be considered the traditional moral-values viewpoint, the tolerance disappears and it results in a termination."

Barber's case became a cause célèbre among groups on the "pro-family" religious right, one of which boasted that more than 200,000 of its members sent emails to Allstate demanding that Barber get an apology and his job back.[6] The head of another group, which launched a fund-raising campaign to help Barber's family, said Barber was "bold in proclaiming his faith and taking a stand for what he feels is correct scripturally" and added that "part of the responsibility of the Christian community is to support people that undergo persecution for their faith, whether it's here or in another country."[7] In February 2006, Barber and Allstate settled the lawsuit out of court, with terms not disclosed.[8]

I have described this case at length because it has just about everything: an employee who believes he was fired for private expressive activity unrelated to work; expression that could be construed as religious in nature or political or both; complications involving personal use of company resources for private expression, including an assertion by the employer that that was the real reason for termination; issues related to the publisher of the private speech identifying the employee as affiliated with the firm; allegations that the employee was punished in part as retaliation for earlier harassment charges; charges that the employer was promoting its own political agenda at the expense of employee speech rights; and claims that the employee was being persecuted for his faith. What a stew! No wonder they settled out of court.

Some of the most contested terrain in employee free speech is found at the intersection of expression and civil rights. Employees are protected by civil rights laws against job discrimination based on a variety of personal characteristics. At the federal level, the familiar list of protected categories originally given in Title VII of the Civil Rights Act of 1964 includes race, color, religion, sex, and national origin.[9] Subsequent legislation made it also illegal to engage in employment discrimination based on age (for those over forty) and disability.[10] Civil rights protections in some states go beyond these to include protection against discrimination for such categories as sexual orientation, marital status, ancestry, arrest record, mental disability, or status with respect to public assistance.[11]

The collision between expression and civil rights raises a number of issues, on both sides of the employer-employee divide. Employers, as we saw in earlier chapters, have wide latitude to censor employee speech that they don't like, more so in the private sector than in the public sector (but quite a bit in both). But what if the "speech" is a form of expression tied to one's social identity—identity rooted in one of those legally protected categories such as race, religion, or national origin? In that situation, an employer who acts against the speech incurs legal perils, as Allstate Insurance might have in the Barber situation. On the other hand, what if the employer allows provocative expression and other employees perceive it as insulting or offensive? Or just annoying? There is no law that protects insulting speech on the job and no obligation for employers to tolerate it. Employers are obligated to stop or prevent harassment on the basis of sex, race, religion, and so forth to occur, so it seems like an easy call to silence employee speech that might be experienced as harassing.

But what happens when one person's legitimate expression, based on a legally protected category, is another person's experienced insult, also based on a protected category? As an illustration, imagine a variation on the Allstate case in which the employee speaks not in an off-the-job Web site but in the office hallway or cafeteria. Imagine that it occurs in a state where sexual orientation is a protected category in employment discrimination law, and that a gay employee finds the speech—which the speaker feels is legitimate religious expression—to be harassing. I suspect that many would react to this scenario by saying, okay, let's just shut everyone up; the workplace is for work, and everyone should do their racial-sexual-religious-ethnic expression after work, off the premises.

That response might have superficial appeal in theory, but it's impractical and even immoral in practice. Boundaries between what is "on the job" and what is "off the job" are increasingly muddled. Can I say what's on my (political/religious/ethnic) mind when I'm at happy hour at a local pub with co-workers? Does it matter if we talked over some business before the conversation shifted? What if my off-work opinionated speech makes my office colleagues apprehensive about trusting me, or just makes them uneasy around me? And what if my religion compels me to share the gospel with co-workers? Can I mention it to them in the hall or the cafeteria? Can I put up a devotional symbol or message in my private work space?

The identities of sex, gender, race, religion, and national origin that an employer might wish we could leave at home are intrinsic parts of who we are, not interchangeable swatches of psychological clothing. If the boss says "wear red, not blue," that's manageable. If the boss says "come to the office as a human, not as a Hispanic Catholic female," that's asking an employee to divorce herself from herself before reporting for work. The law won't let the boss fire her just for being Hispanic, Catholic, or female, but there are limits to how far an employer must go to accommodate expressive activity that flows from these protected categories.

In this chapter I will pursue two separate but related aspects of this kind of workplace expression. The first is the issue of *accommodation* of employee speech related to religion, sex, race, and so forth. How much expression of this kind do employers have to tolerate because of the Title VII and First Amendment issues that might come into play? How do legal requirements differ between public- and private-sector workplaces? The law aside, how much should employers tolerate? Much of the action here, as we'll discover shortly, is in the realm of religious expression. The second aspect is the issue of potential *harassment* that can result from this kind of expression. Here I have in mind the employee who is exposed to speech at work as a listener—whether captively, passively, or indirectly. When does someone else's speech at work related to religion, sex, race, and all the rest create (in mild terms) an unacceptable inconvenience or (in severe terms) a hostile work environment, one that may rise to a legal matter of harassment and discrimination?

These are difficult questions. A lot of expressive activity that gives employers headaches, and that gives employers' lawyers billable hours, is speech that spills into the hot-button intersection between work and civil rights. Avoiding discrimination and harassment are obviously worthy goals, and it's a tightrope one often must walk between harassing speech and free speech. The problem comes when understandably nervous employers listen too closely to understandably cautious lawyers and end up killing free speech, not just discrimination. It's easy to use the problem of discrimination to justify repression of free speech; it's a lot harder to figure out how to keep a workplace both free and fair.

ACCOMMODATING EXPRESSION (RELIGIOUS AND OTHERWISE)

The majority of complaints of employment discrimination protected by civil rights laws are related to the categories of race and sex. In 2005, race (35 percent) and sex (31 percent) were involved in about two-thirds of all employment discrimination charges filed with the federal Equal Employment Opportunity Commission (EEOC), followed by age (22 percent), disability (20 percent), and national origin (11 percent). Religion accounted for only about 3 percent of discrimination filings. The trends in complaints over a period of several years are revealing. In 2005 the total number of charges filed with EEOC for *any* reason was almost 14 percent lower than in 1995, with noticeable declines in complaint volume for race, sex, age, and disability. Two categories showed increases: the EEOC took in 48 percent more complaints about religious discrimination and more about national origin in 2005 than it did in 1995.[12]

Although religion doesn't account for a large proportion of formal discrimination complaints, it is the category that presents the thorniest problems for issues of expression at work. Perhaps that's because religion (unlike sex or race or national origin) is a basic activity given explicit attention and protection in the First Amendment. Also, religion, unlike gender or race, is inherently about communication: efforts to convert people across gender lines are, to say the least, difficult, and efforts across racial lines are silly. And let's not forget that America is a highly religious country. A recent poll finds that over 90 percent of Americans believe in God or a universal spirit; almost 60 percent say religion is very important or extremely important in their daily lives; over half of Americans attend religious services at least monthly and say they read the Bible, Torah, Koran, or other sacred text at least a few times a month; more than four in ten believe the Bible is the actual word of God and should be taken literally; and almost half think that people with strong religious beliefs are discriminated against in the United States.[13] Almost one-third of Americans think there is too little religious freedom in the workplace.[14]

But the main reason religion raises some of the trickiest workplace speech issues is that religion on the job is by definition expressive. A person's religion is rooted in something we can't see or hear or feel—a belief that has no part in a social encounter unless the believer chooses to make it a part. And that requires expression, so the only way religion enters the workplace is when an individual elects to open for others a perceptual window into their religious beliefs. That can occur through words spoken, clothes or symbols worn, or perhaps items used to decorate a physical workspace.

Many difficult situations involving religious expression in the workplace involve grooming or clothing mandated by religious observance, such as facial hair (beards) or head coverings worn by Muslims and Sikhs. Employers will sometimes resist accommodating these forms of religious expression by arguing that a legitimate business interest is behind a prohibition. Courts have agreed, for example, that being clean-shaven can be a legitimate occupational qualification in some food service jobs.[15] In the past few years, New York's Metropolitan Transit Authority (MTA) has found itself embroiled in a series of legal battles with Muslim and Sikh workers over religious head coverings on the job. MTA has been charged with discrimination for forcing bus drivers to wear MTA caps over their hijabs (head scarves) and for requiring Sikhs to wear a blue-and-white MTA logo on their turbans.[16] The Sikhs who filed a complaint see the logo requirement as sacrilegious and contend that co-workers wearing yarmulkes and Yankee baseball caps were not asked to do likewise.

How cases like these will turn out is hard to predict (the MTA complaints are still pending) because the law constructs a subjective and fluid balance between an individual's right to religious expression and an employer's right to run its operations efficiently and harmoniously. An attempt to capture the law in a nutshell would look something like this: employers have to let workers engage in religious expression unless it's too inconvenient, in which case they don't. As usual, the real meaning of what's allowed and not allowed legally doesn't lend itself to a nutshell summary, so a closer look is in order. As usual, there are federal rules but some variation in the states. As usual, there are differences in how it all plays out in public-versus private-sector employment. These complications aren't a sinister force—complexities and contingencies are an inescapable fact of life in litigation—but they have a chilling effect. If workers can't determine whether expression will have a significant cost, they'll stay silent. If employers can't easily figure out which expression will get them into legal trouble, they'll overregulate. And when workers do express themselves and employers object, everyone will spend time and money in a courtroom.

Let's imagine that an employee working as a retail clerk in a store insists on wearing, say, an eyebrow piercing because she's a member of the "Church of Facial Adornment," and the piercing is an established religious symbol for the group. The employer, who prefers that store clerks not wear this sort of jewelry as part of presenting a professional appearance, points to a "no facial jewelry" policy in the employee handbook, and insists that the employee lose the eyebrow ring during work hours. The employee argues that this is religious discrimination in violation of Title VII and tells her boss that unless the store accommodates her wish to wear the jewelry, she'll get a lawyer and sue. The boss tells her she can cover the jewelry during work hours, but she insists that she be allowed to leave it as is, uncovered. Does she have a case? Is this protected religious expression?

The federal employment discrimination law known as Title VII says that an employer cannot discriminate based on religion—which means religious belief or practice—unless the employer can show that "he is unable to *reasonably accommodate*" the employee's observance "without *undue hardship* on the conduct of the employer's business."[17] So how much accommodation is reasonable? And how little hardship gives the employer an out?

The U.S. Supreme Court tackled these questions in a 1977 case involving airline worker Larry Hardison, who wanted Saturdays off to observe the Sabbath. Hardison worked for (now defunct) TWA in a department that operated 24-7, and the airline would have had to violate a union sen-iority system to accommodate his scheduling preference. With no one else to fill the Saturday slot, TWA eventually fired Hardison for not showing up for his assigned shift. Hardison's lawsuit charging religious discrimination under Title VII focused specifically on the issue of reasonable accommoda-tion. The Supreme Court ruled that the airline, by meeting with Hardison to try to find a solution, by agreeing to let him have special religious holi-days off, and by authorizing a union steward to try to arrange a swap of shifts, had gone far enough. The critical sentence in the decision was this: "To require TWA to bear more than a *de minimis* cost in order to give Hardison Saturdays off is an undue hardship."[18] In other words, it's an undue hardship on the employer if the company has to incur more than a minimal or trivial cost. That's a pretty low standard.

So where does that leave our eyebrow-pierced store clerk? Unemployed. Or so a federal appeals court decided in the 2004 case of one Kimberly Cloutier, an employee at a Costco in West Springfield, Massachusetts.[19] Cloutier had several facial piercings and described herself as a member of the Church of Body Modification.[20] After much back and forth, Costco told her she could cover the jewelry while at work with skin-tone-matching bandages. The court found this to be a reasonable accommodation on Costco's part, akin to wearing a shirt to cover a tattoo. It also said that the accommodation Cloutier wanted—a blanket exemption from the facial jewelry policy—would cause Costco to lose control of its public image, so would impose an undue hardship on the company.

It's hard to read about *Cloutier v. Costco* without at least entertaining some questions: So this is a church? Body modification is religious expression that gets First Amendment protection? The court sidestepped this issue by reasoning that since Costco's accommodation was adequate, it doesn't really matter whether Cloutier was expressing "real" religious beliefs or not. Still, the judge who heard the case in federal district court did take time out to acknowledge how thorny these issues can be:

> This decision is not intended in any way to offer an opinion on the sub-stance or validity of the belief system of the Church of Body Modific-ation. While its tenets may be viewed by some as unconventional, or even bizarre, the respect afforded by our laws to individual conscience,

particularly in regard to religious beliefs, puts any deconstruction of the Church's doctrine beyond the purview of the court.[21]

Figuring out whether bona fide religious belief is behind religious expression is a multilayered question. First, is the belief a *religious* belief? The Supreme Court during the Vietnam War addressed this question, outside the context of employment, in a couple of cases about conscientious objector status in the military. In one of these cases, the court interpreted religious belief to

> embrace all religions and to exclude essentially political, sociological, or philosophical views. . . . The test of belief "in a relation to a Supreme Being" is whether a given belief that is sincere and meaningful occupies a place in the life of its possessor parallel to that filled by the orthodox belief in God.[22]

A second case expanded eligibility for conscientious objector status to those whose objections were moral or ethical rather than explicitly religious.[23] Based on these cases, federal EEOC regulations created guidelines for employers by defining "religious practices" as including

> moral or ethical beliefs as to what is right and wrong which are sincerely held with the strength of traditional religious views. . . . The fact that no religious group espouses such beliefs or the fact that the religious group to which the individual professes to belong may not accept such belief will not determine whether the belief is a religious belief of the employee or prospective employee.[24]

Second, does it matter how committed the individual is to their religious belief? This question was at the heart of the case of an Indiana foundry worker named Eddie Thomas, who objected to being transferred from a job making sheet steel to a department making turrets for military tanks. Claiming that his religious beliefs as a Jehovah's Witness prevented him from participating directly in production of weapons, Thomas quit his job; the court case that followed was about eligibility for unemployment benefits. At a hearing he said he was okay with the earlier job, producing steel that might later be used to manufacture armaments, but not with working in the direct manufacture of arms.

Thomas lost his case in the Indiana Supreme Court, which questioned whether the nature and underlying basis of his religious belief was sufficiently clear. "A personal philosophical choice rather than a religious choice," said the court, "does not rise to the level of a first amendment claim of religious expression."[25] But the U.S. Supreme Court saw it differently, rejecting not only the Indiana court's conclusion about Thomas's religious beliefs but also the very idea of a court trying to weigh its validity. Deciding whether something qualifies as "religion," said the Court,

> is not to turn upon a judicial perception of the particular belief or practice in question; religious beliefs need not be acceptable, logical, consistent, or comprehensible to others in order to merit First Amendment protection. . . . Courts should not undertake to dissect religious beliefs because the believer admits that he is "struggling" with his position or because his beliefs are not articulated with the clarity and precision that a more sophisticated person might employ.[26]

The Court also cautioned against weighing an individual's religious beliefs or practices against those of others. In Thomas's case, there was evidence of a Jehovah's Witness co-worker who had no qualms about working on tank turrets, and apparently the Indiana court thought this was important. But courts should not try to figure out whose version of religious doctrine is better or more correct, said the U.S. Supreme Court, because courts "are not arbiters of scriptural interpretation."[27]

Should we read from this decision that anything goes when it comes to religious expression at work that potentially qualifies for First Amendment protection? The Court in *Thomas* said no: "One can, of course, imagine an asserted claim so bizarre, so clearly nonreligious in motivation, as not to be entitled to protection."[28] It didn't venture a definition of "so bizarre" that might guide us in the future. A federal judge in Florida apparently knew bizarre when he saw it, dismissing a man's claim that he suffered discrimination at work for his "personal religious creed" that Kozy Kitten Cat Food "is contributing significantly to his state of well being" and to his "overall work performance."[29] The man's religious devotion to cat food, said the judge, is merely a personal preference that falls outside the protection of Title VII or the Constitution. In a case in the early 1990s that did not involve employment, the Supreme Court had the opportunity to assert that a religion involving animal sacrifice as an integral part of worship is neither bizarre nor incredible.[30] I am unaware of cases involving animal sacrifice in the workplace.[31]

RELIGION IN GOVERNMENT EMPLOYMENT

Religious expression takes on added significance—with added complications—when it occurs in a public-sector workplace. Religion, unlike sex, race, or national origin, gets it own explicit treatment in the First Amendment. Recall from Chapter 2 that government employers are by definition state actors so are bound to follow the Constitution and respect the First Amendment rights of employees. The First Amendment's treatment of religion has two facets. First, the *free-exercise clause* protects an employee's right to religious exercise, including expression, free from interference by a government employer. Second, the *establishment clause* means government employers must avoid letting religious speech or observance in the workplace convey any kind of official endorsement of a religious viewpoint. These two principles can easily collide when a government employee's own religious expression happens to look to outsiders like an official position espoused by the government entity or agency that employs him.

The case of George Daniels, a police officer in Arlington, Texas, is illustrative. Daniels was fired because he wouldn't remove a gold cross pin (symbolizing his commitment to evangelical Christianity) from his uniform, in violation of a department policy. Daniels rejected three possible accommodations offered by the department: wearing a ring or bracelet instead; wearing the pin under his shirt or collar; or transferring to a non-uniformed position. He lost his federal lawsuit when an appeals court ruled that a police department doesn't offend the First Amendment by refusing to allow individually chosen uniform adornments, even religious ones.[32]

If this were a private-sector job—let's say he was a security guard instead of a police officer—the outcome could be the same, but the reasoning behind it would be different. A private employer could, for example, prohibit religious symbols on the company uniform to avoid giving the impression that the business is associated with a particular religious viewpoint. If our hypothetical security guard challenges that rule as discrimination based on religion, the employer's ability to win in court will turn on its ability to show that accommodating the employee's religious expression involves costs that impose an "undue hardship" on the business.

For a public employer, it's not just a matter of showing "undue hardship"; the establishment clause of the First Amendment is also in play. In the case of George Daniels (the actual police officer, not the hypothetical private security guard), the court worried that an officer's private religious expression displayed on duty might give rise to impermissible government establishment of religion: "Visibly wearing a cross pin—religious speech that receives great protection in civilian life—takes on an entirely different cast when viewed in the context of a police uniform."[33] A private employer might prefer not to give outsiders the impression that the firm is connected to some religious viewpoint, but a government agency *must* not give that impression.

In situations involving religious expression by employees in public-sector jobs there is one further wrinkle. Recall from Chapter 4 that for people in government jobs, a key legal test for protection of employee speech is whether a message is on a matter of "public concern," as opposed to private self-interested expression.[34] For example, a city employee who voices concerns about the municipal budget at a city council meeting is engaged in protected speech on a matter of public concern. But when that same worker speaks out to complain about, say, her recent subpar performance appraisal, her complaint is unprotected speech addressing a personal workplace grievance. Speech on matters of public concern is protected unless an employer can show that the expressive behavior significantly disrupts workplace efficiency or harmony or otherwise interferes with the agency's ability to perform its mission. So what about the symbolic display of religious belief? Is that a form of speech on a matter of public concern? Or just private, self-interested expression?

This question has been answered in different ways in different situations. In George Daniels's case (the Texas police officer with the cross on his uniform), a federal appeals court acknowledged that religious conviction is "a matter of great concern" to many people, but it also felt that the symbolic display of religious beliefs is "intensely personal in nature." The court concluded that "it simply is not a matter of 'public concern' as that term of art has been used in the constitutional sense."[35] A different court reached the opposite conclusion in the case of Monte Tucker, a computer analyst in California's state education department and a devout Christian. Tucker's lawsuit challenged an agency rule that said employees cannot display any religious materials outside their own closed offices or cubicles and cannot engage in any religious advocacy during work hours or in the workplace. Reasoning that public-concern speech means expression on just about anything other than internal workplace power struggles, the court here rejected the notion that speech about religion is not speech on a matter of public concern.[36]

Even when speech by a public employee is on a matter of public concern, it still loses its protection if the employer can show that it is excessively disruptive to the government agency's mission or operation. As we saw in Chapter 4, employers have tried to make many kinds of arguments—sometimes successfully, sometimes not—about how worker speech puts mission and performance at risk. Speech that is religious brings the unique risk that the employee's expression will be construed as inappropriate endorsement of religion by the agency. In Monte Tucker's case, the court acknowledged this concern but decided that the rules about religious speech were simply too sweeping a way to deal with it:

> There is a legitimate state interest in preventing displays of religious
> objects that might suggest state endorsement of religion. The state has
> a legitimate interest, for example, in preventing the posting of Crosses
> or Stars of David in the main hallways, by the elevators, or in the
> lobbies, and in other locations throughout its buildings. . . . However,
> banning the posting of all religious materials and information in all
> areas of an office building except in employees' private cubicles simply
> goes too far.[37]

A government agency should avoid the appearance of supporting religion, said the court; it just needs rules that are more narrowly devised to accomplish that, rather than broad prohibitions on employee speech that happens to be religious in nature. Monte Tucker had a job that did not involve meeting the public in his office, so the display of religious symbols in his office raised no establishment-clause problem. In a later case involving a state social worker who did meet routinely with clients in his office, the same appeals court found it entirely reasonable for the employer to stop him from keeping a Bible on his desk or decorating his office with faith-related items.[38]

It's one thing to display prominent religious symbols in a government

office where clients can see them, but what about situations where employees informally converse about matters of faith with recipients of government services? An example is the case of Jo Anne Knight, a nurse consultant for the Connecticut Department of Public Health. During a home visit
with a patient in the end stages of AIDS, Knight shared with the man and
his same-sex partner her religious beliefs about homosexuality and artlessly
remarked that "although God created us and loves us, He doesn't like the
homosexual lifestyle." A complaint filed with the health department by the
two men led to Knight's being suspended for misconduct. In a lawsuit challenging her punishment, Knight claimed violations of rights to both free
speech and free exercise of religion. She lost her case in a federal appeals
court, which arrived at the sensible conclusion that promoting a religious
message while working with a client on state business raises genuine establishment-clause concerns and makes it hard for the state to provide services
in a way that is neutral toward religion.[39]

Situations involving religious expression in the public-sector workplace are,
at the end of the day, about an unavoidable collision between two ideas that
emerge from the same sentence in the First Amendment: the individual's
right to freely exercise religious belief without government interference
and the government's need to preserve religious neutrality in delivering
public services. Government employers have often prevailed in employee
speech cases, as I explained in Chapter 4, because courts are often sympathetic to arguments that employee speech is disruptive to the agency's mission or efficiency. For religious speech, the establishment clause of the First
Amendment elevates the bar that employee speech has to clear to be protected: it must not only not be disruptive but also must not give the appearance that the agency is favoring or promoting some religious viewpoint.
The state's interest in avoiding establishment-clause violations is "compelling," the Supreme Court has said, and can justify discrimination against
speech on the basis of its religious content.[40]

Here courts have also frequently come down on the side of employers,
assuming that an establishment-clause concern about government endorsement of religion trumps a government employee's right to free exercise of
religion on the job. Sometimes, however, judges do stop employers from
going too far, as in the case of the Kentucky public library that banned its

employees from wearing any "clothing or ornament depicting religious, political, or potentially offensive decoration." A woman fired for wearing a cross pendant in violation of the policy won her lawsuit when a federal court decided that her approach to accessorizing "could not be interpreted by a reasonable observer as governmental endorsement of religion."[41]

Overall, though, there is arguably more freedom of religious expression in the private-sector workplace than in government jobs. At a private place of employment where religious expression makes others uncomfortable, an employer has various options short of silencing the speech to accommodate both the rights of the speaker and the sensitivities of the listener. But when religious expression occurs in a government workplace and appears to implicate government as favoring or endorsing the message, there may be no option other than to prohibit the speech altogether.[42] So although private employees generally have less free speech protection than public employees (as we saw in Chapters 4 and 5), they may have more protection for *religious* speech than government employees. From the perspective of principles of secular democracy and the separation of church and state, more protection might not be a bad thing.

TIGHTENING THE ACCOMMODATION STANDARD: WRFA

Some religious groups have long been concerned that the "reasonable accommodation" and "undue hardship" standards make it too easy for employers to get away with quashing employee religious expression. For three decades the federal courts have stuck with the principle that accommodating religious expression poses an undue hardship for the employer if it involves more than a *minimal* cost to the firm. Some states have laws erecting a higher hardship bar for employers to clear to deny a worker's religious speech rights claim. One that does is New York, where the human rights law, like federal law, gives employers an out if accommodating religious expression causes "undue hardship." But New York's law defines that term explicitly as "an accommodation requiring *significant expense or difficulty* (including a significant interference with the safe or efficient operation of the workplace or a violation of a bona fide seniority system)."[43] It also lists factors that go into a determination of hardship for the employer, including financial costs, the number of workers affected, and difficulties associated with a geographically spread out workplace.

For several years, a coalition of religious organizations in the United States has been pushing for a change to federal law to accomplish nationally what states like New York have done locally. This effort has taken the form of a proposed bill in Congress that would define undue hardship the same way New York does—as a "significant expense or difficulty."[44] The Workplace Religious Freedom Act of 2005 (WRFA), which at this writing awaits congressional action, enjoyed sponsorship from both parties in both the Senate and the House. (How often do you find Senators Orrin Hatch, Sam Brownback, Hillary Clinton, Charles Schumer, and John Kerry all on the same side of a social issue?)

The elevated undue hardship standard in WRFA would be far more protective of employee rights to religious expression than the federal government's current de minimis (minimal cost) approach. In fact, the proposed higher standard for accommodating *religion* would match what federal law already requires of employers in cases of *disability*. The Americans with Disabilities Act of 1990 (ADA) says employers must reasonably accommodate a worker's disability unless doing so requires "significant difficulty or expense."[45] In a sense, then, those seeking to raise the bar for an employer's "undue hardship" in coping with religious expression at work believe that religion deserves the same level of accommodation as disability.

There is a potentially serious problem here. ADA confers on the disabled a legal right (to substantial workplace accommodation) that is not available to the nondisabled. This accommodation seems reasonable; there is nothing in the Constitution that says we can't make special provisions in the law for those with physical or other disabilities. But religion is different. It is well established under the First Amendment that government cannot favor religion over nonreligion. The higher undue hardship standard for employers in WRFA would, in a sense, create a special right at work for those with a religious viewpoint or message and as a result may raise constitutional problems and invite a plausible court challenge.[46]

Serious reservations about WRFA have also been expressed by business and civil liberties groups (also not traditional political bedfellows). The U.S. Chamber of Commerce, a national lobby for business interests, worries that the new standard for undue hardship would force employers to impose the religious views of employees on customers and would hamper firms' ability to maintain a work environment free from religious harassment.[47] The American Civil Liberties Union (ACLU) cautions that the WRFA standard would lead to "radically different analyses" of religious accommodation requests, forcing employers to allow excessive and inappropriate religious observance on the job. The ACLU cites the examples of a police officer who might refuse to protect an abortion clinic on religious grounds or a social worker who wishes to use Bible readings instead of secular therapy in prison inmate counseling. Most religious observance cases that now reach the courts involve people seeking time off for religious holidays or accommodation for religious clothing or hairstyles, the ACLU contends, so a better approach would be a narrow bill that addresses just these particular circumstances.[48] The possibility that people of religious faith in public-service jobs could escape critical responsibilities behind a shield of religious observance is deeply troubling and should give supporters of WRFA serious pause.

FREE SPEECH + HARASSMENT = COLLISION

The focus in this chapter has been on when and how employers should accommodate expressive behavior that is somehow related to protected categories in civil rights law: religion, race, sex, national origin, and so on. Most of my examples have been about religion, because religion is the one area of expressive content that is singled out for special protection in the First Amendment and for rules about workplace accommodation in federal and state employment law.

But there is more to employee speech on these kinds of topics than just questions of tolerance and accommodation. Employers are also obligated (legally and morally) to maintain a workplace that is free of harassment. More than twenty years ago, the U.S. Supreme Court made it clear that sex discrimination under federal law exists when unwanted behavior of a sexual nature is offensive or intimidating enough to create a "hostile work environment."[49] Determining that a hostile work environment is present involves weighing various factors having to do with the nature of the offending behavior and its consequences. In an important (and unanimous) 1993 Supreme Court ruling that clarified the standard for a hostile environment, Justice Sandra Day O'Connor listed factors to be examined in a particular situation:

These may include the frequency of the discriminatory conduct; its severity; whether it is physically threatening or humiliating, or a mere offensive utterance; and whether it unreasonably interferes with an employee's work performance. The effect on the employee's psychological well-being is, of course, relevant to determining whether the plaintiff actually found the environment abusive. But while psychological harm, like any other relevant factor, may be taken into account, no single factor is required.[50]

Although the notion of a hostile work environment began as a form of sexual harassment, it also applies to harassment and discrimination based on race, religion, and national origin. Through a principle called "vicarious employer liability," employers are responsible when harassment is committed by someone who occupies a supervisory role.[51] Even if the harasser is not a supervisor, the employer can be held responsible if the improper behavior was foreseeable or was previously brought to the employer's attention but not responded to appropriately.

The problem, from a free speech perspective, is that the genesis of a hostile work environment is typically found in expressive behavior. A workplace that someone experiences as "abusive" in some sexual, racial, ethnic, or religious sense most likely got that way because of the utterances or communications of others. If a judge or a jury or, for that matter, a human resources department, thinks that speech is severe enough to create a hostile work environment based on sex, race, religion, national origin, or some other protected category, then there is harassment. This inevitable collision between speech and harassment has catalyzed a lively debate among legal scholars about whether the law on a hostile work environment amounts to a basic and unacceptable infringement on free speech rights.

On one side of the debate are those who believe that by regulating in rather nonspecific terms a "hostile work environment," harassment law muzzles free speech in the workplace to an extent that offends the First Amendment.[52] The goal of creating a workplace free of discrimination is generally a reasonable one for those who take this view. Their concern is that the vagueness of what is or isn't harassment has a chilling effect on expression. Employers' fear of being accused of harassment results in the silencing of speech that really is harassing as well as speech that isn't. Moreover, with employers in many situations themselves liable for employee speech, they have no choice but to overregulate the expressive activity of those who work for them. Law professor Eugene Volokh, a leading critic of harassment law as a threat to free speech, complains that hostile-environment law "burdens any workplace speech that's offensive to at least one person in the workplace" based on that person's race, religion, sex, or other protected category, even when the speech is "not severe or pervasive enough to itself be actionable."[53]

In rare cases, those accused of harassment have mounted an argument that the First Amendment protects the speech that is said to have created a hostile work environment. A well-known case involved a woman named Lois Robinson, a welder at a Florida shipyard who sued her employer after experiencing pervasive harassment over a period of several years perpetrated by male co-workers and supervisors in the form of posted photos of nude women, derogatory and sexual remarks, obscene graffiti, and other indignities. The federal judge who heard Robinson's case rejected free speech arguments on several grounds, perhaps the most important of which is the basic conclusion that "pictures and verbal harassment are not protected speech because they act as discriminatory conduct."[54]

This decision seems like a fair weighing of the balance between speech and harassment given the outrageous pattern of abuse that the shipyard had forced Robinson to endure for years. I am, however, sympathetic to critics who think the court in this case went overboard in crafting part of the remedy. The judge's final injunction approving the company's new harassment policy mentioned these activities as violations:

> Displaying pictures, posters, calendars, graffiti, objects, promotional materials, reading materials, or other materials that are sexually suggestive, sexually demeaning, or pornographic, or bringing into the JSI work environment or possessing any such material to read, display or view at work. . . . Reading or otherwise publicizing in the work environment materials that are in any way sexually revealing, sexually suggestive, sexually demeaning or pornographic.[55]

The judge's order defined a picture as "sexually suggestive" if it showed a person "not fully clothed" or "posed for the obvious purpose of displaying or drawing attention to private portions of his or her body." The problem here, law professor David Bernstein argues with only a touch of hyperbole, is that it seems to bar employees from reading a Danielle Steele novel or an issue of *Cosmopolitan* on their lunch break, or from listening to Eminem or Britney Spears on a portable music player.[56]

Lois Robinson's case was an extreme one in the sense that the harassment was undeniably severe and pervasive. Critics of hostile-environment law as a threat to free speech like to point to tamer examples, such as complaints about the presence in the workplace of a piece of public art with mildly sexual content or the posting in a work area of a *New Yorker* cartoon or a photo on someone's desk of his spouse in a bathing suit.[57]

These critics also suggest that the problem with free speech and harassment is just as compelling in private-sector employment as it is in the government workplace. The argument goes something like this: Yes, there is ordinarily no state action in a private workplace, which for the most part (as we saw in Chapter 2) can regulate employee speech as it sees fit. However, with harassment law there is a kind of state action because the government, through its hostile-environment regulations, is forcing the private employer to regulate certain forms of speech (the potentially harassing kind). As a result, the state is acting, so the restrictions on employee speech that result from those regulations—even in the private sector—are open to First Amendment scrutiny. At least that's the argument.[58] I am unaware of a court that has yet bought into it.

Some have proposed remedies for the free speech–harassment collision designed to separate speech that is truly harassing from speech that might be offensive to some but is not aimed specifically at harming or humiliating a single individual. Eugene Volokh would create two categories of speech: "directed speech" aimed at a *single individual* on account of her identity (race, sex, religion, and so forth) and "undirected speech" that is intended to communicate to other employees *generally* and perhaps is merely overheard or incidentally heard by the offended person.[59] He contends that the goal of workplace equality is sufficiently advanced by restricting only directed speech—expression that the speaker knows to be offensive and directs toward someone else because of that person's protected status (race, sex, and so forth). He would not place restrictions on undirected speech, even if offensive, bigoted, or pornographic. Volokh believes that his approach eliminates the worst speech that insults or harasses co-workers but preserves rights to expression that may be provocative but isn't necessarily harmful:

> It protects employees from offensive messages without preventing the speakers from getting their messages across to other employees. If a speaker wants to convince his coworkers that women should stay in the home, or that Catholic politicians are not to be trusted, he may still do so. The proposed standard would only prevent him from targeting his speech at a coworker who will likely be offended by it, and this coworker is in any event unlikely to be convinced by the offensive speech.[60]

Law professor Jeffrey Rosen proposes a variation on this theme: do away with the hostile-environment doctrine and let people who are harassed at work by way of directly harassing speech and improper sexual behavior sue offenders under invasion-of-privacy laws. This option, he argues, would let people take action against harassment intended to harm and humiliate but would weed out the "trivial indignities" of workplace speech and conduct that employers and courts spend a lot of time and effort sorting through.[61] These are intriguing suggestions that would, if implemented, ease the tension between free speech and harassment and loosen up restrictions, both legal and managerial, on speech that goes on at work. These are worthy objectives but are not without difficulties.

Consider, for instance, the case of Richard Peterson, a Hewlett-Packard (HP) employee and self-described devout Christian who objected to the company's workforce diversity initiatives. Believing he had a duty "to expose evil when confronted with sin," Peterson started displaying in his cubicle (visible to co-workers and customers) large posters with scriptural passages that could be interpreted as condemnations of homosexuality, including the well-worn "abomination" passage from Leviticus. Asked by his managers to cease and desist, Peterson told them that he viewed HP's diversity campaign as intended to target heterosexual and fundamentalist Christian employees. He was ultimately fired when he refused to remove the posters, and unsuccessfully sued HP in federal court to get his job back. Recognizing that this kind of nondirected speech can nonetheless create an intimidating and hostile environment, the appeals court said the company has no obligation to allow an employee to post messages intended to demean and harass co-workers.[62]

The suggestions made by Volokh and Rosen for solving the collision between harassment law and free speech seem to assume that when expression of a sexual, racial, or religious nature is not directed with harmful intent at a particular individual, it runs little risk of creating an intimidating, abusive, or discriminatory workplace for others. Presumably Volokh and Rosen would say that messages like Richard Peterson's at HP are the kind that should be frowned upon but not acted upon legally by an offended co-worker. Weeding out trivial slights from the realm of actionable harassment is a worthwhile goal, but the line between merely annoying and harmfully harassing is not an easy one to draw.

On the other side of this argument are legal scholars who say that the conflict between harassment law and the First Amendment is overblown. Although conceding that some employers may be overly cautious and restrict speech that isn't harassing, they say that harassment regulations, given their structure and established procedures, don't require such cautiousness because the standard for a hostile environment is not as vague as critics contend. Suzanne Sangree points to several factors that make it unlikely that the hostile-environment doctrine will snare innocent employers and innocent speech:[63] First, employers cannot be held liable for harassment unless they had notice and refused to take remedial action, so employers are unlikely to be caught unaware. Second, a key element of harassment law is the requirement that the offending speech or behavior is "unwelcome," which draws a boundary around a limited sphere of expression and puts a burden on the victim to communicate the fact that it's unwelcome.

Sangree rejects the notion that employers will overregulate to avoid liability, limiting core political speech that would be otherwise protected. She argues that speech that has an intent to undermine equity in the workplace by discriminating is not protected speech and that this is the kind of speech that hostile-environment regulation is likely to curtail. She does concede, though, that a net thrown around speech creating a hostile environment will inevitably have some holes in it:

> Admittedly, some speech, which is arguably political, such as messages of the inferiority of women, which does not rise to the level of harassment, and which is not expressed in the form of low-value speech, will

inevitably be chilled by risk-averse employers. The extent of this chilling, however, is not substantial.[64]

Sangree also argues that market forces will help keep companies from over-regulating speech, because overregulation would undermine morale to the economic detriment of the firm. Overall, she says, the danger that harassment rules and policies will chill protected speech "is vastly outweighed by the invidious discrimination prohibited by hostile environment law."[65]

Perhaps courts are capable of drawing a distinction between speech that is merely offensive to someone and speech that is truly harassing. A recent example is found in a case involving the television comedy series *Friends*. A writer's assistant on the show, Amaani Lyle, filed a lawsuit charging that writers' use of sexually course and vulgar language, including discussions of their own sexual experiences, amounted to harassment based on sex under California law. The California Supreme Court denied her claim, finding that harassment law does not outlaw "sexually course and vulgar language or conduct that merely offends."[66] Noting that the offensive speech was generally not directed at Lyle, the court said that nondirected speech can harass but "is less offensive and severe than conduct that is directed" at an individual.[67]

The *Friends* case outcome calls to mind Eugene Volokh's argument that distinguishing between directed and nondirected speech is a way to resolve the conflict between harassment and free speech. But others reject this distinction as a way to salvage harassment law while keeping the spirit of the First Amendment intact. The problem, says law professor Mary Becker, is that harm can result whether the speech is directed at an individual or spread to multiple listeners. "A few mild directed remarks would be much less harmful than pervasive non-directed hostile or abusive speech," writes Becker, and "both can be used to make women feel they are not welcome in the workplace."[68] She also argues that the line between directed and nondirected speech would be difficult in practice to define. If someone posts something generally offensive that targets a group to which you belong near your cubicle, is that directed or nondirected speech?

A good way to crystallize the two sides of this debate over harassment and free speech is through the lens of one particular underlying issue: what lawyers call the "captive-audience doctrine." When the court in the case of Lois Robinson (the shipyard worker) found that her co-workers' expression created a hostile environment, it relied in part on the idea that government can regulate speech to protect the rights of others who are captive listeners, unable to easily escape the message. "The free speech guarantee admits great latitude in protecting captive audiences from offensive speech," the court said.[69]

Those, like Eugene Volokh, who see harassment law as a threat to free speech, think the court in *Robinson* got it wrong; they argue that the captive-audience doctrine is meant to apply to people in their homes. (The Supreme Court, in a landmark case about Federal Communications Commission [FCC] rules regulating vulgar radio broadcasts, said the home is a place where one's "right to be left alone plainly outweighs the First Amendment rights of an intruder.")[70] Volokh contends that if captivity means an inability to avoid offensive speech, then we are all captive every day, and people at work, like people everywhere else, frequently have options to avoid hearing or seeing offensive messages (although not always). In public one cannot avoid insults altogether, he says, and the same is true in the workplace.[71]

Those on the other side of the issue question whether it's really so easy for employees to escape harassing speech, given the reality of power dynamics in the modern workplace. Law professor Jack Balkin puts it this way:

> Few audiences are more captive than the average worker. It is true, in theory, that one does not have to be subjected to racist or sexist speech on the job—one can simply shield one's eyes or ears, or failing that, one can decide not to show up for work anymore. But this will mean that one's employment also will end.[72]

In other words, employee interests are inescapably trumped by the need to have and hold a job. Employment, as Balkin puts it, is "yoked together with the hostile work environment," so the argument that one can avoid insulting or distasteful speech without consequences is unconvincing.

In the final analysis, this is a debate in which both sides have a point, but in which both sides also seem to exaggerate the persuasive force of that point. Does the law protecting people from a hostile work environment infringe on free speech in the workplace? Sure it does, because hostile environments are often a result of expressive activity. Do some employers overcompensate by creating rules and norms that chill some speech that doesn't really create a hostile environment? No doubt, although that may be more a product of faulty (if well-intentioned) legal advice than legitimate prudence. Are employees a captive audience deserving protection from abusive expression? Often yes, but we needn't assume that people are incapable of telling the difference between the annoying and the abusive.

The greatest impact on freedom of expression in the workplace comes not from how courts decipher the conflict between harassment and speech but from how employers do. Matters involving employee speech end up in court when managers make decisions that lead employees to hire attorneys and file lawsuits. But for every time that happens, there are no doubt countless occasions where managers make decisions and set policies that do not incite conflicts and lawsuits. The choices that managers make about the kind of workplace culture for expression they would like to foster, and about the steps they are willing to take to protect expression and civil rights in the workplace, will determine how much speech occurs and how much is chilled. Given a faith-at-work movement that some see as a significant shift in the boundary between religion and business, these choices are especially prominent (and difficult) in the area of religious expression.[73]

Civil rights laws that safeguard workers from discrimination on the job have defined a major battleground for the exercise of free speech at work. These laws can be an important source of protection against workplace injustice, but their power to remedy those injustices is diluted by the presence of the basic employment-at-will rule. With no requirement that there be a legitimate cause for discipline or dismissal, clever employers can find ways to punish workers for who they are or what they say without risking serious legal consequences. A simpler strategy, though, is to pursue lawsuit avoidance through overregulation of speech in the workplace. Firms that overregulate are merely doing what their lawyers suggest. Here, for example, are a prominent Oklahoma law firm's guidelines for handling workplace speech related to Title VII concerns. In an employment law newsletter article, the firm advised employers to ensure "that the following topics are never permitted in the workplace":

- any reference to any part of an employee's body
- any reference to an employee's race, ethnicity, or religion
- any reference to an employee's disability
- any reference to an employee's sexual habits
- any jokes of a sexual nature or ethnic jokes
- any pornography or nude pictures of any kind
- any joking requests for sexual favors, risqué dress, or suggestive acts
- any vulgar language with possible sexual connotations
- any harassment or jokes directed at one gender, ethnicity, or religion, regardless of content
- any e-mailing or forwarding of e-mails containing any of the above[74]

This advice seems well intended, in a prudish sort of way, and it might well successfully limit the volume and severity of harassment claims. But it takes scarcely an instant to think of examples of harmless, innocent speech that would be caught in this policy's expansive web of prohibition. Who would want to work at a place where such an uncompromising speech code is literally and rigorously enforced?

EIGHT

Speech in the Digital Age

MEG SPOHN TAUGHT CLASSES at the Westminster, Colorado, campus of DeVry University, a for-profit company, until Monday, December 12, 2005, when she was called into a dean's office, fired on the spot, and escorted to her car by someone from human resources. Spohn was told she was being sacked because of disparaging comments in her personal online blog about DeVry and its students. Spohn, who characterized any nonpositive comments she might have made about DeVry as "water-cooler kvetching," insists she never disparaged students online. She was fired without any warning, discussion, or disciplinary procedure, and DeVry never identified any specific posted content as the cause of her trouble.[1] Spohn later wondered if the culprit might have been a cranky blog entry nineteen months earlier in which she called a required online DeVry training session "useless CRAP" and "bullsh*t," and added: "Several hours of my online time that I could have been doing something meaningful like looking at porn, GONE!"[2]

A couple of weeks after losing her job, Spohn had these thoughts about the online activity that got her in trouble:

> My blog is just about what's going on in my life and what I'm thinking about. It never occurred to me that my thoughts would offend somebody, never mind get me fired. As far as I knew, until a couple of weeks ago, I had security by obscurity anyway. Why would anybody even care what I was noodling about? My firing was utterly surreal to me.[3]

Her comments here will strike some as naive. Of course your online speech broadcast to a potential audience of millions, even if reaching an actual readership of merely dozens, can get you into trouble if a suspicious (and perhaps humorless) employer finds out and disapproves. And you should know that obscurity is a flimsy basis for security in a world of Web crawlers and search engines. But naïveté aside, did Spohn's pungent online speech—creative self-expression for the digital age—so offend the sensibility of a large corporate enterprise as to justify a swift and unforgiving vocational beheading?

Computers, networks, digital media, and information technology, over the last generation, have obviously transformed work and workplaces in massive ways. To cut to the chase, I can sum up the effects of the last quarter-century's worth of technology on free speech in the workplace in four short sentences. One, people have access both at work and off-work to expanding channels and opportunities to express themselves about matters both related and unrelated to their jobs. Two, with distribution through digital networks, these channels easily reach wide audiences both inside and outside the firm. Three, these audiences inevitably include employers, who grow increasingly apprehensive about the flow of information in new forms and formats they cannot easily control. Four, employers often overreact by treating harmless extracurricular employee speech through digital channels as a hazardous obstacle to productivity and the firm's success.

This is, admittedly, a stylized version of the connection between information technology and employee speech. It assumes that as advances in technology bring new digital outlets for expression to people's offices, factories, homes, and pockets, managerial reactions will be reflexively fearful and punitive. And examples of employer overreaction, most notably in a number of situations where individuals have found themselves out of a job (or experiencing difficulty getting a job) because of their online activities maintaining Web pages and blogs, aren't hard to find. But examples where the individual called on the carpet or fired for online expression is not a victim of employer overreaction so much as a victim of his own bad judgment are also plentiful.

Examples at the extremes aren't the ones that really matter. On one extreme, consider a firm that punishes or fires an employee who maintains a harmless Web site or blog that is truly and completely unrelated to work—say, a person who writes about a hobby or a favorite sports team. A firing of this type would be reprehensible, but there's no evidence that it occurs with any frequency.

On the other extreme are employees who in their online expression about work disclose proprietary information, make threats or harassing remarks, or engage in clearly inappropriate invasions of co-workers' privacy. Rob Smith, for example, was fired from his job as a supervisor at Kerr-McGee for his incendiary blogging, which included statements that "the n-word was sometimes deserved," that his "company's workplace violence seminar was ridiculous," and that he kept "a three-foot piece of stainless steel pipe behind [his] desk and that was all [he] needed."[4] Smith expressed consternation that he was terminated without warning and in the absence of a corporate policy about off-work writing—he later called his firing "cowardly, dishonest, undignified"—but I suspect that few would object when an employer elects not to tolerate that sort of speech.[5]

A less abusive example, one that didn't seem like a gross miscarriage of justice, occurred in 2005 when Google acted against Mark Jen for his blogging about the company. The twenty-two-year-old Jen, who had been working at Google for less than a month, posted commentary on financial results and future products that apparently hadn't yet been made public.[6] In a reflective post to his blog shortly after being fired, Jen seemed to come to lowercase grips with his error in judgment:

> i should've waited a little longer and felt the company out a bit more
> before i started blogging at length. in retrospect, that is good advice
> and a lesson learned. i was just too excited. i felt like i was joining
> a small start-up family; i thought i was going to start new initiatives
> and improve existing ones; i thought i could jump in the deep end
> and immerse myself in the revolutionary development environment;
> i thought i could make connections to real people in the outside world
> and get first hand feedback; i thought google would love it. i thought
> wrong.[7]

Most of the cases—the interesting ones, anyway—where employees get in trouble for their online activity fall somewhere between the extremes: The expressive activity involved does have something to do with job or employer but doesn't seem to involve a concrete threat to the vitality of the enterprise in the form of disclosure of propriety information, invasions of co-worker or customer privacy, or openly scathing commentary about the organization. Instead, they involve people simply expressing themselves about something and someplace where they spend many of their waking hours—their jobs—in ways that a corporate PR person probably wouldn't.

For this, if they happen to work for the kind of employer that greets uncontrolled employee expression with knee-jerk anxiety, they put jobs and careers in serious peril.

FLY ME TO THE UNEMPLOYMENT LINE

One well-publicized example occurred in 2004 when Delta Air Lines fired flight attendant Ellen Simonetti because of the contents of her personal blog, Diary of a Flight Attendant. Simonetti had been blogging about her life and her work (using the pseudonym "Queen of Sky" and masking the airline's identity) for about nine months without interference from Delta. The situation changed when Delta objected to the inclusion in the blog of some very mildly provocative photos of herself in her flight attendant uniform on an aircraft.[8] (According to news reports the Delta logo was visible in one photo.)[9] Simonetti described the motivation behind her online enterprise:

> The reason I started my blog in the first place was as a form of therapy. I had lost my mother in September 2003 to cancer and that hit me hard. It was much easier to write about my feelings than talk about them. Now, my employer was telling me that the very thing that had gotten me through those tough times, my blog, could cost me my career. I felt my rights were being infringed upon. And I decided to fight back.[10]

As an at-will employee—Delta flight attendants are not unionized— Simonetti had no legal recourse on free speech grounds. The airline, as a private-sector employer, had the legal right to fire her simply because it didn't like her off-work expressive activity (or even if it did like it!). Simonetti claims, however, that Delta has taken no similar action against some male airline employees with blogs that include photos of uniformed workers and mild sexual content. She initially filed a discrimination complaint with the EEOC and in 2005 filed a federal sex discrimination lawsuit against the airline.[11]

Simonetti's situation is a good illustration of the large gray area for individual employee expression that has been created by information technology and the Internet. The situation is not one in which the employee was engaging in off-work speech that had nothing whatsoever to do with her job. Simonetti wrote periodically about her travels, with tidbits of information and commentary about the life and work of a flight attendant.[12] The online photographs that irked the airline—assuming that a reader of her blog could figure out which airline she worked for—might well have sounded alarms at many employers accustomed to having complete control over corporate image, branding, and reputation. But the idea that Simonetti's expressive activity actually did or would have a tangible negative effect on Delta's image or reputation is, frankly, far-fetched. It is a measure of corporate intolerance for free expression and dissent that an employer would regard this very mildly subversive off-work behavior by an experienced employee as a firing offense.

Michael Hanscom earned similar zero-tolerance treatment from Microsoft in 2003. When he included on his personal blog a photo of some Apple computers in a receiving area at the firm's Redmond, Washington, campus, he was fired from his position as a contract worker in the copy shop.[13] In posting the photo, Hanscom was apparently offering up little more than a touch of gentle irony, given the longtime competitive rivalry between the two companies for dominion over the nation's virtual desktops. He says he was careful to crop the picture so that it gave no indication of the location in the shot, but his accompanying comments indicated that the receiving area was in the same building as the copy shop where he worked. Hanscom surmised that this made him and his blog a security risk, and he was summarily sacked despite offering to remove the offending post.[14]

Hanscom's plight raised more eyebrows than it otherwise might have because the company that canned him, Microsoft, is itself a tech-savvy empire with a reputation as a reasonably progressive employer. A security risk is a legitimate reason for an employer to act against employee speech, but the firm's swift and uncompromising ax in response to an isolated and seemingly small mistake in judgment seemed like a harsh response. Microsoft, for its part, was among the earliest firms to embrace blogging as a business tool for product development, marketing, and employee communication. "Blogging is a natural extension of what is in our corporate DNA," a Microsoft executive said in 2005, when there were over a thousand company employees blogging.[15]

One well-known Microsoft employee-blogger, Robert Scoble, authored a personal blog for several years featuring commentary on the company and its industry with a balanced critical style that generated a wide audience of loyal readers. When he left Microsoft in mid-2006 to join a startup, a Reuters story described Scoble's approach to corporate blogging as a para-doxical dance between the roles of personal commentator and informal corporate flak: "Using his blog as a soapbox, Scoble came to personify a new style of corporate honesty in which he publicly spoke his mind on controversial topics. He was often willing to judiciously criticize Microsoft or praise its most fierce competitors."[16] The reference here to "a new style of corporate honesty" seems a bit overwrought, given that many, if not most, employers appear far more inclined to censor or kill extracurricular employee commentary on the firm than encourage it. But Scoble had noth-ing but praise for Microsoft's approach to his expressive activity: "No one at Microsoft has complained to me about my views for a very long time. In fact, the harsher I got the more support I got."[17] Certainly, Microsoft wouldn't have encouraged (or at least looked the other way from) Scoble's blogging if it didn't think that it reaped benefits from his widely read com-mentary. As Doc Searles, author of *The Cluetrain Manifesto* and a keen observer of Internet trends and their impact on business, remarked, "There is no HR metric for figuring the worth of a worker like Scoble."[18]

Blogging is not the only form of communication through digital technol-ogy that gives people new ways to express themselves—and to get in trou-ble with their employers for expressing themselves. It does, however, seem to be getting most of the attention at the moment.

A blog is, of course, just a particular sort of Web site, one that tends to (but need not) follow a set of conventions of form and structure, although there are no hard and fast rules and many variations. A typical blog (short for "Weblog") has the look and feel of a journal, with dated entries shown in chronological order, the most recent at the top. Blogs usually are a col-lection of brief entries, measured in sentences or paragraphs rather than pages. Blogs often have a feature that allows readers to post comments in reply to individual entries; some blog owners allow posting openly without censorship, while in others the owner of the blog screens comments before they appear.

The diarylike quality of a blog's typical structure makes it widely appealing as a vehicle for personal online written expression. Free and simple-to-use blogging software makes it widely available. Without any knowledge of how the World Wide Web actually works or how the programming languages behind Web pages function, a person can create a new blog from scratch in minutes and publish new entries to it instantly. Many blogs are group projects, with several people posting entries rather than just a single individual. Blogs can be handy as focal points for maintaining communication among groups of people, which makes them appealing for a variety of political, professional, and community purposes.

For my purposes in this book, the remarkable aspect of the growth of blogging is its appeal for individuals seeking a digital soapbox for self-expression. The opportunity to publish one's observations, thoughts, and opinions, instantly available to anyone on the planet with an Internet connection, is apparently irresistible to many. In the spring of 2006, the blog search engine Technorati was tracking over 35 million different blogs worldwide—a sixty-fold increase in three years—with roughly 75,000 new blogs created each day.[19] Within the United States, according to a study by the Pew Internet and American Life Project, 12 million adults were involved in keeping a blog in 2006, and 57 million adults were reading them.[20]

For many individuals who have latched onto blogging as a way to speak their inner thoughts to a waiting world, the casual informality of this diary-like medium seems to make them overlook the risks that someone with authority over them, like a parent or an employer, is looking on. When that happens, an innocent offhand comment intended to do nothing more than let off some steam after a tough day becomes an alarm bell calling into question the blogger's judgment or stability. An administrator at Harvard University named Norah Burch learned that the hard way when her employer discovered her blog, which included sentiments like this one: "I am two snotty e-mails from professors away from bombing the entire Harvard campus." After losing her job, Burch said, "I'm not dangerous and I don't wish anyone harm or malice and I don't even dislike anybody. I just had momentary frustration and the blog was a good way to get it out so I can get on with things."[21]

The solution for employees who write online about work, some would say, is easy: just don't do it. That's Heather Armstrong's advice. She has the dubious distinction of being one of the earliest and best-known examples of an employee fired for blogging, from her job as a Los Angeles Web designer in 2002. In her blog, called dooce, Armstrong wrote from time to time about her co-workers, not by name but with seemingly inadequate discretion. (Exhibit A: her blog entry a few weeks before she was fired, titled "Reasons the Asian Database Administrator Is So Fucking Annoying.")[22] Armstrong says she lost her job after someone anonymously emailed executives to tell them of the "unsavory things" she had written on her Web site.[23] The lesson she took from the experience and passes on to others: "Never write about work on the Internet unless your boss knows and sanctions the fact that you are writing about work on the Internet."[24] Armstrong may have lost her job, but she gained an eponym: An online slang dictionary defines the verb "dooce," as "to be fired from your job because of the contents of your weblog."[25]

Although blogs may be the latest thing in online employee venting, they are hardly the first thing or the only thing. Before blogs there were—and still are—message boards that invited current, former, and prospective employees to post and discuss anonymously. Among the best known of these are the many company-specific discussion boards maintained at Vault.com, where users have been sounding off about their workplaces since 1998.[26] A team of researchers at universities in Australia and the United States, analyzing thousands of comments posted at Vault.com, found that company insiders are more likely to post messages with negative emotions than outsiders, suggesting that employees are eager to find opportunities to vent dissatisfaction with work and workplace and are willing to use visible online channels to do so.[27]

ADVICE AND CONSENT

Attorneys advising employers about how to cope with the brave new digital world of blogs, Web sites, message boards, newsgroups, wikis, instant messaging, and all the rest would likely approve of Heather Armstrong's advice: just don't do it. A number of published commentaries by employment lawyers advise firms to beware the blog, and offer a range of (predictable) suggestions on how to keep the beast caged, or at least tamed.[28] Much of what the lawyers are telling employers is perfectly reasonable: Make it clear to employees that online speech that is defamatory, harassing, abusive, or a breach of confidentiality is, just as in offline speech, out of bounds. Ensure that blogging or other online activity doesn't interfere with work commitments. Require employee-bloggers to respect copyright laws and abide by them. Consider spelling out in company policies specific provisions about blogs, message boards, Web sites, chat rooms, and other forms of online expression, and designate someone in the company to act as a point person for employee questions and clarifications.

Attorneys are tendering other pieces of stock legal advice, however, that might seem reasonable at first glance but that represent causes for serious concern from a free speech perspective. For example:

Improper content can range from postings that are disrespectful to your company to those that are completely unrelated to your employees' job but still reflect on you. . . .

Prohibit workers from disparaging the company, co-workers, customers, or competitors either by name or implication. . . .

Make it understood that you expect bloggers to treat the company and your employees, customers, and competitors with respect.[29]

Respect is a wonderful thing and a perfectly acceptable virtue to cultivate in the workplace, but it is a rather vague standard for the regulation of off-work speech. Threats to punish any speech that might "reflect" on the company and blanket bans on disparagement "either by name or implication" have the ring of a chilling, zero-tolerance approach to expression that puts employees on notice that their off-work speech is wholly owned by their employer.

Other pieces of advice would have employees seek prior approval from the company for personal expression that is both legal and harmless. For example: "Require employees to request permission from their supervisor (or other designated company official) to provide a link from their sites to the company's website."[30] Although a single link is a small thing, this kind of requirement is a gratuitous infringement on a person's discretion to express themselves away from the job in a way that may well have nothing to do with the firm's image or reputation.

Employers are also told by lawyers that employees who write about the firm, its customers, or its competitors "must make it clear that the views expressed in the blog are theirs alone."[31] It's eminently sensible for an employee who finds herself in a situation where job-related speech might reasonably be construed as a statement on behalf of the employer to offer a disclaimer that dispels this impression. So, for example, it offends no principle of personal liberty when a person who publishes an article on some work-related topic, and whose employer is identified in the byline, includes (as we often see) a disclaimer that the writer's views are not those of her employer. But it is a needlessly stern form of compelled speech for an employer to say to employees: if you comment about your work, even occasionally and mildly, you must constantly and explicitly distance yourself from your employer. The individual who sells her time and labor to an employer has no reasonable expectation that management "speech" on some matter of public interest (as often occurs) will be accompanied by a disclaimer that the opinions expressed are those of the firm, not its employees as individuals. There is no legitimate, ethical reason (beyond the firm's self-interested desire for efficient control) that an employee should be forced to submit to such a disclosure requirement in her own personal, off-the-job expressive activity.

The suggestion that employers put in place a policy about online punditry is a particularly good one, but few companies have figured out how to do it right. Vague mandates to treat people with respect and avoid doing harm to the company can be viewed as little more than veiled reminders that we can interpret these guidelines any way we like and fire someone if we don't like what he's saying anytime we want. One company with a thoughtful approach is Sun Microsystems.[32] Although Sun is encouraging employees to blog on its servers about product and industry issues, it doesn't try to caution people away from free speech about their life at work: "It's perfectly OK to talk about your work and have a dialog with the community, but it's not OK to publish the recipe for one of our secret sauces." Instead of a specific list of dos and don'ts, Sun goes with constructive guidelines for effective blogging (be interesting; expose your personality; write about what you know; be clear, complete, and concise). The company concedes that the point here is to forfeit corporate control over employee speech, not tighten it: "By speaking directly to the world, without benefit of management approval, we are accepting higher risks in the interest of higher rewards." This sort of corporate "theory" of online free speech doesn't amount to an endorsement of an expressive free-for-all at the work-place, but it does show that it's possible to imagine that employee free expression and corporate goals need not be incompatible.

YOUTHFUL INDISCRETIONS

There is an inescapable demographic angle to the hoopla around employee speech on the Internet: young workers are more likely to get in trouble for online speech, because young workers are more likely to engage in online speech. To be sure, the overall generation gap in online activity in the United States is shrinking: it is no longer the case, for instance, that young people are vastly more likely to use the Internet than older Americans. Survey data from the Pew Internet and American Life Project, which tracks trends in online activity, show only a modest drop-off in use of the Internet among people in their thirties and forties compared to those in their twen-ties (the gap grows more noticeable for people in their fifties and beyond). Among those who are online, there are few if any meaningful differences between age groups in use of the Internet for such things as email, obtain-ing news, product research, and online purchases.[33]

But there are clear generational differences in expressive activity online, including blogging. Pew data show that in 2005, 20 percent of Americans between the ages of eighteen and twenty-nine had created blogs, compared to just 9 percent of those in their thirties, and 3 percent of those in their forties.[34] People in their twenties are more than twice as likely as people in their forties to read blogs or use text messaging.

The generational differences are not just because younger workers are more likely to be online or creating blogs. Younger people are more likely to be living their lives online, broadcasting the intimate details of their existence through blogs or social networking Web sites such as MySpace, Facebook, and Xanga. They come to the workplace less savvy about the risks of online personal expression for job and career; unsurprisingly, the examples I've mentioned of people who have gotten into trouble were more likely to involve bloggers in their twenties rather than older workers. (Mark Jen, the blogger who lost his job at Google, looked back on the incident as "a great learning experience.")[35] Naive to the awkward collision between youthful online exhibitionism and the reality of an adult life at work, twentysomethings bring to the job, as one *New York Times* writer put it, "an innocence and nonchalance about workplace rules and corporate culture."[36]

Having grown up in an online culture where intimate disclosure is commonplace, many workplace novices come with a history—a traceable searchable archive of all those personal thoughts and intimate details (often with photos!) published on the Web, ready and waiting for a prospective employer with curiosity and a search engine. One job-seeking UCLA senior who wasn't getting much in the way of interview action from recruiters Googled himself at a friend's suggestion; he says the interviews started coming once he removed a satirical online essay titled "Lying Your Way to the Top" that he had previously posted on a Web site.[37]

According to the Society for Human Resource Management, less than 10 percent of HR professionals in 2005 were reading job candidate blogs before making hiring decisions.[38] That number is likely to be rising quickly, however, given employment attorneys sharing advice like this with corporations:

> Before hiring your next employee, perform a Web search to see if they have a blog and, if so, read it. Chances are that a candidate's blog will be far more telling than any reference you'll receive from past employers. Neutral job references are the norm, and your shining star may reveal much more on her blog than she did in the job interview.[39]

People with hiring authority are not just reading, they're also listening. Nate Fulmer lost his job in the accounting department of a laboratory supply firm in South Carolina when people at the office discovered his podcast—an audio program he and his wife, Di, were producing and posting online. Their episode of the "Nate and Di Show" devoted to disenchantment with organized religion drew an unpleasant reaction from Nate's conservative Christian boss, and a pink slip to go with it, even though he never mentioned his employer in the show. The lesson Di drew from the experience: "If you live in a place like South Carolina, be careful what you say."[40]

In fact, to judge by what college placement officers are hearing from hiring companies, the likelihood that an employer will check out an applicant's online past is probably already a good deal higher than has been reported. One of the most popular social networking sites for university students is Facebook, which requires collegiate users to have a campus email address to view the personal profiles of others at the same university. That requirement should keep their pages hidden from employers' prying eyes, yes? No. According to one university career services director, companies will sometimes ask college interns—who have the right kind of email address— to do online background checks on prospective employees.[41] In other cases, employees who recently graduated keep may be hanging onto their college email address so that they can do this as well.

Using readily available search tools to uncover intimate details of the personal lives of employees and job applicants may turn into business as usual for an emerging voyeuristic-industrial complex, and it's easy to place the blame with individuals who make the "mistake" of expressing themselves online with insufficient restraint. A more thoughtful approach to our expanding lives in an online information society, however, leads to a more cautious judgment: this is a tricky area for the health of free expression. I mentioned earlier the chilling effect on even mildly critical speech regarding one's job or employer that overly sanctimonious corporate blogging policies can have. Now we're talking about chilling just about *any* form of speech by way of the threat that some employer sometime will ferret out of cyberspace some indiscreet bits and bytes from your less-than-wholesome past. There is, by the way, an intriguing paradox in play here: many new employees and prospective employees who are living their lives online are too young to fully understand adult workplace culture they are entering, while many managers and employers who are checking out the online lives of their newest employees are too old to fully grasp digital culture.

As with so many issues of employer regulation of personal expression, this one allows us to arrive easily at the obvious cases: perhaps it isn't a good idea to pepper one's MySpace page with photos of oneself passing out drunk with a prostitute while bribing a Congressman at a white supremacist convention. But in the conceptual gulf between that sort of escapade and a photo showing oneself, say, with a hammer in hand at a Habitat for Humanity project site lies a vast terrain of behavior whose meaning is open to widely varying interpretations. What one potential employer perceives as evidence of an impressive commitment to social activism, for instance, another might see as the telltale sign of a alarmingly subversive persona.

Refreshingly, there are some employers who refuse to take the Google-bait. Explaining her firm's reluctance to data-mine into the dark online recesses of job applicants' pasts, Maureen Crawford Hentz, who manages talent acquisition at Sylvania, told a reporter, "I'd rather not see that part of them. I don't think it's related to their bona fide occupational qualifications."[42] For firms that do mine the Web for information about job applicants, it seems sensible to use what surfaces in an enlightened way and to avoid jumping to conclusions about character and potential based on isolated online postings by young adults just entering the workforce.

PROFESS FOR SUCCESS

What about cases where online activity *does* include content that's relevant to one's qualifications? One sphere of employment in which online expression, especially in the form of blogging, has created a stir is the world of academe—professors (like yours truly) at colleges and universities. Higher education is unusual in the context of the issues I have been discussing because professors, especially those with appointments at research universities, are essentially paid to communicate ideas to the outside world. Although scholarly journals and meetings have been the traditional outlets for professional academic communication, the online world of blogs and Web sites provides irresistible vehicles for expression for many professors, for both professional and more personal content. Among academics in the various disciplines, scholars in law seem especially taken with blogs as a vehicle for expression and communication. One survey estimated that more than 300 law professors were blogging in late 2006, an increase of over 50 percent from a year earlier; many of the bloggers were prominent scholars at some of the nation's most prestigious law schools.[43]

Opportunities for online expression have natural appeal here because the life of an academic, especially one seeking tenure or promotion at a research-oriented institution, is in many ways an extended exercise in self-promotion. Advancement occurs not solely based on the objective volume of someone's research output but also as a result of the informed perceptions of its quality by a professor's scholarly community. Faculty handbooks and policy documents at research universities routinely mention the development of a national or international reputation in one's scholarly field as the basis for a favorable tenure decision. Academics like to think that the articles or books we publish cultivate that reputation on their merits, and they do, but with so many aspiring academics publishing a vast quantity of research of varying quality, reputation will at times precede readership rather than follow it. Academics have discovered that blogs, Web sites, newsgroups, and listservs are efficient vehicles for "getting one's name out there," and as every politician knows, name recognition is the first step to success.

The political machinations of the pursuit of tenure aside, blogs and other online channels have proved to be terrific vehicles for building and maintaining scholarly community. Group blogs involving professors with shared professional interests, for example, give rise to lively exchanges that can be more timely and vibrant than is otherwise possible in the slow, deliberate world of traditional scholarly publishing. Groups of separate, related blogs written by professional colleagues who read one another's sites can accomplish the same thing, as do listservs. According to political scientist and group-blog contributor Henry Farrell, "Academic blogs offer the kind of intellectual excitement and engagement that attracted many scholars to the academic life in the first place, but which often get lost in the hustle to secure positions, grants, and disciplinary recognition."[44] We find in cyberspace scholarly communities in any number of disciplines that make interaction among academics a more frequent thing and, incidentally, allow people outside the field, or outside academia entirely, to look on and even participate. To a certain extent, all of this has had a healthy, even democratizing, effect on the metaphorical ivory tower.

But academics, like the other people I've been discussing in this chapter, inevitably have to seek employment and sometimes wish to move on to something new. Academics, like others, sometimes can't resist the urge to move beyond their narrow domain of scholarly expertise and post online their feelings, political opinions, life stories, or photos of their kids. And increasingly, academics, like everyone else in any market for a job or promotion, find themselves being evaluated by others with power over their fate who have a search engine and know how to use it.

In most cases where people lose their jobs because of online expressive activity, we hear only the individual's side, because employers retreat (understandably) behind confidentiality on personnel matters. For academics we often find even less transparency because the tenure and promotion process is frequently a black box even to the person denied promotion. So when Daniel Drezner, a political scientist and well-known blogger, was denied tenure in 2005 by the University of Chicago, it was hard to know what role his blogging may have played. One of two professor-bloggers to be denied tenure at Chicago that year (the other was a physicist), Drezner had opened his very first blog entry in 2002 by saying, "I shouldn't be doing this. I'll be going up for tenure soon."[45] Three years later, the day after he received the bad news, he took up the question of whether blogging played a role in his tenure outcome in a post on his blog (where else?):

> I dunno, perhaps, probably not, maybe, I guess so, a little, could be, I seriously doubt it, and who the hell knows? Any decent social scientist must allow for multiple causes, so it's not necessarily an either/or question. At the moment, I simply lack the data to confirm or deny any explanation.[46]

Several months later, after moving on to another university (with tenure), Drezner mused about the effect his blogging might have had on the colleagues at Chicago who judged him: "I found that some of my colleagues overestimated the time and effort I put into my blog—which led them to overestimate lost opportunities for scholarship."[47]

Professors invite trouble if their extracurricular speech starts to look like curricular preaching on subjects of dubious academic merit. In 2006, Kevin Barrett, a lecturer at the University of Wisconsin, inspired calls for his dismissal when it came out that he is part of an online group that believes the World Trade Center was destroyed on 9/11 as part of a plot by the U.S. government and has shared this belief with students. The university's provost decided to keep Barrett on staff in the name of academic freedom and "the free exchange of ideas." But while academic freedom gives a professor the right to study what he wants and to talk about provocative ideas in the classroom, wrote Stanley Fish in a *New York Times* op-ed piece about the Barrett case, it doesn't give him the right to recruit students to a political agenda.[48] Controversies about professors and their politics are, of course, as old as universities themselves. What is new is how digital technology blends the political and the professional sides of one's life in an online stew of personal identity, bringing these kinds controversies to the surface more readily and inviting wider audiences to look on and even (as Barrett discovered) to try to censor.

As constructive as blogs and other forms of informal online expression can be for academics to disseminate ideas and foster discussion, they can turn into a liability if colleagues (who may ultimately sit in judgment) take it as a signal that someone is more of a limelight seeker than a serious scholar. "Whether online or off," observes Robert Boynton of NYU's journalism department, "the kind of accessible and widely read work that brings an academic public recognition is likely to draw the scorn and suspicion of his colleagues."[49] A professor at a midwestern college writing (anonymously) about an academic search to fill a professorship at his institution put the risks of this kind of speech in clear perspective:

> You may think your blog is a harmless outlet. You may use the faulty logic of the blogger, "Oh, no one will see it anyway." Don't count on it. . . . Our blogger applicants came off reasonably well at the initial interview, but once we hung up the phone and called up their blogs, we got to know "the real them"—better than we wanted, enough to conclude we didn't want to know more.[50]

The occupational pitfalls of online expression are clearly not limited just to new college graduates with MySpace pages.

THE MAIL EGO

Most of this chapter has focused on the free speech travails of blogging that offends the policies or sensitivities of employers. Bloggers are an easy target because they personify the idea of free-wheeling, instantaneous, one-to-many electronic expression. But while a significant number of people are giving blogging a test drive, and a growing number of employers are wrestling with its benefits and risks, other forms of digital communication present their own workplace free speech hazards. Email, in particular, has been around a lot longer, and is used by many more people for both work-related and personal communication. Unlike blogging or other uses of the Web, email contents aren't publicly available for anyone to find, although someone armed with a large list of recipients can air a message to a wide audience.

Email and other messaging technologies (such as instant messaging) are "private" in the sense that recipients are individually designated. Nonetheless, a person's control over her email-based speech is only as predictable as the actions of message recipients. The store-and-forward capability that makes email such an appealing productivity tool erodes the sender's control over who ultimately receives a message. To be sure, a lack of control over one's audience is hardly new to the digital age; a copy of a private message on paper could always be produced for an unintended audience—the boss, a competitor, the district attorney, and so on. Email, though, makes this possible with minimal effort and at virtually no cost. All that stands between you and the unwanted recipients of your "private" message is someone else's push of an email *forward* button. Also, when we use email for communication that might otherwise have occurred by phone or face-to-face, more of our speech assumes a written form that can escape our control over audience and consequences.

One striking illustration of that loss of control involved Laurie Garrett, an award-winning science writer for at the New York newspaper *Newsday*. After attending the World Economic Forum in Davos, Switzerland, in 2003, Garrett sent a 2,100-word email to a handful of friends sharing her informal comments and personal observations about the doings in Davos. Within several days, the email had been forwarded many times, stripped of its headers and her last name, and posted to archived Web sites and lists, sparking wide discussion and speculation about who wrote it and whether it was some sort of hoax.[51] When Garrett became aware of the digital distance her "private" email had traveled, she reacted publicly on a large community Weblog: "To my deep embarrassment, and acute sense of invaded privacy, all of you—thousands of strangers—are dissecting my personal letter. I would never have written for public consumption in such a sloppy, candid, opinionated flip tone. This was never intended for your eyes."[52] Garrett, a Pulitzer Prize–winning journalist, may not have suffered an employment consequence as a result, but it's a compelling example of the public risks one takes with supposedly private email correspondence.

Another who took that risk was Jonas Blank, a summer associate at a white-shoe law firm. Blank inadvertently sent an email describing his day to a few dozen recipients, many of whom were partners at the firm: "I'm busy doing jack. Went to a nice 2hr sushi lunch today at Sushi Zen. Nice place. Spent the rest of the day typing e-mails and [gabbing] with people."[53] Unsurprisingly, his breezy, eyebrow-raising missive made wider rounds, forcing him ultimately into a public declaration that he was "thoroughly and utterly ashamed and embarrassed." Notwithstanding his digital faux pas, Blank landed a full-time job at the firm anyway. A column on careers in the *Wall Street Journal* that recounted Blank's story used his happy ending and similar examples to make the point that in some business settings, "unmitigated gall can be more marketable than galling."[54] Well, maybe. Free speech is a beautiful thing, but chutzpah remains a dodgy career strategy.

Because email is privately directed rather than publicly readable, the speech it contains has a different relationship to employer control than expression in a blog or elsewhere on the Web. An individual using a personal email address, as opposed to one on his employer's network, is in a better position to shield his speech from his employer—subject, of course, to the discretion and trustworthiness of message recipients. But in jobs where email is conveyed through an employer-owned network, the employer has the unfettered ability to read anything and everything. Many employers resist the urge to do so, preferring to give employees the same level of privacy they generally expect when using a telephone at work. According to one recent survey, however, more than one-third of large American companies employ people specifically for the purpose of reading others' outbound email, and close to half use text-scanning software to search messages for indications of inappropriate communication.[55] Almost one-third of companies surveyed said they had fired someone in the past year for breaking a rule about use of email.

Firms seem most concerned with email that breaches confidentiality and releases proprietary information. But employees also risk punishment for more personal forms of self-expression. In many cases employees have gotten in trouble for sharing inappropriate content through a company email system—the kind of humorous or risqué material that has become a staple of the workplace inbox. The ones that make the news tend to involve extreme violations of good judgment and common sense, as when First Union Bank in North Carolina fired seven employees for circulating an email that included videos of sexual activity, or when the city of Tampa disciplined forty-four municipal employees, nineteen of them with the police department, for using email on work computers to share sexually explicit photographs.[56]

With email now a thoroughly commonplace vehicle for personal and professional communication, employers can't realistically expect to apply a strict business-use-only policy to email use. One study of corporate email behavior in late 2005 found that almost a quarter of all messages in employees' inboxes were not work related, and only 28 percent of employees say they never forward jokes, photos, video clips or other nonwork content to co-workers.[57] The use for jokes and other frivolity aside, email is often how you make a lunch date, check to see if the car is ready, or confirm a medical appointment, so it makes no more sense to have zero tolerance for personal email or Internet use on company time as it would to prohibit all personal phone calls.

Most employers get this; many firms with formal policies on the use of electronic communication seem to be striving for a balance that would allow reasonable personal use. Hewlett-Packard, for example, tells employees that they "may occasionally use HP's telephone and computer systems to send or receive personal messages, to access Internet materials that are not directly business-related, or to create personal documents or files."[58] Pfizer couples its acknowledgment that personal use is inevitable with a warning:

> Although you may use your Pfizer computer for incidental private use, you have no expectation of privacy in e-mail received in your Pfizer inbox. Pfizer owns both your computer and all information stored on it. Pfizer may review any of those materials at any time. Remember also that e-mail creates a permanent electronic record. So be careful when using e-mail and avoid risky behaviors like using strong language or passing rumors or commenting on someone else's area of expertise in personal or business-related e-mails.[59]

Policies like these straddle the divide between personal and work-related communication using employer technology. Sometimes, as in the case of Rolf Szabo in October 2002, the line is hopelessly blurred.

Szabo, a twenty-three-year veteran at Kodak, received an email forwarded from his supervisor regarding the company's participation in the Human Rights Campaign's annual Coming Out Day for people who are gay, lesbian, bisexual, and transgendered. (Perhaps you can guess where this is going.) The corporate email urged supervisors and employees to be supportive of co-workers who choose to come out at work and reminded them of Kodak's equal employment opportunities policies. Szabo replied with a one-sentence email: "Please do not send this type of information to me anymore, as I find it disgusting and offensive."[60]

Perhaps that message in itself would be enough to draw at least a disapproving frown from an employer committed to equality based on sexual orientation, but Szabo transformed molehill into mountain by sending his response to all one thousand recipients of the original email. He was fired after refusing to sign a document containing an apology and outlining future steps to prevent it from happening again. A Kodak spokesperson said Szabo was canned not for holding a particular belief but because sharing it in a mass email "created the potential for a hostile work environment."[61] Szabo's situation drew notice from religious conservatives; the head of one Christian lobbying group called it "political correctness gone berserk."[62]

The politics of "political correctness" aside, probably few would fault a company for preferring that the mass-distribution capability of its email network not be hijacked by an individual's incendiary rhetoric. Employers overreach, however, when they try to shut down unfriendly speech that doesn't even come from an employee. Consider, for instance, the case of *Intel v. Hamidi*, in which former Intel employee Kourosh Hamidi sent emails criticizing the company to a number of current employees—35,000 of them.[63] Although his messages came through Intel's email network, he breached no computer security barriers, and he offered to remove anyone who requested it from his list. Intel sued Hamidi under a legal theory of trespassing and prevailed in a lower court, but the California Supreme Court reversed in favor of Hamidi.

The ruling was in large part a complex reading of the law on trespassing, but in a welcome blow against unbridled corporate censorship, the court rebuffed Intel's argument that Hamidi's efforts to communicate with current employees inflicted tangible economic harm on the company. Intel claimed that it suffered a loss of productivity when employees spent time reading and reacting to Hamidi's messages. Under certain circumstances, a principle of autonomy does give someone a right not to listen to an unwanted message, but the court said that right doesn't justify a sweeping legal barrier to outside communication directed to Intel's corporate email addresses. Hamidi, said the court, had "no more invaded Intel's property than does a protester holding a sign or shouting through a bullhorn outside corporate headquarters, posting a letter through the mail, or telephoning to complain of a corporate practice."[64] I will gracefully refrain from mentioning the irony of a system where business interests in the name of marketing (and free speech!) lobby for the right to fill our inboxes with unwanted messages but object vociferously when individuals use similar means to direct free speech at their employees.[65] Or perhaps I won't.

The overall picture I have painted in this chapter is one of employers struggling with the opportunities and threats in play when employees express themselves through technology and new media. We must keep in mind that the channels may be new, but much of the expression isn't. People have been sharing the insight that "my co-workers are crazy and my boss is a jerk" for as long as there have been co-workers and bosses. The technology accelerates this sort of conversation and, of course, make it easy to widen its audience—to the entire planet, in theory, when one chooses the Web. But then again, some of the speech *is* new, and it can be explained with varying degrees of cynicism.

The highly cynical explanation: many find the prospect of a ready audience for one's personal musings to be an irresistible temptation to speak, even on subjects in which they previously had no serious interest or viewpoint. This temptation seems to explain a sizable piece of the blog phenomenon. The mere opportunity to be heard by many (even if the likelihood of that happening is slim) compels self-expression for its own sake. It's an updating of Descartes for the digital age: I am, therefore I blog. This explanation assumes the worst in people's self-expressive impulses: an egotistical delusion of self-importance and a narcissistic craving to be heard. We don't know how much online expression is motivated this way; I know of no poll that asked people "Do you blog for egotistical, narcissistic reasons?" Let's also keep in mind that most people don't create blogs at all.

A far less cynical take: there is new speech and more speech because technology changes the very nature of the people's social ties to other individuals, to institutions (including workplaces), and to community and society. Being networked doesn't just generate an audience for the narcissist in us; it generates engagement for the citizen in us. A person blogs his passionate views on the war or on the economy or on the industry he works in, not merely because the Internet generates a potential audience but because it builds a community of ideas and practice to join. This logic builds on theories of the First Amendment that I discussed in Chapter 6: digital media expands the "individualist" aims of free speech, namely personal autonomy and self-fulfillment in the pursuit of the good (and free) society.

Obviously cyberspace is populated with both the narcissistic and the engaged (including some who simultaneously occupy both terrains). Howard Rheingold, an early and influential commentator on the Internet who is credited with coining the term "virtual community," anticipated the possibility that virtual communities could turn out to have real benefits for the good society, or merely illusory ones: "Virtual communities could help citizens revitalize democracy, or they could be luring us into an attractively packaged substitute for democratic discourse."[66] Corporations and other employers, wrestling with all of this new speech, for the most part exhibit little interest in democracy. The U.S. system of employment is built, both legally and economically, on a logic of efficiency and control, not collective self-government. Employers, as we have seen in many of the examples in this chapter, are more apt to perceive threat than opportunity in the avenues for digital expression that their workers are navigating.

In a rich and provocative essay on digital speech and democratic culture, Law professor Jack Balkin argues that the digital age alters not just the form and content of personal expression but the very meaning of free speech, the values it serves, and its relation to democratic society. The realities of more interactivity, mass participation, and creative transformation that come with the Internet, he argues, lead to new forms of social conflict, especially around who owns and controls information. Balkin is thinking mainly at the level of society, but clearly something analogous is playing out in microcosm in the digitally infused workplace:

> At the very moment when ordinary people are empowered to use digital technologies to speak, to create, to participate in the creation of culture, and to distribute their ideas and innovations around the world, businesses are working as hard as possible to limit and shut down forms of participation and innovation that are inconsistent with their economic interests.[67]

The result is a workplace paradox for the information age: On one hand, all of this marvelous technology invests individuals in a free society with new and compelling expressive powers. On the other hand, meanwhile, employers conditioned to elevate efficiency interests over all others recoil from what they see as a new set of threats to their economic autonomy, producing in many cases more of a chill on employee speech than might have existed in the first place.

Rachel Mosteller, a reporter for a daily newspaper in North Carolina, wrote this on her personal blog one day:

> I really hate my place of employment. Seriously. Okay, first off. They have these stupid little awards that are supposed to boost company morale. So you go and do something "spectacular" (most likely, you're doing your JOB) and then someone says "Why golly, that was spectacular." Then they sign your name on some paper, they bring you chocolate and some balloons. Okay two people in the newsroom just got it. FOR DOING THEIR JOB.[68]

The next day she was fired. As in the rest of her blog, Mosteller refrained from identifying herself, her employer, her co-workers, or her location. "I didn't think of it as a problem," she said.

NINE

Managing Expression inside the Workplace

People have an obligation to dissent in this company. . . . I mean,
I sit up here on the 50th floor, in the library. I have no idea what's
going on down there, so if you've got a problem with it, speak up.
And if you don't speak up, that's not good.

—Jeffrey Skilling, former CEO of Enron[1]

CORPORATE EXECUTIVES ARE ACCOMPLISHED PRACTITIONERS of the
art of talking the talk of openness, free speech, and dissent in the workplace.
Fortunately for the rest of us, journalists are accomplished at the sort of
petard-hoisting that results when quotations like this are dredged up.
Enron, to be sure, isn't a representative example of workplace culture or,
for that matter, workplace anything. Its swift financial collapse, organizational implosion, and managerial fall from grace set it apart from anything
we might regard as the typical corporate experience. But if Enron isn't typical, Jeffrey Skilling's comment about free speech and dissent is: a familiar if
hollow genuflection to principles of openness and heterodoxy.

Delegation, participation, and communication have been common
themes in business school classrooms and executive training sessions for
decades. I do not contend that it's all a sham, fronting for ever-expanding
corporate tyranny, or that all employers and workplaces are wholly unforgiving of free expression or employee dissent. Without doubt, we find a
good amount of variation in how employers approach (and tolerate) expressive activity by workers. These variations are a product, at least in part, of
trends in the art and science of management on such issues as worker
autonomy, involvement, voice, justice, and ethics. But do these developments in management thinking amount to meaningful developments, or
are they just the latest tools of management control that build the illusion

of a liberated workplace? The answer is, both explanations are correct. Employers may genuinely want workers to be engaged, committed, and satisfied, but on their (the employers') own terms—not too engaged (because we only want your ideas if they conform to corporate values), not too committed (because we may compel you to believe and say things you don't like), and not too satisfied (because we could do away with your job on a moment's notice).

Much of what happens to employees who exercise rights to free expression results from the actions and decisions of supervisors, managers, executives, and business owners, not judges. A big emphasis in the book has been on what the law has to say about an employer's ability to regulate or punish expressive activities—how courts and legislatures wrestle with the clashes between employer power and employee speech that come before them. I've described a number of situations where a managerial decision leads an employee to call a lawyer or a reporter. But, of course, most situations don't end up in courts or newspapers; they stay inside the organization, under the sway of employer rules and policies, managerial whims, and an organization's culture. In this chapter, I discuss some key strains of management thought and behavior that illuminate how issues related to employee speech play out inside workplaces. I will also look at some representative examples of formal corporate policies toward expressive activity. The picture that emerges is a managerial culture in the American workplace that eagerly claims to value fairness, open communication, and expressive freedom but easily compromises these ideas in the name of management power, corporate efficiency, and market supremacy.

THINKING ABOUT MANAGEMENT THINKING

Modern management theory over the past half century can be read broadly as movement toward collaboration and participation in the accomplishment of work. I will not suggest, however, that these lofty words describe the direction that all workplaces in the American employment economy have taken. Plenty of jobs remain hopelessly deskilled, plenty of workplaces retain a culture of rigid hierarchy, and plenty of American workers find their employment to be a numbing and alienating exercise in drudgery. But in the broader culture of conventional management wisdom, as it plays out in business school classrooms, management textbooks, and leadership training experiences, the trend for many years has been to wean managers off pure command-and-control thinking and onto the concepts (or buzzwords, if you prefer) of employee participation, involvement, and empowerment.

Beginning with new approaches to "socioemotional" leadership after World War II, this kind of new management thought has appeared in many flavors and has gone by such labels as "open systems," "organization development," "corporate culture," "participative management," "self-directed teams," and "transformational leadership," to name just a few.[2] It's easy to be cynical about a lot of what passes for trends in management science: are these approaches really legitimate advances in employee self-actualization and the humanism of the market-capitalist workplace or just a series of boardroom fads masking the enduring goals of employee compliance, conformity, complacency, and efficiency?

The short answer is both: Clearly, many workplace cultures are far less bureaucratically rigid and more accommodating to employee input, needs, wants, and goals than they were a generation or two ago. But at the same time, American employers remain fiercely protective of the near-consummate power they enjoy over their workforce courtesy of U.S. employment law, and they are willing to put abundant legal and financial resources into defeating regulatory threats to their economic or moral autonomy. It also isn't clear that the management "innovations" that capture popular imagination really do what their promoters would like us to believe. Take the classic notion of employee participation in decision making, which was for years widely regarded as a path to elevating worker performance and satisfaction. A hard look at research evidence indicates that these effects may exist, but at such low levels as to be of little practical significance.[3]

Connecting the evolution of modern management with the topic at hand—free speech at work—invites a paradox. Movement away from old-school notions of bureaucracy and alienation in favor of cultures of employee participation and involvement makes workplaces more hospitable to free expression. After all, if authority structures are flatter, work teams are more common, and employee input is more encouraged, then expressive activity within the workplace, on work-related issues at least, ought to expand, right? Certainly communication networks at work are wider and busier, especially given new forms of digital technology that expand interaction among employees who may not be in the same location (or on the same continent). New tools for interaction are especially relevant for people in managerial jobs, who tend to have larger discussion networks and more ties with others at work.[4] So can we assume that more interaction and wider patterns of communication translate into freer expression?

Not necessarily. In many workplaces, speaking up is still seen as pointless or even dangerous, contributing to what management researchers call a climate of "organizational silence."[5] Silence happens, according to these researchers, when people fear that speaking up will lead them to be evaluated negatively or will damage workplace relationships.[6] Silence is detrimental, not just for workers, who can lose a sense of control, commitment, or value to the firm, but also for employers, who may find their decisions and strategies undermined by limited information, a diminished ability to detect and correct errors, and a lack of negative feedback from below.[7] Managers who preach collaboration can still find themselves running laboratories of employee silence if those who work for them believe that only "positive" contributions are desired and that disagreement is an invitation for reproach rather than reward.

That collaboration and silence are simultaneously possible points to an important observation made some years ago by organization theorist William G. Scott: a more cooperative workplace is not the same thing as a freer workplace. In an insightful essay on workplace liberty and justice, Scott describes Western management thought as perched on a basic assumption that different groups and classes all share an interest in achieving organizational goals. With this assumption of class harmony, the essential purpose of management is to "design and lead cooperative systems so that human betterment and excellent organizational performance are joint outcomes."[8] The problem is that freedom, including freedom of expression, is more apt to elicit conflict rather than to enhance cooperation. As a result, says Scott, freedom presents a challenge to conventional management thinking: "How can liberty be reconciled with mutuality of interests because liberty tends to heighten conflict in organizations?"[9]

Scott goes on to point out that liberty has meaning as a significant organizing principle in employment only if firms see the enhancement of individual character and self-determination as part of their core purpose.

They generally don't. Although some firms may mention these sorts of aims in corporate value statements or human resources policy documents, employers are unlikely to take them very seriously except as a means to achieving "real" organizational purposes related to productivity, efficiency, and prosperity. Employers aren't necessarily sinister, just instrumentally motivated. Public opinion surveys on employee morale bear this out, showing that workers are cynical about the commitment employers have to employees' welfare. A national poll in 2005 found that 59 percent of workers described themselves as loyal to their employers, but only 26 percent saw the firm as loyal to its employees. And only 40 percent described the morale of their workplace as good or excellent.[10] Modern approaches to management and new forms of communication might elevate the volume of workplace interaction, but that interaction doesn't necessarily translate into a happier workplace, or one more hospitable to freedom of expression.

One strain of management psychology that is particularly relevant to free expression at work is known as "organizational justice." The term refers generally to the study—typically by management academics and social psychologists—of the role of "fairness" in the workplace. Fairness as a management value has a lengthy pedigree, going back at least as far as Chester Barnard's 1938 classic, *The Functions of the Executive*.[11] For many years the idea of fairness in the workplace was mainly connected to *outcomes*—the fairness of pay or promotion opportunities, for example, and the rules and conditions that lead people to view allocations of these things as fair.[12] The focus changed with the publication of an important book in the 1970s by two psychologists, John Thibaut and Lauren Walker, on the subject of the fairness of *processes* in legal and organizational disputes.[13]

Thibaut and Walker introduced the study of "procedural justice"—the fairness of the processes used to resolve a dispute—to the fields of conflict resolution and organizational behavior. The study of organizational justice became one of the most commonly explored topics in human resources management and organizational behavior, with published research studies numbering in the hundreds.[14] Researchers have looked at the fairness of a wide variety of processes, such as those related to hiring and promotion, performance evaluation, the setting of pay, grievance handling, and drug testing. Although it's difficult to sum up such a large body of research in a sentence, I can say generally that employees who perceive that workplace procedures are fair are more likely to be satisfied with their jobs, to be committed to the organization, and to make extra contributions over and above job requirements. Evidence also links these justice perceptions with better work performance and with reduced levels of negative behaviors, such as workplace theft.[15]

This concept of justice in the workplace is important for a discussion of free speech because there is a connection between expressive activity and the beliefs held by workers that a workplace is procedurally fair. That connection is found primarily in a concept known as "voice," which refers to having opportunities to provide input about an upcoming decision. One of the most robust findings in studies of organizational justice is that having a chance to give input elevates perceptions that procedures are fair.[16] This so-called voice effect may well make a procedure seem fairer because the opportunity to speak gives individuals a chance to influence the outcome of the decision. Interestingly, however, studies have shown that it can make people think the procedure is better even when they know that they *cannot* affect the outcome.

In a compelling demonstration of this phenomenon, researchers ran an experiment where a performance goal was to be set for a work task that participants in the experiment would perform.[17] The "outcome" here was the decision as to how difficult the goal should be. After learning and practicing the task, some participants were invited to give input on what the goal should be before the actual goal was set. Others were told that the goal had already been set, what that setting was, and that it would not be changed, but they were invited to give input anyway. A third set of participants was not invited to provide any input and was simply told what the goal would be. (In all cases, the goal was set at the same level.) After doing the task, the researchers asked participants to evaluate the fairness both of the procedure used to set the goal and of the decision outcome: the goal itself. Those in the first group—able to voice an opinion before the decision—saw both the procedure and the outcome as fairer than the other two groups did. That's no surprise. What is interesting here is that individuals in the second group—able to voice an opinion but have *no effect* on the decision—rated both the procedure and the outcome as fairer than those who had no opportunity to give any input.

The opportunity to weigh in doesn't have the same effect in all situations; other studies have identified specific circumstances when the voice effect does and doesn't work. Generally, though, people value the chance to speak up about issues that potentially affect them. They value that opportunity, not just because having a say might turn the outcome in their favor but also because of the personal satisfaction that comes from being able to speak one's mind. Research also shows that people derive significant social benefits from being treated fairly by groups and organizations: they are more apt to trust those making decisions, to feel good about their own social standing in the group or organization, and to cultivate a sense of commitment to perform on behalf of the group.[18]

These findings point to substantial benefits when employers treat employees and workplace issues and disputes in ways that are procedurally fair. Of course, most of these benefits accrue to employers, not to employees. Sure, the evidence suggests that workers are generally happier with their situations and feel better about their standing in the organization when they think that procedures are fair, and that's certainly worth something. But I know of no evidence that organizational policies promoting fairness make the individuals within smarter or otherwise better humans or improve their pay or advancement prospects. From an applied standpoint, research on justice in the workplace is less about actual fairness than it is about managing employees' *perceptions* of fairness, which means identifying the levers of management that can inflate those perceptions and understanding the consequences for organizational goals of doing so. We might think, in a big-picture sense, of justice as a critical piece of democratic self-government and the "good society," but in the hands of autocrats—including employers in a system governed by the idea of employment at will—justice can be the means by which conflict is submerged and collaboration is enforced. As William G. Scott points out, we find systems of justice in even the most tyrannical institutions because justice "requires individual obedience to the established cooperative order."[19]

Some of this background on the study of justice in the workplace might give the false impression that procedural justice—the notion that the fairness of procedures matters—was invented in the twentieth century. Actually, concerns about the fairness of procedures have been around at least as long as the Bill of Rights and the concept of due process in the Fifth

Amendment (not to mention the Magna Carta). What late-twentieth-century students of management figured out was that some elements of due process confer efficiency and productivity advantages for employers, and incidentally might make the workplace a bit more pleasant for workers.

Due process is critical in an analysis of free speech at work because without it an employee punished for her speech has no right to any sort of hearing before an impartial authority or any guarantee that there was a reasonable basis for the action taken against her. As I discussed in depth in earlier chapters, there are some just-cause protections against being fired arbitrarily in government employment. Public-sector workers also enjoy First Amendment protections when their speech on matters of public interest doesn't undermine their employers' efficient operations. However, for most employees who work in the private sector and are subject to the ruthless charms of employment at will, no such protections are in play.

The management research on procedural justice gives employers tools to leverage employee satisfaction and commitment, but it hasn't made workplaces into laboratories for due process. Without genuine due process—which means both protection against being punished or fired without legitimate cause and guarantees of procedural fairness—expressive liberty at work gains little from the science or practice of organizational justice.[20] For employers, the absence of a due-process requirement is efficient—to a point. Firing someone for their speech without the niceties of a procedure allowing challenge or redress saves time and money. But when a termination turns into a wrongful termination lawsuit, it becomes a unpredictable and potentially costly enterprise. This explains why, as I mentioned in Chapter 5, it was *employers* in Montana who backed that state's unique just-cause dismissal law as a substitute for employment at will.

For workers, a lack of due process amounts simply to powerlessness at the hands of an employer's arbitrary discretion. And even given an option to challenge legally an employer's decision (for instance because the employee works for the government, or lives in Montana), the price of doing so is high, in time, money, and reputation. For an employee who finds himself in a labor market lacking readily available job alternatives, the costs are especially severe, heightening the incentives to self-censor. The courts afford due process once a lawsuit is filed, but the best option for everyone concerned is a fair procedure with a just-cause standard *inside* the firm—

precisely what management theorists who advocate procedural justice would advocate, but which has not become a necessary feature of the American employment system.

SPEAKING IN (CORPORATE) CODE

One avenue for insight into how employers manage expression is the obvious one: look at what they say they do. Most large firms in the private sector have created business codes of behavior that indicate, with varying levels of detail, the expectations of the firm regarding appropriate behavior by employees. These codes, which go by various names ("code of conduct," "code of ethics," and "code of business practice" are common titles), are a useful vantage point for looking at corporate policy on certain aspects of free speech by employees. Many of these codes also address how the company sees its obligations to other stakeholders, such as customers, suppliers, and communities, and articulate the preferred way that the firm and its employees should behave in those stakeholder relationships.[21] In U.S. corporations, codes of conduct grew in popularity during the 1990s, after Congress enacted corporate crime sentencing guidelines. These guidelines allow for a significant reduction in the fine or penalty imposed in some corporate crime convictions if the firm can show that it has an effective compliance program in place and that a business code is one part of such a program.[22] Recent estimates indicate that as many as three-fourths of large U.S. firms have one of these codes in place.[23]

The employee conduct issues that come up most frequently in these codes are those related to fraud, corruption, discrimination, and other forms of bad behavior. An academic paper in the *Journal of Business Ethics* a few years ago analyzed the content of business codes at the world's 200 largest companies (most of which were U.S. firms).[24] It revealed that roughly half of these codes mentioned conflicts of interest, receipt of improper gifts, bribery, harassment, insider trading, and the use of proper accounting principles. The issues having to do with expressive behavior identified in this study were all about speech that employees were supposed to avoid: disclosure of confidential information, racist insinuations, tasteless or obscene jokes, verbal abuse, treatment of others with disrespect, and a category of behavior labeled "gossiping/ridiculing/insulting."

A closer look at these corporate codes reveals that many of them lay out the firm's policies and attitudes toward other important aspects of employee speech. In a systematic study of the codes of conduct of major U.S. firms, PhD student Amanda Carrico and I examined many publicly available codes for firms that made the Fortune 500 list of America's largest companies (by revenue).[25] We looked for evidence of corporate policies and guidelines that both encouraged and frowned on employee speech. We were especially interested in policies regarding expressive activities by employees that occur outside of work, given that extracurricular speech is frequently the kind that lands people in hot water with their employers.

The form of employee speech most commonly promoted in these codes is in the realm of whistleblowing. You don't generally find that word— "whistleblowing"—actually used, but a large majority of firms (upward of two-thirds) include in their codes explicit language inviting workers to voice concerns about rules violations, ethical lapses, or other forms of wrongdoing that they observe or suspect. Virtually all the codes that encourage this kind of communication also explicitly promise that retaliation (a word most of them do use) against those who do speak up will not be tolerated.

Many firms offer in their codes a general statement valuing employee input and open communication at work. These statements often have the look and feel of platitudes rather than of serious attempts to engineer a cultural tolerance for free expression. Typical of these kinds of statements is one found in Boeing's Ethical Business Conduct Guidelines: "An open and honest culture is one in which all employees feel free to share opinions and perceptions in a professional manner in order to resolve issues."[26] Or this from AT&T's Code of Conduct: "Differing opinions and expressions of concern are welcomed. While we may disagree with one another, we know that healthy debate is important."[27]

Companies put more energy and ink into statements in their codes about the kinds of "open communication" that they would rather *not* see in the workplace. Given the legal risks associated with racial, sexual, or other forms of harassment and discrimination, just about every code articulates a prohibition on harassing speech. Many describe in general terms the categories of expressive actions that create a hostile work environment; an example is the code at energy giant ConocoPhillips, which mentions "overt advances . . . demeaning comments, jokes, language, and gestures."[28] Some, like the transportation company Ryder's Principles of Business Conduct, are disarmingly specific in identifying troublesome expression:

> using degrading or stereotypical words or actions in jokes, cartoons, insults, tricks, pranks or horseplay related to sex, race . . . or any other class protected by law . . . using sexually suggestive or mocking comments which describe an individual's body or attire . . . whistling or "cat calls" . . . making graphic or verbal commentary about an individual's body, sexual prowess or sexual deficiencies . . . mocking, ridiculing or mimicking another's culture, accent, appearance or customs . . . displaying sexually suggestive or provocative pictures or objects . . . displaying an individual's actual physical body or parts of the body in a graphic manner . . .[29]

Some codes contain curiously worded passages that come off as efforts to identify other undesirable (but not harassing in the legal sense) forms of employee speech. Pharmaceutical distributor AmerisourceBergen, for instance, tells employees in its Code of Ethics and Business Conduct "Do not use business communications as a platform for negative personal opinions or speculation."[30] The retailer Target in its Business Conduct Guide cautions employees to communicate always with the "the brand" first and foremost in mind: "Each team member is responsible for maintaining the company's image when communicating with others. You can enhance or hurt the company's image with every written, verbal or electronic communication."[31] I don't wish to read too much into these statements; after all, just as with upbeat platitudes about "open communication," the link between code-of-conduct pronouncements and day-to-day workplace reality may well be tenuous, if not imaginary. There is, though, in these kinds of vague passages a not-so-veiled implication that anything said could lead to trouble, so be sure to think *really carefully* before saying much of anything.

Many firms treat these codes of conduct as a convenient opportunity to remind employees that regardless of the kind of expressive behavior they are undertaking, they should harbor no illusion of a right to privacy when they communicate using workplace tools or systems, even for allowed personal uses. In legal disputes over violations of privacy, it is often relevant whether an individual whose privacy "rights" are at stake had a reasonable basis to expect privacy in the first place.[32] Accordingly, firms use these codes (or separate policy documents on the use of communications systems) to make it perfectly clear that there is no expectation of privacy. Wal-Mart's Statement of Ethics leaves little to chance: "Associates have no expectation of privacy as to the use of Wal-Mart communication tools, and Wal-Mart has the right to and does monitor your communications tools, including their content, and your usage of such tools."[33] Private employers are allowed under U.S. law to disabuse employees of any and all notions that their personal communications during the workday might merit a shred of privacy. However, some firms are willing to stop short of the full big-brother-can-and-definitely-will-watch-you treatment. Automotive supplier Tenneco, for example, injects a for-cause hurdle into its policy: "The Company has the right to review e-mail messages or files when there is reasonable grounds to suspect abuse."[34]

We find some interesting variations in how employers use these codes to regulate the personal expressive activities of their employees, especially after-work involvement in civic and political activities. Corporate employers are understandably explicit and strict about regulating political activity by employees while they are *at work* or using company resources. They face the risk that campaign regulators might treat those activities as "in-kind" corporate political contributions, a risk compounded by the fact that direct corporate contributions to candidates are illegal in federal elections and in some state and local elections. As a result, many codes of conduct include language barring employees from campaign-related activity that occurs during the workday, on employer property, or through the company's communication systems.

Political activity outside the workplace is a different matter. As I discussed in Chapter 5, although there are laws protecting one's right to vote (and to vote for the candidate of one's choice) from employer interference, relatively few states have broad protections for other kinds of off-work political activity. Many Americans would probably be alarmed to discover that many employers can, if they wish, regulate their employees' private political activity. No doubt few companies do this overtly. In fact, treatment of outside political activity in corporate codes of conduct tends to start with some sort of broad, sunny remark of encouragement, like this one from Target: "Team members may participate and contribute to political organizations or campaigns. In fact, in the interest of healthy communities and a strong political system in our country, team members are encouraged to do so."[35] Most would probably find this kind of corporate effervescence to be essentially harmless, but there is something just a bit paternalistic, or at least cloying, about learning in a manual of ethics or conduct that your employer deigns to honor your right as a citizen to participate in democracy and civil society.

Employers do seem to worry that employees' personal, off-the-job political activity will be linked to or reflect on the company, so they use language in their codes to put some distance between employees' speech and the firm's—or, more precisely, obligate employees to create that distance. A gentle and reasonable approach is found in Hewlett-Packard's Standards of Business Conduct, which asks employees to refrain from leading others to believe that their personal views are those of the firm: "While you are encouraged to participate in your community and the political process, you may not create the impression that you are speaking or acting for HP."[36]

More troubling are passages in codes of conduct that seek to put a kind of corporate gag order on the individual, compel unnecessary disclaimers from the employee, or otherwise impose vague limits on acceptable political activity. In the gag-order category we find the policy of telecommunications company Verizon, which insists that employees "ensure that any personal political testimonials, endorsements, other statements or lobbying activities *do not reference our employment with the company* or imply its support for our position."[37] An example of a policy that appears to mandate employee disclaimers separating personal views from those of the employer is found in the Cardinal Health Ethics Guide: "In the conduct of their personal, civic, and political affairs, employees should *at all times make clear* that their views, actions, gifts and contributions are their own and are not those of Cardinal Health."[38] For perplexing vagueness, there is Disney's admonition to employees that they can participate as private citizens in politics unless it "would give rise to an improper appearance of partiality."[39]

We should not overinterpret the specific language of these codes, which, after all, are attempts to put in writing some fairly abstract rules and principles around business conduct that will always be open to interpretation in specific cases. Also, we can detect the presence of lawyers around the code-of-conduct drafting table: many provisions are less about coaching nuanced ethical judgments and more about creating the policy backstory for actions later that might look like discipline or termination. For employees working at-will, of course, no backstory is really needed. Employers may use these codes to craft an image of the firm as ethically thoughtful, consistent, or reasonable, but under employment at will, arbitrary discipline or termination for expressive activity requires no supporting argument from these kinds of policy documents.

But even with those caveats, we find in many of these codes the documentary evidence of employer wariness (if not outright intolerance) of free expression at work. Asking employees to be sure their political speech is not easily construed as the employer's is certainly reasonable. But requiring employees to always make certain that their expressive activities are explicitly distinguishable from corporate discourse, "or else," has the look and feel of intimidation, not friendly advice on how to be a good employee.

This is especially perilous turf for employees who in their off hours really do take their employers' kindly advice and become involved as political or community activists. An activist who is careful to avoid mentioning her place of employment as she becomes a public figure in community affairs is still at some point apt to have her employer named in a media report; after all, members of the press identify people in the news by age and occupation routinely, even when those pieces of information are unrelated to why they are making news. And in any event, why shouldn't someone making news as a political activist or community leader be identified by her work and workplace? For many of us, our work is a huge part who we are, one we don't shed nights and weekends. Selling employers our time and our energy need not mean that we also must sell our identity.

Much of what I've been discussing here relates to employee speech the corporate employer would rather avoid, or avoid being associated with. The other side of the coin is compelled speech—the message an employer might coerce from its employees. A potentially insidious form of this, one that often draws some attention in these business code documents, is the giving of money to political candidates through company-sponsored political action committees (PACs). Firms cannot contribute corporate funds to federal candidates, but election law does allow them to create and administer PACs, aggregating donations from individual employees and using those funds to make contributions to campaigns.[40] Corporate PACs, already a common campaign finance vehicle, grew in popularity after the 2002 passage of federal campaign finance reform that regulated corporate soft-money donations. In 2003, the number of PACs overall declined, while the number of corporate PACs increased, and by 2004, over half of companies in the Standard & Poor's 500 Index had PACs.[41]

Employers with corporate PACs often mention them in discussions of political activity in codes of conduct, usually asserting that contributions are strictly voluntary. The most broadly worded statements go further, stressing no connection whatsoever between political participation and terms of employment. An example is ConocoPhillips' statement: "No direct or indirect pressure in any form is to be placed on employees to make any political contribution or participate in the support of a political party or the political candidacy of any individual."[42] Coca-Cola puts it more succinctly: "Your job will not be affected by your choices in personal political contributions."[43]

But how voluntary are PAC contributions, really? How comfortable are people with employer reassurances that a job or one's standing in the firm is unaffected by the choice of whether to play along (or not) with a PAC contribution appeal? Not very, according to Bill Allison of the Center for Public Integrity, a Washington-based campaign finance watchdog group. "There is pressure in corporations to be a team player," Allison says, and "if you're an ambitious employee in lower levels of management, you may feel that donating is in your interest."[44] A survey by *CFO Magazine* (a publication geared, you will not be shocked to learn, to senior financial executives) found that almost a quarter of respondents at the level of corporate vice president or higher felt that not giving to the PAC would be detrimental to their career, and another 15 percent were not sure.[45] Corporations have been known to give "public" recognition to PAC contributors at meetings of executives; that'll surely alleviate the pressure to give. One need hardly be a conspiracy theorist to entertain the hypothesis that a lot of "voluntary" political contributions in the workplace fall somewhere well short of being genuinely voluntary.

The same, incidentally, can be said of contributions to charitable giving campaigns, such as the ubiquitous United Way, in the workplace. Employers routinely pressure workers to help them achieve high levels of participation in these campaigns, which can lead to donations to agencies whose mission, even though "nonpolitical" to qualify for tax-exempt status, can easily embody a civic or political message. Many United Way campaigns fund the Boy Scouts of America, for example, even though the Scouts discriminate openly on the basis of sexual orientation.[46] United Way policies typically assert that employer coercion is inappropriate; for example, this one is from the United Way of the Bay Area (which by the way refuses to include the Boy Scouts among its affiliated groups): "Any semblance of pressure (whether real, implied or perceived) is contradictory to our operating standards."[47] But as we've seen with corporate PACs, saying there's no pressure to participate doesn't easily translate into employee perceptions that no pressure exists.

Criticizing corporate power as a threat to the republic is almost as old as the republic itself. Thomas Jefferson warned of the "aristocracy of our moneyed corporations," Abraham Lincoln fretted that "corporations have been enthroned," and Franklin D. Roosevelt feared for liberty "if the people tolerate the growth of private power to a point where it becomes stronger than their democratic state itself."[48] These and other pithy observations about the perils of capitalism could segue nicely into an agitated sermon on how evil corporations and their management practices are sapping democracy through a frontal assault on the First Amendment and the Bill of Rights.

But I don't see value in overstating the case. America's employers—the people who run our corporations, but also the people who hire and supervise millions working in public-sector jobs and nonprofit organizations—aren't conspiring to repress workers as some sort of sinister collective assault on the Bill of Rights. I suspect that virtually all of them as individual citizens think the First Amendment is a pretty good idea. As employers, however, they are taking what the law and conventional economic morality give them: the right to be reflexively suspicious of employee behavior that departs from managerial expectations or usual practice. What looks at times like unfettered and arbitrary corporate power is often just managerial habit, abetted, of course, by the whispers of attorneys about the legal risks that lurk in every corner of tolerance for employee freedom. In this environment, productivity and performance can withstand little interference from the messy spontaneity of free speech. Shortly before the 2006 midterm elections, a *New York Times* article about political conversations in the workplace quoted one CEO: "Nothing belongs at work that becomes disruptive or impacts performance."[49] One imagines that his firm operates without humans.

In *False Prophets*, a critical examination of management wisdom over the last century, business historian James Hoopes points to a common tactic for diluting worker fears about management power: "Make corporate life seem freer than it is."[50] Hoopes is not himself pushing for a freer workplace; he'd like managers to see their top-down power for what it is, accept its necessity for corporate efficiency, and understand that communication in a work-place is not the moral equivalent of free speech in a democracy. The point of leadership, in this view, is to encourage communication in light of man-agerial power, not to dilute that power in order to foster communication or some gauzy notion of workplace democracy.[51]

Easier said than done. The lure of managerial privilege, coupled with an employer-friendly legal system, creates for too many employers an irresistible preference for imperiousness over judiciousness. Christine Carpanzano of Glen Ellyn, Illinois, learned this first-hand when she lost her job selling train-ing programs for a community college to local businesses. After voicing objections to a company slush fund created by a hidden charge built into cus-tomer accounts, Carpanzano's employer apparently couldn't resist some free speech of its own: a remarkably indiscreet note in her file that read "We need to terminate. Need a reason."[52] A jury in her successful lawsuit against the college gave her 300,000 reasons.

The Case for Freer Expression

It is necessary to recognize the powerful forces that impel men towards the elimination of unorthodox expression. Most men have a strong inclination, for rational or irrational reasons, to suppress opposition.

—Thomas I. Emerson[1]

EMERSON IS RIGHT. His observation, from the opening pages of his masterful 1970 book, *The System of Freedom of Expression*, captures a noxious managerial impulse to silence workplace speech rather than to understand, accommodate, or tolerate it. But managers aren't the only ones who fall victim to the impulse to silence opposition; Emerson is actually describing just about all of us. However tolerant and open-minded we imagine ourselves, the fact remains that opposition is uncomfortable, and reconciling differences of opinion is hard work. We are more apt to surround ourselves with viewpoints we like and discount those we don't like. Walter Lippmann writes in a famous 1939 essay that "a good statesman, like any other sensible human being, always learns more from his opponents than from his fervent supporters."[2] Nicely put, but who has the time? As sensible humans with busy schedules and a preference for social harmony, most of us put more effort into avoiding opposition than into learning from it.

I say this not to justify the erosion of free expression in and around the workplace but to put it in context. No doubt we can find some employers who are motivated by a toxic blend of greed, power, and despotic arrogance and who define the workplace as their personal fiefdom of control, conformity, and productive efficiency. The worst of these practice what researchers have labeled "abusive supervision"—managerial brutishness that elicits from employees significant anxiety about their jobs, workplaces, and even their lives as a whole.[3] It would be silly, however, to pin the American workplace's unfriendliness to employee speech on these kinds of bosses.

The managerial ranks of employers are populated mainly with sensible humans—with busy schedules and a taste for social harmony—and most of them probably think the First Amendment and the Bill of Rights are pretty reasonable things.

The issue is not troglodytes running the workplace. Instead, it's a legal and economic system under which employers don't just buy a person's labor; they also reserve the right to rent an employee's conscience, ideology, and social identity. As a result, employers don't think about free speech much: employers put little energy into free speech and other civil liberties because the law for the most part gives them a pass. They also don't think much of it: at times when they can't avoid contemplating free speech—like when they're dragged into court for infringing upon it or confronted with a legislature that wants to force them to worry about it more often—they will typically go to great lengths and deploy serious resources to preserve their ability to not think much about free speech. As journalism professor Lawrence Soley thoroughly documents in his book *Censorship, Inc.*, the opportunities for corporations to silence speech by employees, consumers, and activists are "limited only by the imaginations of corporate executives and their attorneys."[4]

A generation ago, many thought that the American workplace might be headed toward a future where employees had more rights on the job and more freedom from arbitrary employer tyranny. A remarkable 1971 survey showed overwhelming support for some due-process protections for employees against the capricious acts of management. We're not talking about the opinions of unreconstructed socialists or starry-eyed leftists here; this was a survey of subscribers—more than 3,400 of them—to that most established of management establishments, the *Harvard Business Review*.[5]

The participants in the survey were asked about the fairness of firing a person "for the good of the company," with no hint of fraud or misconduct by that person and giving him no opportunity to defend himself. Three-fourths of respondents said that this is "very unfair, should never be done," while less than 2 percent thought it was appropriate for the good of the firm. Only 6 percent said they would themselves do something like this occasionally if it was for the good of the company. A large majority also said that employees should have the right to know all the allegations behind a decision to fire them. (Being a creature of its time, this survey also shed light on the pivotal question of how managers should cope with the "hippy dresser." Fifty-two percent said he should be told "we'd like to have him stay with us but not if he looks like a hippy.")

These findings are striking (except maybe the one about hippy couture) because they paint a picture of broad dissatisfaction among the managerial class with the basic premise of our employment system: the employer's right to fire anyone, at any time, for any reason. Might the presence of this sentiment thirty years ago have foreshadowed workplace liberalization? *Harvard Business Review* executive editor David Ewing at the time thought so:

> Within the management castle, as well as out in the woods and fields, there is growing support for employee rights. . . . The notion of a "bill of rights" for corporate employees has been advocated in the Harvard Business Review and will doubtless find its way soon into other management journals. . . . There is growing impatience with the concept that anywhere, in any organization, rights of free speech and free press should be suspended.[6]

Ewing said a "new mood is coming over organizations," one that will encourage corporations "to be the servant of the republic as well as of its stockholders."[7] Management professor Kenneth Walters wrote in the *Harvard Business Review* in 1975 about "the banding together of employee groups who refuse to work for organizations that condition employment on the sacrifice of basic rights."[8] Walters saw (or thought he saw) movement away from employment at will as a harbinger of "fundamental changes in employee rights."[9] In a particularly dramatic vision of a coming workplace-rights utopia, management professor Jay Forrester argued in a 1965 article that corporations need "constitutions" to limit their power and establish employee rights, just as public legislative bodies are subject to a national constitution.[10]

So what became of this worker-centric optimism from the 1960s and 1970s? Where did the trajectories of liberal management theory and expanding employment rights go astray? The simple answer is that they ran headfirst into late-twentieth-century market capitalism. Civil rights and civil liberties were growth industries in the period during and following the Vietnam war, but the 1980s and 1990s were more about deregulation and indulgence than injustice. Regulatory walls came tumbling down in many industries, Congress ceased to be consistently friendly to the labor movement, union membership plummeted, MBA programs expanded rapidly, privatization ran rampant, global free trade took root as an economic religion, and the executive suite became a fashionable place to be seen again.

We can point to some signs of progress on employee speech rights since Gerald Ford pardoned Richard Nixon, but they come with serious qualifications. Whistleblower protections as a matter of law have spread from rare to everywhere, but availing oneself of those protections remains legally challenging, financially costly, and markedly hazardous to one's career health. A few states have adopted statutory protections for off-work behavior or political activity, but only a few, and courts all too frequently buy employer arguments about disruptive threats to workplace harmony. As I observed in Chapter 3, the harsh rule of employment at will has been chipped away in many states through exceptions based on public policy, but almost nowhere is free speech recognized as a public-policy exception.

In public-sector employment, the Supreme Court expanded workplace speech rights for a while during the sixties and seventies but eventually arrived at a balancing test that has left judges siding routinely with employers. In the private sector, the doctrine of state action (discussed at length in Chapter 2) remains as powerful as ever, which means virtually no protection for individual rights against private employers who choose tyranny and repression as their guiding management principles. Although for a time the Court saw value in protecting some expression on private property, by the 1990s the Court had fully returned to a clear preference for property rights over expressive rights. Under the plain meaning of state action, writes constitutional scholar Erwin Chemerinsky, "the private institution always wins and the individual fired or disciplined by it for expression always loses."[11]

Freedom of expression in the workplace is excessively and needlessly limited, as a matter of both law and management practice. An argument for this position begins with a few basic assumptions. First, freedoms to think, speak, and act are paramount values for a free society. Second, guarantees of due process are indispensable to the existence of a just society. Third, work is not merely something people do between intervals of "real life"; it's where people to a meaningful extent live out their lives. Accordingly, freedom of expression and guarantees of due process do not lose their significance, for both the individual and for society, when someone goes to work or otherwise spends a lot of time in a nonpublic setting. But at the same time, a free society also means giving private institutions, not just individuals, a large measure of freedom from government interference.

We naturally think of issues involving rights at work as arising from tension between two opposing ideas: the job-related needs of individuals (for such things as financial security, occupational advancement, and self-determination) and the efficiency-related goals of employers (such as productivity, growth, and prosperity). A more complete picture emerges, however, if we imagine these rights occupying terrain between *three* ideas in tension: individual wants, employer goals, and the aims of a self-governing democratic society. This three-way view pulls us past a parochial market view of employment—beyond the simplistic notion that work is merely a negotiated exchange of labor for capital, and democracy is something you worry about nights and weekends. It confronts us, instead, with a bigger idea: that freedom of speech, the nature of work, and the quality of democracy are intertwined. When employers silence or chill employee speech, they aren't just shaping their organization's culture, they are undermining "democratic culture"—a society in which ordinary people can actively participate to lower barriers of rank and privilege and to develop influence over the institutions and forces that shape their futures.[12]

This way of thinking about the significance of free speech at work raises three crucial issues. The first is how to balance an individual's right to personal expression in a deliberative democracy that values free speech against an employer's right to run a business as it sees fit in a market economy that values free enterprise. The second, given my earlier, lofty assertions about connections between work and democracy, is understanding how limits on workplace expression tarnish the larger civil society within which employers and employees exist. The third is describing in realistic legal and managerial terms what an expansion of expressive rights on and off the job would look like.

A BALANCING ACT

In the discussion in Chapter 6 of theories of free speech and the First Amendment, I talked about individualist approaches that locate the value of free expression in personal autonomy, fulfillment, and self-realization.[13] These values are impaired in a system that lets employers heavily curtail free expression. Censorship, repression, and similar limits to free speech in society as a whole seem obviously to threaten these values, but does it follow that limits to *workplace* expression have a similar effect? If so, then workplace intolerance for free speech interferes with basic rights to autonomy of belief and expression.

To put it another way, the experience of liberty depends in part on the experience of liberty at work. It is in connection with their jobs and workplaces that many people encounter meaningful adult interaction and experience social engagement, so the idea of political and cultural overlap between life and work is unremarkable. Ethically speaking, basic moral rights such as freedom of choice, autonomy, and privacy are more important than the boundaries of organizations and their rules or customs. Business ethicist Patricia Werhane calls these rights "so basic and inviolable that every human being possesses them despite his or her particular social, political, historical, or even cultural situation."[14] In this sort of incorruptible libertarianism, basic moral rights deserve respect in most situations, winning out over competing interests such as the economic and property rights of corporate and other employers.

The counterweight to a focus on individual rights is market liberalism— the logic of free enterprise as the foundation for individual liberty rather than as a threat to it. A market view suggests several grounds for giving employers a free hand to limit worker speech: the firm's "right" to seek profits without putting those profits at risk by the behavior of an employee; the employer's "right" to manage the internal dynamics of a business as he sees fit; the employer's "right" to cultivate the loyalty and trust of workers; the firm's "right" to create and preserve an image or reputation; and a firm's "right" to its own expressive activity.[15] I hasten to add that the logic behind these "rights" isn't driven solely by a narrow admiration of markets for their own sake. If the goals of a healthy society include economic prosperity and stability, then a relatively free hand for employers to manage productivity and efficiency may work to promote important public interests.

That market view doesn't, however, put employee rights and employer interests on equivalent moral footing. I put the "rights" of corporations and employers in quotation marks because they are not rights of the kind that protect individual civil liberties. Although some libertarians regard private property ownership as a natural right, a corporation's "property right" interest in particular ways of doing business is a contrived privilege, one that has meaning only in relation to the acts of government that create the privilege and enforce it. "A corporation is an artificial being," Chief Justice John Marshall wrote almost two centuries ago, "invisible, intangible, and existing only in contemplation of law."[16] Because a corporation is merely a "creature of law," said Marshall, it has no properties or attributes except those conferred upon it by its charter. By the early twentieth century, courts and legislatures had morphed the corporation from a government-enabled entity into a legal version of a "person," with autonomy to hold assets, conduct business without interference, and go to court.[17] Even so, what corporations have acquired are legal privileges, not moral authority, which is the exclusive province of sentient beings.

The enactment of laws—an action taken by *individuals* who exercise their rights of conscience and belief and speech in collective acts of self-government—is what grants to employers their ability to enter into contracts and do business in certain ways. Other laws—generated also by *individuals* acting in concert through systems of representative government—make it possible for employers or property owners to anticipate the support of public institutions to enforce their "rights" (such as the police officer who confronts a trespasser, or the court that hears a contract dispute). The law has come to treat corporations as if they were persons in one key way: through the Supreme Court's endorsement of a right to corporate speech over the past thirty years. In doing so the Court has limited the power of government to stop corporations from airing their views in the so-called marketplace of ideas. This right allows employers to "speak," but it doesn't enable them able to reap the intrinsic human value of free speech. Justice Byron White made this point forcefully in a dissenting opinion in one of the Court's landmark corporate free speech cases:

> The principal function of the First Amendment, the use of communication as a means of self-expression, self-realization, and self-fulfillment, is not at all furthered by corporate speech. It is clear that the communications of profit making corporations are not "an integral part of the development of ideas, of mental exploration and of the affirmation of self." They do not represent a manifestation of individual freedom or choice.[18]

Declaring that corporations aren't humans is a reasonably satisfying way to escape the moral trap of granting "human rights" to organizations, but it doesn't do much to sort out the conflicts among individual rights, employer interests, and societal goals. How, for example, do we measure a system such as employment at will that favors employers against an employee-friendly alternative like a requirement of just cause for dismissal? These are obviously competing claims: either we have employment-at-will rules that let you fire someone for no reason, or we have just-cause dismissal rules requiring a valid reason. Yet both systems appeal to similar underlying values: autonomy and fairness.[19] These values underpin the employer's claim to ownership and free enterprise, and they are also behind the employee's desire for job security and due process. So whose values win out?

One solution is found in the logic of the marketplace. When an employer and a worker agree on a job, a wage, and working conditions, the party giving up rights—typically the employee—is (in theory) compensated for rights foregone. This sort of market-wage explanation is convincing, however, only if the integrity of a working free market for labor is assumed. But that's an assumption with a number of problems. Business ethicist Michael J. McCall, among others, points to common imbalances between employer and worker that make the act of hiring a true market transaction in name only. Firms will often have far more *knowledge* than individuals about the background labor market in which they are striking a deal. Firms will often have more *power*, with the individual depending more on the job than the firm is dependent on the individual employee. And employees will commonly be at a disadvantage related to *mobility*—finding it harder to replace a job with a comparable alternative than it will be for the firm to replace the employee.[20] Workers at the mercy of these labor-market imbalances have no choice but to put more effort into hanging on to a job than exercising on-the-job rights, much less trying to test or expand those rights.

But even if the market for labor did work the way free markets are supposed to, without harmful imbalances of knowledge and power, it would still be wrong to treat employer-employee tension over free speech in the same way we treat tussles over economic rights. Fans of employment at will praise it on efficiency grounds as a system that gets it right most of the time. Its worth "should not be judged by the occasional cases in which it is said to produce unfortunate results," writes law professor Richard Epstein in an influential defense of employment at will, "but rather by the vast run of cases where it provides a sensible private response" to labor difficulties.[21] This perspective, I contend, is inadequate for a system of free speech. There are some human dimensions of social life—freedom of expression among them—for which economic efficiency and equilibrium are not acceptable benchmarks. When an employee's speech is silenced by the actions of a powerful institution—an employer-at-will, perhaps, or a court siding with an employer—far more speech may be chilled than just the expressive act at hand. In matters of civil rights and civil liberties, the "occasional cases" that in Epstein's stoic phrasing "produce unfortunate results" are often the ones that matter most.

As we saw repeatedly in earlier chapters, the hard cases pull courts into the balancing game—weighing an individual's right to expressive activity against an employer's ability and discretion to conduct business as it wishes. The courts get involved more frequently in government employment, where workers actually have some legitimate First Amendment rights in the workplace to be weighed, but balancing does come up in a number of situations involving expressive activity in the private-sector workplace as well. In public employment cases, the U.S. Supreme Court has defined the government employer's interest in unnecessarily strong terms. Employee speech oversteps its bounds, and can be censored or punished, if it offends discipline or harmony, erodes personal relationships, diminishes loyalty or confidence, or interferes with (in theory) any aspect of the enterprise.[22] With such vague and sweeping legal grounds available for employers to disallow speech, we should not be surprised that employees usually come up on the short end of the balancing test in workplace speech cases.

Balancing of this sort is ethically troubling because it assumes that an employee and an employer deserve to be treated with moral equivalence—that they have equally valid moral claims to autonomy and free choice. If an employment relationship is nothing more than a free market exchange of capital and labor, then perhaps moral equivalence is reasonable. But when employment is viewed as a broader mix of interests involving individuals, organizations, and the (presumably free) society in which they are embedded, a new balance makes sense. The virtues of economic independence and well-functioning markets take a back seat to higher-order values of individual liberty and democratic self-government. An individual's rights to freedom of belief, association, and expression take precedence over the economic autonomy of an organization acting in the role of employer.

This is how it works, at least on paper, in countries where there are legal protections resembling civil rights protections for political viewpoints: an individual's rights take precedence. I am referring here to "political opinion" as a category that is protected, like race, sex, religion, and so forth, against discrimination or termination in employment. This protection, as I mentioned in Chapter 5, appears explicitly in conventions of the International Labor Organization and in the domestic labor law in some countries, but (with a few state-law exceptions) not in the United States.

Legal protection for political opinions would have the effect of giving political expression moral priority. Outside the workplace, political expression is treated by both U.S. courts and legal theorists as speech deserving of the greatest protection. In the workplace, however, an individual's right to expression and an employer's right to sustain efficiency or morale are essentially equivalent moral claims to be balanced. And that's true only in the public sector, where the balancing test applies. (And as I have noted, the balancing test tends to favor employers when it is applied.) For most private-sector employment situations, there is no imperative to balance competing interests. The illusion of employment at will is that a free market for labor gives both parties—employer and worker—equal rights to walk away. The reality is that with imbalances of knowledge, power, and mobility, employer interests usually win out over individual expressive rights.

SOCIETY, CIVIL AND OTHERWISE

A compelling argument that freedom of expression matters, and that there ought to be more of it, goes well beyond effects on just the workplace. Expanding employee rights is a good thing from the employee's perspective and may or may not seriously harm employer interests, depending on how "expansive" the expansion is. Treating free expression in the workplace as a question of balance between employee liberty and management autonomy is important, but inadequate, because it overlooks the connection between rights at work and the character of the broader society within which work exists. I have in mind here the effects of workplace expression on political society—which is to say on the health and well-being of our (small *d*) democratic institutions. But I am especially concerned with the effects of workplace expression on "civil society," which refers generally to the nature of community life and social order apart from the workings of organized government.[23]

"Civil society" is a term that for many political theorists and historians invokes Alexis de Tocqueville's two-volume study of the American people, politics, and society published in 1835 and 1840, *Democracy in America*. An important piece of Tocqueville's survey of nineteenth-century American democracy is his discussion of associational life—people's involvement in voluntary civil and political organizations. Tocqueville sees this as not just a feature of democracy but the very essence of it:

> The most natural privilege of man, next to the right of acting for himself, is that of combining his exertions with those of his fellow creatures and of acting in common with them. The right of association therefore appears to me almost as inalienable in its nature as the right of personal liberty.[24]

Tocqueville's analysis ranges across many diverse aspects of American government and society. *Democracy in America* is, however, often singled out for its treatment of associations and civil society because Tocqueville marveled at the depth of associational life he observed firsthand. "In no country in the world," he writes, "has the principle of association been more successfully used or applied to a greater multitude of objects than in America."[25]

Involvement in voluntary associations builds political community by joining together shared beliefs held by people who might not otherwise come to know one another. Freedom of speech and assembly are critical mechanisms for making this involvement happen.[26] In his studies of Americans' membership in voluntary civic organizations—everything from PTAs to environmental groups to bowling leagues—social scientist Robert Putnam argues that involvement in these activities enhances social trust and limits opportunism. The result, in theory, is a society with greater civic impulses to solve problems collectively, building healthier democracy. Putnam's widely cited book, *Bowling Alone*, chronicles a late-twentieth-century decline in participation by Americans in civic associations and laments the harmful effects of that decline on civic engagement and the state of democracy.[27]

Are employer limits to free expression contributing to a decline in civic engagement? In broader terms, is an employment system built on market capitalism and employment at will at odds with liberty and democracy in broader society? The way to answer that question is to look at how workplace expression and civil society are connected.

One way to see that connection is to consider the idea of a workplace that tolerates generally uninhibited conversation among employees. Conversation isn't typically a major workplace goal, but work inevitably provides a venue for conversation. Work is, of course, where many people spend a lot of their time, but, more important, for some it's where primary opportunities for social interaction arise. It's where people may form social ties with other adults that lead to involvement in formal and informal associations beyond work. For many people, it's one of the few places where these ties cross the racial, cultural, and ethnic boundaries that otherwise divide communities.[28] Interactions at work, therefore, are a crucial way in which people amass what sociologists call "social capital": the social obligations, expectations, and connections that make it possible to act cooperatively with others for mutual benefit.[29]

Work and the workplace, therefore, open up for many a key path to participation in associational life—in civil society in the Tocquevillian sense. Such opportunities become more important as Americans spend ever-increasing amounts of their time working.[30] But limits to freedom of expression throw obstacles on that path. When employees encounter harsh reactions to their expressive activities at work or after work, or when they self-censor because of the fear of likely reactions, then interactions and relationships at and around work that might build social capital are less likely to occur.

The dynamics here are, I will confess, a bit abstract: more "social capital" leading to expansion of one's "associational life" and a healthier "civil society." Let me suggest more concretely that relationships and conversations at work influence the broader political life of individual employees, and by extension communities. Social scientists who study public opinion and political behavior have shown convincingly that political attitudes both come from and are transmitted through the informal groups and social networks that people belong to, both in and out of workplaces.[31] These relationships are important for a robust democratic system because evidence shows that informal friendship groups create a protective environment for people with views that deviate from conventional or majority viewpoints.[32]

A person's working life on the job and political life outside of work are also connected by the idea that work encourages or even "teaches" people to be political. A study in the early 1990s showed that the authority structures people experience at work explain their participation in campaigning, voting, protest, and other forms of political behavior. The study's author, Richard Sobel, speculated about how employees "learn to be political" at work:

> Those who do not participate in work decisions, or participate only in decisions affecting their own jobs, do not learn skills that carry over to the political sphere: avoiding office or shop politics may lead to avoiding politics outside, while being political at work encourages being political in the community. The quality of political life may, then, depend on the quality of work life.[33]

The flip side of this argument would be that silence or noninvolvement at work discourages political or civic activity beyond the workplace. Management researchers who study silence in the workplace say that employees are reluctant to speak up when they assume nothing good will result, or they fear that they will put themselves at risk.[34]

But what about employers and workplaces that foster not silence but *conformity*? Alexander Meiklejohn, the celebrated twentieth-century free speech theorist, writes that "a citizen may be told when and where and in what manner he may or may not speak, write, assemble, and so on. On the other hand, he may not be told what he shall or shall not believe."[35] That distinction between speech and belief is clear enough, but it overlooks the possibility that being directed what to say will over time coerce changes in beliefs and attitudes. We know from a long tradition of attitude research in social psychology that behavior consistent with particular attitudes can generate those attitudes and enhance their strength.[36] The point here is that employers who compel worker speech, whether through routine organizational communication or through calculated propaganda, aren't just manipulating workplace messages (as is their prerogative) but may also be undermining individual rights to autonomy of belief.

Employer pressure to be silent, or to conform with a favored viewpoint, sets a trap for a civil society whose health depends on dissent, because it takes a forceful individual to break free of coerced conventional wisdom. The pressure that people who hold minority views feel to suppress their opinions is what German political scientist Elisabeth Noelle-Neumann writes of when she discusses the notion of a *spiral of silence* in public opinion. The "spiral" is a cycle of fear and self-censorship that results from a threat of isolation and ostracism. People have the confidence to speak out when they think their opinions are shared, writes Noelle-Neumann, but people in the minority are cautious and silent, "reinforcing the impression in public of their side's weakness, until the apparently weaker side disappears completely except for a small hard core that clings to values from the past, or until the opinion becomes taboo."[37]

The problems this spiral can pose for effective democracy and civil society are significant and readily apparent. Effective democratic self-government is difficult to sustain if disincentives for opposition and dissent are so powerful. In his remarkable book about the conflict between social pressures and genuine belief, *Private Truths, Public Lies*, economist Timur Kuran warns of the dangers of widespread "preference falsification," the act of misrepresenting one's desires because of social pressures to say otherwise. Among these dangers is an inability to see disadvantages in the status quo:

> The disadvantages may once have been appreciated quite widely. Insofar as public discourse excludes criticism of fashionable political choices, however, their shortcomings will tend to get forgotten. And in the process members of society will lose their capacity to want change. The status quo, once sustained because people were afraid to challenge it, will thus come to persist because no one understands its flaws or can imagine a better alternative.[38]

In sum, an unrepressed climate for workplace expression is related to the health of democracy and civil society in a number of ways. The approach that employers take to individual expressive rights is potentially connected to the quality of the social ties people cultivate at work, the associational activities they engage in at and beyond work, their forms and levels of political activity and civic engagement in their communities, and even the larger environment for dissent and opposition in political and civic affairs. A lot more than just work, it seems, happens at work.

FREER SPEECH

I've explained throughout this book how the American legal system and regular management practice in tandem are diluting basic individual rights to autonomy of thought and expression. I am not suggesting the presence of an active conspiracy by lawyers and managers to deny freedom of expression to the American worker or to diminish the role of free speech in society. The culprit, instead, is a confluence of legal, political, economic, and managerial forces that make the workplace unfriendly, and growing unfriendlier, to free expression. Our legal system, by imagining that employers and workers have equal power and by denying the importance of civil liberties in the private sector, leaves employees with hollow rights on the job. The current tilt of our political system, which is far more responsive to corporate interests than to those of the American worker, ensures that labor rights will remain hollow for some time to come. Economically, rising inequality and diminishing job security mean that free and fair markets for labor are more imaginary then ever. Meanwhile, managers are trained and taught to regard control, efficiency, and the bottom line as paramount moral principles. Together, these disparate forces come together to infringe on the civil liberties of individual workers, and impair the broader social-civic enterprise in which work and workplaces exist. How do we reverse course here and halt the erosion of expressive rights at work? Let's start with the law.

Any conversation about the legal side of unleashing free speech in the American workplace begins with the employment-at-will doctrine that forms the foundation for the U.S. system of employment law. Employment at will is the most significant potential source of large-scale leverage for reducing threats to free expression at work. The most important change that could occur legislatively would be to put in place just-cause dismissal rules, effectively doing away with employment at will. A just-cause requirement would limit the grounds for firing an employee and would provide workers with a procedural right to challenge a dismissal. To make this happen, states could enact statutes in the mold of Montana's Wrongful Discharge Act or the Model Employment Termination Act that would protect employees from arbitrary dismissal.[39] Besides protecting employees from being fired for unacceptable reasons, such as expressive activity that harms no genuine employer interest, these measures would provide some assurance that procedures available to an employee to challenge a dismissal (or demotion or other serious job consequence) would be fair.

The combination of a just-cause requirement for firing and a due-process requirement for handling employee challenges would give workers a "property right" in the continuation of their job, creating a situation where they could be disciplined or fired only for good reason and through fair procedures.[40] This combination, if available to every public and private employee, would go a long way toward protecting rights to free speech at work. Employers would lose some freedom to hire and fire (especially fire) as they see fit, but they would benefit from a reduction in the unpredictable risks and large awards that come with wrongful-discharge law under employment at will. Employers would also be better off if a worker who challenges a disciplinary action unsuccessfully is less inclined to escalate to a lawsuit because she sees the internal process as procedurally fair.

Wholesale elimination of the at-will principle in employment law is long overdue but pragmatically isn't likely in the foreseeable future. There are, however, ways to imagine incremental reform given that the actual workings of employment at will vary from state to state and are based on many smaller-scale elements of common and statutory law. On the common law (judicial) side, courts could (and should) expand opportunities for employees to succeed in wrongful-discharge cases by expanding exceptions to employment at will. As I discussed in Chapter 3, most states recognize at least some public-policy exceptions, preventing employers from firing someone where doing so would violate an important public-policy principle. Remarkably, free speech doesn't qualify. It's a bedrock principle of liberal democracy, a protected basic right in every state constitution, and the leadoff civil liberty in our federal constitution, yet a public-policy exception to employment at will for free speech is nowhere to be seen in state employment law. In states where exceptions to employment at will are found in common law (as opposed to legislatures), judges can and should carve out a free speech exception for expressive activity unrelated to one's job or workplace.[41] Employers would be forced to endure more speech by employees, including speech that deviates uncomfortably from the employer's preferred point of view, and they would face a higher hurdle to clear to prove that worker speech interferes with business interests. These costs seem tolerable, however, when weighed against the merits of giving workers more rights as citizens shopping around the marketplace for ideas.

Just-cause and due-process protections would effectively unravel the employment-at-will doctrine. Less dramatic, but perhaps more feasible in the near term, are other available reforms that need not amend the basic premises of employment law. One possibility is to build some solid protection for employee political speech and activity against employer retaliation into state law. As I explained in Chapter 5, this protection exists in varying form in the laws of some states, but few statutes are sufficiently strong and sweeping in their coverage. A good model is California's law, which bars employers from any action that would influence employees to engage in or refrain from engaging in "any particular course or line of political action or political activity."[42] Louisiana also gets it right, giving employees the right to "participate in political activities of any nature or character" without fear of job-related punishment or retaliation.[43] Adding language of this sort to employment law in all states would do much to insulate political speech from workplace-related infringements.

The other long-overdue statutory solution is expanding the presence and reach of so-called lifestyle discrimination laws that bar employers from punishing off-work employee conduct that is legal and poses no significant threat to an employer's business. As I discussed in Chapter 5, several states have narrow versions of these laws limited to consumption of certain products—mainly tobacco and alcohol—but only a handful of states have laws with broad language protecting, in theory, just about every after-work pursuit, including expressive activity. The typical wording found in these laws lets employers retain some control over off-work conduct if they can show that the behavior harms them. North Dakota's law, for instance, says that employees' off-work activities are protected as long as they don't conflict with "the essential business-related interests of the employer" or with a "a bona fide occupational qualification" related to an individual's job.[44] The issue for employees, of course, is how courts weighing cases brought under these laws will parse and apply a phrase like "essential business-related interests." Given the deference that courts often show toward employers in so-called "balancing" situations, lifestyle discrimination laws, while helpful and clearly necessary, clearly are no panacea.

Even better than lifestyle discrimination statutes would be laws specifically protecting free speech rights on the job. There are existing models: as I discussed in Chapter 5, laws on the books in Connecticut and South Carolina appear to extend the First Amendment to the private-sector workplace.[45] The operative word is "appear," however, because the laws in these two states qualify as models by their language but not by their implementation. Courts hearing cases brought under these laws have tended to sympathize more with claims by employers about how speech threatens their interests than with the free speech interests of employees who are punished for expressing themselves.

Balancing employee claims against employer interests is the heart and soul of *public*-sector employee speech cases when they reach courtrooms, and there is room here for improvement in how that balance plays out. The test in federal law for determining whether employee speech deserves First Amendment protection starts with the question of whether the speech in question addresses an issue of "public concern," which is a matter of "political, social, or other concern to the community."[46] If it does—and that's a big if, given how easy it is to find gray areas in the definition of public concern—then the question is whether an employee's speech impairs the mission, efficiency, morale, or workplace harmony of the agency she works for. Case law over the years since this two-part test was first fashioned suggests a high tolerance by the courts for employer claims that employee speech is disruptive, and a rather narrow view of the kind of speech that rises to the level of "public concern." The remedy here is straightforward: courts hearing public-sector cases should interpret the public-concern test expansively and should look with more skepticism than they have in the past on employer claims that speech is disruptive.

Flawed though that two-part test may be, it is at least available as a source of protection for speech by government employees. Not so for the far larger number of workers in the private sector. The culprit is the constitutional principle of state action—that violations of First Amendment rights matter legally only when the state is doing the violating. Some critics of state action argue that the distinction between public and private actions is illusory: even private actors must rely routinely on state action (law enforcement, the courts, and so on) to prevent other private actors from interfering with their "private" rights.[47] Weakening or eliminating the state-action requirement would accomplish the worthy goal of elevating private-sector speech rights to the rough equivalent of those available to workers in the public sector.

The irrational blur of the public-private distinction comes into focus when you see it in practice. Consider the logic in a 1960 Supreme Court ruling overturning an Arkansas law that forced public school teachers to identify organizations to which they belonged or contributed:

> To compel a teacher to disclose his every associational tie is to impair
> that teacher's right of free association, a right closely allied to freedom
> of speech and a right which, like free speech, *lies at the foundation of a*
> *free society*. . . . Such interference with personal freedom is conspicuously
> accented when the teacher serves at the absolute will of those to whom
> the disclosure must be made—those who any year can terminate the
> teacher's employment without bringing charges, without notice, with-
> out a hearing, without affording an opportunity to explain.[48]

Nothing here suggests that the risks to the integrity of a free society hinge on the teacher's public (versus private) employment status. If anything, the dangers decried by the Court are particularly acute in the private sector, where being fired "without notice, without a hearing" is now, almost a half century after this opinion, far more likely to occur.

Realistically, though, the potential significance of dismantling the state-action principle is matched by the sizable odds against it happening any-time soon. Some of the most compelling published arguments by eminent legal scholars for weakening the state-action requirement are now old enough to drink,[49] and there are no indications that federal courts have developed an urge to chip away at the requirement. This is unfortunate. With First Amendment and other basic rights being enforced only in pub-lic settings, our constitutional system is arguably out of touch with the real-ity of lives lived under the substantial control of large private institutions.[50] The climate for expression at and around the private-sector workplace would benefit markedly from dilution of the requirement of state action in constitutional law. (So would the legal profession benefit, when the passing of state action into the dustbin of legal history opens new opportunities to bring constitutional-rights claims against private parties.)

Making the private sector look like the public sector won't do much good, however, unless courts are willing to give workers a fair shake, rather than deferring too easily to employer concerns about the effects of speech on workplace efficiency. Several suggestions I've made here—lifestyle discrimination laws, statutes extending the First Amendment to the private workplace, reinterpreting the public-concern standard in public employment—still leave courts with the obligation to weigh free speech claims against those efficiency and productivity concerns. We need a shift of this balance of interests: rather than deferring by reflex to employers' stated concerns about efficiency, courts should compel them to show that worker speech is genuinely and substantially harmful. Such a shift might well increase the number of lawsuits, and employers would have difficult choices to make about whether and how to regulate speech that they wish wouldn't occur. But although there might be some costs in efficiency, litigation, and even morale at the outset, the change in the legal landscape for speech claims would force smart employers to rethink whether a punitive approach to provocative speech is necessary or desirable. In time, they would come to see that although free speech can be messy and complicated, it need not necessarily be silenced to preserve the economic vitality of the enterprise.

Of course, speech sometimes isn't merely "messy"; it's insulting, bigoted, or discriminatory. As I discussed in Chapter 7, one narrow area of law that has had a large effect on workplace expression is found in the civil rights laws regulating a "hostile work environment." Some are justifiably concerned that well-intentioned efforts to curb harassment at work based on sex, religion, race, and national origin have a chilling effect on free speech. This effect occurs, critics say, because of difficulties defining what speech will or will not contribute to a hostile environment, leading attorneys to advise employers to overregulate the expressive activity of employees. Others respond that the law isn't as vague as critics make it out to be. I tend to agree, but the fact that employers need not overregulate doesn't mean they aren't taking the legal advice given to them and overregulating speech anyway.

I mentioned in Chapter 7 some proposals to reform the notion of a hostile environment as a way to remove the incentive for employers to silence so much speech.[51] One proposal is to distinguish situations involving unpleasant speech that isn't aimed at specific individuals from cases where individual workers are targeted directly by harassing speech. Victims of direct harassment could anticipate legal remedies while employees who engage in more general or undirected speech of a racial, sexual, or religious nature would be entitled to some protection. It isn't clear that this strategy would cope adequately with situations where workers or managers create a harassing environment without directing their taunts or invective toward a single individual. Workplace harmony is hardly served when racist or sexist messages are floated around the office rather than directed at specific targets. But employee liberty interests are also sacrificed under current rules when lawyers see shutting down all potentially provocative expression as the way to avoid lawsuits. Proposals to tame the hostile-environment doctrine merit serious attention as a way to reduce the temptation by employers and their attorneys to err on the side of censorship.

There is no reason American workers can't have plenty of freedom of expression in and around the workplace. They can have it today. The law doesn't so much throw up obstacles to employee free speech as it offers up opportunities for employers to restrict expression. Many employers seem to welcome those opportunities. (To be fair, many don't.) Situations where employees are disciplined or fired for expressive behavior mainly occur not because of legislatures and judges but through the actions of employers who see expressive acts as threatening harmony, prosperity, or reputation. Laws change slowly, but managers can change their policies and practices toward employee speech much more quickly. They could do it today.

My argument here is not a manifesto for anything goes—the right to speak about anything at any time. After all, employee expression can pose a genuine threat to legitimate employer interests, and a functional free-enterprise system need not require employers to tolerate speech of that sort. It's alarming, however, when people are punished on the job not because their speech concretely jeopardizes employer interests but because their actions trigger needless employer fears about the effects that might occur. We have built in the American economy a management culture so dependent on predictability and control that even remote threats to the established order are treated with suspicion and dealt with harshly. The American legal systems of employment law and corporate governance largely excuse employers from worrying about how their actions square with constitutional values or human rights.

The result—the state of play as to free speech in the American workplace—is a managerial impulse to limit rather than encourage or tolerate expression. Perhaps for some employers this impulse is the product of a pathological loathing for treating employees with fairness and dignity or for the First Amendment or for motherhood and apple pie or for all the above. For most, though, it's an impulse that feeds off the economic and political system in which it thrives, a system where work is work and society is something you do after work.

Reforming the managerial impulse to control or silence employee expression begins with a change in employer mind-set about the intersection between free speech and employment. The prevailing approach to workplace relationships based on the concept of employment at will begins with the assumption that an employer "owns" an employee's time at work and commitment to the job. As a result, the employer is entitled to protect itself against employee actions that could inflict harm on the employer, even if that harm is highly provisional or even imaginary. As a practical matter, this prerogative gives employers nearly unfettered discretion to define what acceptable employee behavior looks like, both on and off the job. Seen in its worst light, it's a system in which employees trade not just labor for wages, but also basic liberties for wages. Free speech rights are precarious, if not meaningless, when firms reflexively treat employee expression (sometimes with a hair trigger) as an avoidable nuisance, a legal liability, a challenge to reputation, or a threat to commercial prosperity.

It's time for changes in the mind-set of those who make judgments on employers' behalf about how, when, and why expressive employee behavior will be tolerated. Changes in the law of the sort I am proposing would compel managers to rethink their approach to employee rights. Still, reversing the erosion of free speech rights in the American workplace is more apt to happen through persuasion than compulsion. More attention is paid now to matters of ethics and social responsibility in the education of managers and in journalism about the workplace than at any time in the past few decades. But although business ethics might seem for the moment a growth industry, and a worthwhile one at that, focusing everyone's attention on doing right and doing wrong won't by itself have much effect. A broader, more substantial, and more difficult need is for employers to reframe their roles in society, from seeing themselves as servants to a labor market economy to imagining themselves as collaborators in a vibrant democratic society. Many have observed (although someone said it first)[52] that we do not live in an economy but in a society, a point of telling insight that drops off the radar during the working day inside the market religion of America's employment-at-will system.

More freedom of expression for American workers does not mean turning workplaces into debating societies or free-for-alls for hostility and harassment. Employers will always retain the ability to encourage and reward job performance, and accommodating expressive behavior need not be incompatible with critical organizational goals. Yes, free speech can be messy; a freer workplace for speech does compel employers to accept and tolerate more unpredictability, and even to sacrifice a bit of efficiency in the name of expressive freedom. This doesn't have to be an unfair or excessive burden: innovations in workplace culture frequently carry a modest price tag in efficiency or productivity. The particular "innovation" I have in mind is important and worthwhile not simply because freedom of speech fulfills some abstract notion of the good society (which it certainly does) but because of its critical role in promoting some very concrete goals: individual autonomy and creativity, constructive workplace dissent and decision making, and an engaged citizenry that doesn't have to sacrifice civic engagement for job security.

Needless curbs on employee speech are more than just inconveniences for the individuals involved; they contribute to the debilitation of civil society and consensual democracy. Legal reforms can go a long way toward reversing these effects, but real progress will happen when employers arrive at judgments—at mind-sets—that the success of the enterprise is not so easily threatened by employees' acts of artistic, literary, political, or just idle expression. The law gives employers the right to err on the side of silencing expression that might conceivably raise concerns. Management discretion, civic responsibility, and common sense present an attractive alternative: looking with nuance and care at the busy intersection where individual expression, workplace interests, and a free society come together.

Acknowledgments

Several years ago I began to think about connecting the focus of my academic research and teaching (power, conflict, and politics in work organizations) with a central theme in my extracurricular, quasi-activist life (civil liberties and democracy in a free society). This book is an offspring of that union. My ability to put serious time and energy into this sort of unconventional subject (for a business school academic) is in no small measure a result of the welcoming and energizing climate for interdisciplinary ideas at Vanderbilt University and its Owen Graduate School of Management.

I am grateful to Vanderbilt and the Owen School, especially the school's dean at the time, Bill Christie, for letting me arrange a research leave in 2004–05, during which time I completed much of the research for the book. Thanks also to my colleagues in the organization studies group at the Owen School for providing a stimulating environment for research, teaching, writing, and thinking: Professors Ray Friedman, Bart Victor, Dick Daft, Neta Moye, Tim Vogus, and David Owens.

The book wouldn't have come together without the skillful and sophisticated touch of my editor at Berrett-Koehler, Johanna Vondeling, who often seemed to understand what I was trying to do more than I did. She has an uncanny ability to mix direction and encouragement in a way that makes the writing better and the argument sharper and keeps the writer energized. I appreciate also the efforts of many others at Berrett-Koehler: Jeevan Sivasubramanian, Kirsten Frantz, Michael Crowley, Marina Cook, Ian Bach, Tiffany Lee, Ken Lupoff, Robin Donovan, Rick Wilson, and Dianne Platner. Under the direction of the wise and talented Steve Piersanti, BK lays claim to a publication model that is unusually collaborative and author friendly, and it turns out they pull it off. It is hard to imagine a publishing outfit—or a group of people—with whom I'd rather be associated. I am also grateful to David Peattie of BookMatters, who managed production, Bea Hartman, who was responsible for the typeface choices and interior design, and Mike Mollett, whose first-rate copyediting significantly improved the manuscript.

The ideas and arguments in the book benefited a great deal from insightful comments by many who read the original proposal, draft chapters, or an earlier version of the manuscript: Tom Bateman, Erwin Chemerinsky, Matt Brody, Ingrid Fulmer, Dan Cornfield, Richard Lloyd, Nathan Goates, Jason Stansbury, Mark Brody, Megan Barry, David Hudson, Michelle Barrett, Lisa Sitkin, Jo Ellen Green Kaiser, Jathan Janove, and Glenn Solomon. I acknowledge also many helpful suggestions offered by colleagues at seminars and colloquia I have given on this topic at several universities in the United States and in Australia. I am especially indebted to Amanda Carrico, a doctoral student at Vanderbilt, whose research assistance was, in a word, indispensable. Many thanks also to Hedy Weinberg, who teaches me constantly what it really means to be a committed civil libertarian.

Much of the book was drafted during a sojourn in Summit County, Colorado, in 2006. My time and productivity there were lubricated by the kindness and hospitality of the folks at Liquid: Owner Dave, Alex, Bill, John, Ryan, and Nate. I revised the manuscript during an extended visit to Melbourne, Australia, one of the planet's great cities (where the coffee is better than just about anywhere else). I am grateful to Mara Olekalns at the University of Melbourne for making that possible.

My thanks to the several literary agents who turned me down for representation. I'll be hanging on to your share.

In several places in the book (especially Chapters 6, 9, and 10), I draw from and expand on my article "The Cringing and the Craven: Freedom of Expression in, around, and beyond the Workplace," in *Business Ethics Quarterly* (vol. 17, no. 2, 2007). I am grateful to the journal and its publisher for permission to do so.

I ceaselessly appreciate Joyce Brody Skodnek's love, support, and DNA. This is for Megan and Max, who have an unmistakable and always salutary inclination to express themselves freely.

Notes

INTRODUCTION

1. Clyde L. Stancil, "Moulton Woman Says She Lost Job for Sporting Kerry Sticker on Car," *Decatur (AL) Daily*, September 12, 2004, http://www.decaturdaily.com/decaturdaily/news/040912/sticker.shtml (accessed July 7, 2005).

2. Associated Press, "Woman Fired for Kerry Sticker Hired by Democratic Campaign," *Associated Press State & Local Wire*, September 15, 2004, http://www.lexis-nexis.com/ (accessed July 1, 2006). See also Timothy Noah, "Bumper Sticker Insubordination," *Slate*, September 14, 2004, http://www.slate.com/id/2106714 (accessed July 7, 2006).

3. Free speech is protected in the *First* Amendment in the Bill of Rights that was ratified in 1791, but the Bill of Rights originally proposed in the First Congress had twelve amendments. Only the last ten of these were ratified; what we call the First Amendment was actually James Madison's third. See Akhil Reed Amar, *The Bill of Rights: Creation and Reconstruction* (New Haven, CT: Yale University Press, 1998), 8–9. Franklin D. Roosevelt, *Annual Message to Congress*, January 6, 1941, The American Presidency Project at the University of California at Santa Barbara, http://www.presidency.ucsb.edu/ws/index.php?pid=16092 (accessed May 11, 2006).

4. *Palko v. State of Connecticut*, 302 U.S. 319 (1937), 327.

5. David A. Strauss, "Freedom of Speech and the Common-Law Constitution," in *Eternally Vigilant: Free Speech in the Modern Era*, ed. Lee C. Bollinger and Geoffrey Stone (Chicago: University of Chicago Press, 2002), 33.

6. *Press Briefing by Ari Fleischer*, Office of the Press Secretary, The White House, September 26, 2001, http://www.whitehouse.gov/news/releases/2001/09/20010926–5.html (accessed June 30, 2006). In a 2004 letter to the editor of the *New York Times*, Fleischer said his comment was misunderstood; see Ari Fleischer, "A Briefing by the Former Press Secretary" (letter), *New York Times*, March 24, 2004, Late Edition, A20. His attempt to reinvent the controversial remark was less than persuasive; see Timothy Noah, "Ari Fleischer Rides

Again," *Slate*, March 24, 2004, http://www.slate.com/id/2097761/ (accessed September 13, 2006).

7. Jonah Bloom and Douglas Quenqua, "Fleischer Should Retract Comment," *PR Week*, October 8, 2001, http://www.lexis-nexis.com/(accessed June 30, 2006).

8. Julie Mason, "Prop. A Leader Leaves Job, Says City Official Interfered," *Houston Chronicle*, July 10, 1998, http://www.chron.com/CDA/archives/archive.mpl?id=1998_3068252 (accessed July 1, 2006).

9. Steven A. Holmes, "Broker Asserts Political Views Drew Pressure," *New York Times*, July 10, 1998, A10.

10. Ibid.

11. Edward Blum, "An Insulting Provision," *National Review Online*, May 2, 2006, http://www.nationalreview.com/ (accessed July 1, 2006).

12. See, for example, http://www.speakerscorner.net/ (accessed July 3, 2006).

13. See, for example, Robert Phillips, R. Edward Freeman, and Andrew C. Wicks, "What Stakeholder Theory Is Not," *Business Ethics Quarterly* 13 (2003): 479–482.

14. Patricia H. Werhane, *Persons, Rights, & Corporations* (Englewood Cliffs, NJ: Prentice-Hall, 1985), 61.

15. Program on International Policy Attitudes, "20 Nation Poll Finds Strong Global Consensus: Support for Free Market System, but Also More Regulation of Large Companies," *World Public Opinion*, March 21, 2006, http://www.worldpublicopinion.org/pipa/articles/btglobalizationtradera/154.php (accessed July 3, 2006).

16. "Survey by Gallup Organization," November 17–November 20, 2005, retrieved from the iPOLL Databank, The Roper Center for Public Opinion Research, University of Connecticut, http://www.ropercenter.uconn.edu (accessed July 3, 2006).

17. Nicholas Wade, "Protection Sought for Satirists and Whistleblowers," *Science* 182 (1973), 1002–1003.

18. *Novosel v. Nationwide Insurance Company*, 721 F.2d 894 (1983).

19. Timothy Noah, "Can Your Boss Fire You for Your Political Beliefs?" *Slate*, July 1, 2002, http://www.slate.com/id/2067578/ (accessed July 3, 2006).

20. Associated Press, "Supreme Court Upholds Firing of Man Who Refused to Put Flag Up at Work," Archives of Television Station WTNH, New Haven/Hartford, CT, October 4, 1999, http://archivesearch.wtnh.com/news/1999/oct/10041999-flag.html (accessed July 6, 2005) .

21. Todd Wallack, "Beware If Your Blog Is Related to Work," *San Francisco Chronicle*, January 24, 2005, C1. Park's comments on her firing appeared on her Weblog at http://troutgirl.com/blog/index.php?/archives/46_Shitcanned.html and http://troutgirl.com/blog/index.php?/archives/48_Consequences.html (accessed February 21, 2005).

22. I will at various points in the book draw connections between free speech and the quality or health of our "democracy." I do so aware that the American system of government literally takes the form of a republic rather than a pure-form democracy. As James Madison observed in *Federalist* No. 14, "in a democracy, the people meet and exercise the government in person; in a republic, they assemble and administer it by their representatives and agents. A democracy, consequently, will be confined to a small spot. A republic may be extended over a large region." With electoral and legislative institutions designed to inject democratic processes into a republican system, the United States is (or strives to be) a democratic republic. My comments about the state or quality of "democracy" refer to the effectiveness of that enterprise, which emerges from the ability of citizens to safeguard liberties and advance policy interests through the instruments of public debate, free association, and deliberative government.

23. David W. Ewing, *Freedom Inside the Organization* (New York: E. P. Dutton, 1977), 5.

CHAPTER ONE

1. Steven Breyer, audio interview with Nina Totenberg for *All Things Considered* (full interview, at 17:30), *National Public Radio*, http://www.npr.org/templates/story/story.php?storyId=4929668 (accessed July 10, 2006).

2. Laurie Manfra, "The Ethics of Rugs," *Metropolis Magazine*, January 16, 2006, http://www.metropolismag.com/cda/story.php?artid=1762 (accessed July 13, 2006).

3. Geoffrey R. Stone, Louis M. Seidman, Cass R. Sunstein, Mark V. Tushnet, and Pamela S. Karlan, *The First Amendment*, 2nd ed. (New York: Aspen, 2003), 360–361.

4. Breyer, audio interview.

5. I am reluctant to use the term "desecration" except in quotation marks because it is a politicized label, one with ideological bias, for actions that use the flag as a vehicle for symbolic expression. Desecration by definition is the act of depriving something of its sacred character. In a secular democracy, it is troubling to lend the notion of "sacredness" (religious veneration) to a national symbol.

6. Robert Justin Goldstein, "Flag-Burning Overview," *First Amendment Center*, June 28, 2006, http://www.firstamendmentcenter.org/speech/flagburning/overview.aspx (accessed July 14, 2006).

7. *Halter v. Nebraska*, 205 U.S. 34 (1907), 42. The beer bottler who brought the case, Halter, didn't argue that free-speech rights were at stake; his challenge to the Nebraska law was focused on issues of state power (can a state regulate the use of the national flag?) and equal protection (is it fair to outlaw use of the flag in advertising but allow it in books, magazines, and pamphlets?). The Supreme Court, in a nutshell, said yes and yes.

8. Justice Louis Brandeis: "There is nothing in the Federal Constitution which forbids unions from competing with non-union concerns for customers by means of picketing as freely as one merchant competes with another by means of advertisements in the press, by circulars, or by his window display." *Senn v. Tile Layers Protective Union*, 301 U.S. 468 (1937), 481–482. For a historical review of related developments, see Ken I. Kersch, "How Conduct Became Speech and Speech Became Conduct: A Political Development Case Study in Labor Law and the Freedom Of Speech," *University of Pennsylvania Journal of Constitutional Law* 8 (2006): 271–284.

9. *United States v. O'Brien*, 391 U.S. 367 (1968), 376.

10. *Spence v. Washington*, 418 U.S. 405 (1974), 410–411.

11. *Texas v. Johnson*, 491 U.S. 397 (1989), 416.

12. "Flag-Burning Amendment Fails by a Vote," *CNN.com*, June 28, 2006, http://www.cnn.com/2006/politics/06/27/flag.burning/index.html (accessed July 10, 2006).

13. Charles Babington, "Senate Rejects Flag Desecration Amendment," *Washington Post*, June 28, 2006, A1, http://www.washingtonpost.com/wp-dyn/content/article/2006/06/27/ar2006062701056.html (accessed July 10, 2006).

14. *Berger and Barhight v. Battaglia*, 779 F.2d 992 (1985), 999.

15. *Tindle v. Caudell*, 56 F.3d 966 (1995), 970.

16. So has the U.S. Supreme Court. See Melville B. Nimmer, "The Meaning of Symbolic Speech under the First Amendment," *UCLA Law Review* 21 (1973): 33.

17. Thomas I. Emerson, *The System of Freedom of Expression* (New York: Random House, 1970), 17.

18. C. Edwin Baker, *Human Liberty and Freedom of Speech* (New York: Oxford University Press, 1989), 51.

19. Cynthia L. Estlund, "Free Speech and Due Process in the Workplace," *Indiana Law Journal* 71 (1995): 114 (emphasis added).

20. Richard Lippke, "Speech, Conscience, and Work," *Social Theory and Practice* 18 (1992): 238 (emphasis added).

21. The discussion of forms and contexts of workplace expression here draws in part on Randy J. Kozel, "Reconceptualizing Public Employee Speech," *Northwestern University Law Review* 99 (2005): 1007–1051. Although Kozel's focus is on public employment, he offers insights on categories of expressive behavior that are relevant for employer reactions in both public and private sectors.

22. *Drake v. Cheyenne*, 891 P.2d 80 (1995), 82 (emphasis added).

23. *Rigsby v. Murray*, 1991 Tenn. App. LEXIS 471 (1991), 6 (emphasis added).

24. Kozel, "Reconceptualizing Public Employee Speech," 1035–1037, distinguished between *intra-office speech* directed specifically at an audience within the place of employment (supervisors, co-workers, or patrons) and *extra-office speech* that is directed outside the office or employment community. He subdivides extra-office speech into three subtypes: (a) speech that is unrelated to the organization, (b) speech that is related to workplace or vocation but provides no specific information about the employer, and (c) speech about the employer that serves a watchdog or whistleblowing function. These are useful categories, but taken together they conflate topic, audience, and function.

25. Sacha Cohen, "Shhh, They're Talking Salary," *USA TODAY*, December 20, 2002, http://www.usatoday.com/money/jobcenter/jobhunt/salary/2002–12–20-salary-talk_x.htm (accessed October 18, 2006).

26. Thomas Jefferson, *An Act for Establishing Religious Freedom*, January 16, 1786, Library of Virginia, http://www.lva.lib.va.us/whatwedo/k12/bor/vsrftext.htm (accessed June 17, 2006).

27. *West Virginia State Board of Education v. Barnette*, 319 U.S. 624, (1943), 642.

28. *Drake v. Cheyenne*, 891 P.2d 80 (1995).

29. Paul Frisman, "Fired Worker Wins, So to Speak," *Connecticut Law Tribune*, October 25, 1999, http://www.lexis-nexis.com/ (accessed July 21, 2004).)

30. *Roberts v. United States Jaycees*, 468 U.S. 609 (1984), 622.

31. Paul Cerkvenik, "Who Your Friends Are Could Get You Fired! The Connick 'Public Concern' Test Unjustifiably Restricts Public Employees Associational Rights," *Minnesota Law Review* 79 (1994): 425–453.

32. David W. Ewing, *Freedom Inside the Organization* (New York: E. P. Dutton, 1977), 93.

33. Patricia H. Werhane, *Persons, Rights, & Corporations* (Englewood Cliffs, NJ: Prentice-Hall, 1985).

34. David Yamada developed this argument in some detail in an article on the role of private-sector worker speech in a post-industrial employment economy, and I draw on his points here. See David C. Yamada, "Voices from the Cubicle: Protecting and Encouraging Private Employee Speech in the Post-Industrial Workplace," *Berkeley Journal of Employment and Labor Law* 19 (1998): 8–21.

35. Jelle Visser, "Union Membership Statistics in 24 Countries," *Monthly Labor Review*, January 2006, 43–45.

36. 348 NLRB No. 39; see also Steven Greenhouse, "Labor Board Broadens Definition of Supervisors," *New York Times*, October 4, 2006, A16.

37. Barbara Rose, "Union Leaders Assail Labor Ruling," *Seattle Times*, October 4, 2006, http://seattletimes.nwsource.com/html/businesstechnology/2003287853_nurseslabor03.html (accessed October 21, 2006).

38. Kevin L. Keller, "Brand Synthesis: The Multidimensionality of Brand Knowledge," *Journal of Consumer Research* 29 (2003): 595.

39. Karl D. Speak, "Brand Stewardship," *Design Management Journal* 9 (1998): 33.

40. See, for example, Bradley J. Alge, "Effects of Computer Surveillance on Perceptions of Privacy and Procedural Justice," *Journal of Applied Psychology* 86 (2001): 797–804; William S. Brown, "Technology, Workplace Privacy, and Personhood," *Journal of Business Ethics* 15 (1996): 1237–1248.

41. Yamada, "Voices From the Cubicle," 17.

42. Patricia Wallace, *The Internet in the Workplace: How New Technology Is Transforming Work* (Cambridge: Cambridge University Press, 2004), 55–57.

43. Among those who have made an argument connecting activity at work with community and political identity are Kate E. Andrias, "A Robust Public Debate: Realizing Free Speech in Workplace Representation Elections," *Yale Law Journal* 112 (2003): 2448–2449; Cynthia L. Estlund, "Free Speech and Due Process in the Workplace," *Indiana Law Review* 71 (1995): 112–114; and Vicki Schultz, "Life's Work," *Columbia Law Review* 100 (2000): 1888–1892.

44. "Survey by the Marlin Company and Harris Interactive," May 22–May 29, 2003, retrieved from the iPOLL Databank, The Roper Center for Public Opinion Research, University of Connecticut, http://www.ropercenter.uconn.edu (accessed July 19, 2006).

45. Developing this argument, Cynthia Estlund calls work "an important arena of social and civic life." Cynthia Estlund, *Working Together: How Workplace Bonds Strengthen a Diverse Democracy* (Oxford: Oxford University Press, 2003), 31.

46. Schultz, "Life's Work," 1928–1929.

CHAPTER TWO

1. James Madison, "James Madison's Speech to House of Representatives Proposing Bill of Rights," *The James Madison Center at James Madison University*, http://www.jmu.edu/madison/center/main_pages-/madison_archives/constit_confed/rights/jmproposal/jmspeech.htm (accessed June 16, 2006).

2. AFL-CIO, *Workers Rights in America: What Workers Think About Their Jobs and Employers* (Washington, DC: AFL-CIO, 2001), 17.

3. Cynthia L. Estlund, "Freedom of Expression in the Workplace and the Problem of Discriminatory Harassment," *Texas Law Review* 75 (1997): 689.

4. The ability to file a lawsuit against a government employer for a constitutional violation actually varies depending on the branch of government involved. State and municipal employees have a clear procedural path to mounting such a claim under the federal law known as Section 1983 (42 U.S.C. § 1983). This option is not available to federal employees. The Supreme Court has held that civil service rules created by Congress provide sufficient procedural opportunities and safeguards for federal workers with constitutional complaints about their employers, so it has declined to offer federal workers a judicial remedy. *Bush v. Lucas*, 462 U.S. 367 (1983); see also *Correction Services Corp. vs. Malesko*, 534 U.S. 61 (2001), 68.

5. Michael L. Wells, "Section 1983, the First Amendment, and Public Employee Speech: Shaping the Right to Fit the Remedy (and Vice Versa)," *Georgia Law Review* 35 (2001): 969–975.

6. 42 U.S.C. § 1983.

7. Karen M. Blum and Kathryn R. Urbonya, *Section 1983 Litigation* (Washington, DC: Federal Judicial Center, 1998), http://www.fjc.gov/public/pdf.nsf/lookup/sect1983.pdf/$file/sect1983.pdf (accessed June 14, 2006), 5–6.

8. Ch. 74, § 2, 1 Stat. 596 (1798).

9. For a concise review of these legal and constitutional developments, see Jack M. Balkin, "History Lesson," *Legal Affairs*, July/August 2002, http://www.legalaffairs.org/issues/july-august-2002/review_balkin_julaug2002.msp (accessed May 12, 2006).

10. Ch. 114, § 1, 18 Stat. 335 (1875).

11. *The Civil Rights Cases*, 109 U.S. 3 (1883).

12. Although *The Civil Rights Cases* are widely regarded as the key judicial origin of the state-action doctrine, there was a hint of the doctrine articulated by the Court's opinion in an earlier case, *United States v. Cruikshank*: "The fourteenth amendment prohibits a State from depriving any person of life, liberty, or property, without due process of law; but this adds nothing to the rights

of one citizen as against another." 92 U.S. 542 (1875), 544. A clearer statement followed in another case four years later: "The provisions of the Fourteenth Amendment of the Constitution . . . all have reference to State action exclusively, and not to any action of private individuals." *Virginia v. Rives*, 100 U.S. 313 (1879), 318. See Erwin Chemerinsky, "Rethinking State Action," *Northwestern University Law Review* 80 (1985): 507 n. 16.

13. *The Civil Rights Cases*, 109 U.S. 3 (1883), 17.

14. Ibid., 58–59.

15. Balkin, "History Lesson." As Balkin explains, the 1964 Civil Rights Act might also have been found unconstitutional unless the Supreme Court was willing to overturn *The Civil Rights Cases* ruling. In the end, however, the 1964 act survived constitutional challenges with a defense on different grounds: as a legitimate form of regulation of interstate commerce. Following the New Deal, federal courts granted the government wide latitude to enforce economic regulation. Five months after the 1964 act was signed into law, the Supreme Court ruled that it fell within the regulatory power of Congress under the Commerce Clause. *Heart of Atlanta Motel, Inc. v. United States*, 379 U.S. 241 (1964).

16. Geoffrey R. Stone, Louis M. Seidman, Cass R. Sunstein, Mark V. Tushnet, and Pamela S. Karlan, *The First Amendment*, 2nd ed. (New York: Aspen, 2003), lxxiii.

17. For a review of these cases see David M. Rabban, *Free Speech in Its Forgotten Years* (Cambridge: Cambridge University Press, 1997). Contrary to the conventional view that the nineteenth century was a dormant period for First Amendment law, Rabban points to substantial debate and litigation on free speech between 1800 and 1917 as deserving of historical attention.

18. *Marsh v. State of Alabama*, 326 U.S. 501 (1946), 509.

19. *Jackson v. Metropolitan Edison Co.*, 419 U.S. 345 (1974), 352.

20. Alynda Wheat and Ellen Florian, "Company Town," *Fortune*, April 14, 2003, http://money.cnn.com/magazines/fortune/fortune_archive/2003/04/14/340928/index.htm, (accessed May 13, 2006).

21. *Nixon v. Condon*, 286 U.S. 73 (1932); *Smith v. Allwright*, 321 U.S. 649 (1944); *Terry v. Adams*, 345 U.S. 461 (1953).

22. *Evans v. Newton*, 382 U.S. 296 (1966).

23. *Burton v. Wilmington Parking Auth.*, 365 U.S. 715 (1961), 725.

24. *Amalgamated Food Employee Union Local 590 v. Logan Valley*, 391 U.S. 308 (1968), 319.

25. *Lloyd Corp. v. Tanner*, 407 U.S. 551 (1972).

26. Ibid., 580.

27. *Hudgens v. National Labor Relations Board*, 424 U.S. 507 (1976).

28. Ibid., 539–540.

29. *Pruneyard Shopping Center v. Robbins*, 447 U.S. 74 (1980).

30. See Jennifer Niles Coffin, "The United Mall of America: Free Speech, State Constitutions, and the Growing Fortress of Private Property," *University of Michigan Journal of Law Reform* 33 (2000): 625–633, for a review of some of these individual state approaches. See also Josh Mulligan, "Finding a Forum in the Simulated City: Mega Malls, Gated Towns, and the Promise of Prune-yard," *Cornell Journal of Law and Public Policy* 13 (2004): 533–562.

31. *New Jersey Coalition against War in the Middle East v. J.M.B. Realty Corp.*, 138 N.J. 326 (1994), 374.

32. *Rendell-Baker v. Kohn*, 457 U.S. 830 (1982), 842, 843.

33. See, for example, Daphne Barak-Erez, "A State Action Doctrine for an Age of Privatization," *Syracuse Law Review* 45 (1995): 1174–1186.

34. John Fee, "The Formal State Action Doctrine and Free Speech Analysis," *North Carolina Law Review* 83 (2005): 585

35. Chemerinsky, "Rethinking State Action," 505 n. 10; Michael Wells, "Identifying State Actors in Constitutional Litigation: Reviving the Role of Substantive Context," *Cardozo Law Review* 26 (2004): 99–125.

36. Charles L. Black, Jr., "Foreword: State Action, Equal Protection, and California's Proposition 14," *Harvard Law Review* 81 (1967): 69.

37. Julian N. Eule, as completed by Jonathan D. Varat, "Transporting First Amendment Norms to the Private Sector: With Every Wish There Comes a Curse," *UCLA Law Review* 45 (1998): 1551 n. 49.

38. William P. Marshall, "Diluting Constitutional Rights: Rethinking 'Re-thinking State Action,'" *Northwestern University Law Review* 80 (1985): 558–570.

39. Chemerinsky, "Rethinking State Action."

40. Gary Peller and Mark Tushnet, "State Action and a New Birth of Free-dom," *Georgetown Law Journal* 92 (2004): 789.

41. Cass R. Sunstein, "State Action Is Always Present," *Chicago Journal of International Law* 3 (2002): 465–469.

42. Barak-Erez, "A State Action Doctrine."

43. Paul Starr, "The New Life of the Liberal State: Privatization and the Restructuring of State-Society Relations," in *Public Enterprise and Privatization*, eds. John Waterbury and Ezra Suleiman (Boulder, CO: Westview Press, 1990), 22–54; see also Mary Bryna Sanger, "When the Private Sector Competes," Reform Watch Brief #3, *The Brookings Institution*, October 2001, http://www.brookings.edu/comm/reformwatch/rw03.htm (accessed September 18, 2006).

44. Charles A. Reich, "The Individual Sector," *Yale Law Journal* 100 (1991): 1429.

CHAPTER THREE

1. The term "common law" has a second meaning: the body of law on contracts, torts, and property that has its origins in English royal courts and that forms the conceptual basis for much of American civil law. James Gordley, "The Common Law in the Twentieth Century: Some Unfinished Business," *California Law Review* 88 (2000): 1817.

2. Given these variations, I hasten to caution that comprehensiveness is not the goal in my discussion of employment at will. The cases and examples I mention in the following pages are illustrative, but in no way exhaustive.

3. Patricia H. Werhane and Tara J. Radin (with Norman E. Bowie), *Employment and Employee Rights* (Malden, MA: Blackwell, 2004), 56.

4. H.G. Wood, *A Treatise on the Law of Master and Servant: Covering the Relation, Duties and Liabilities of Employers and Employees*, 2nd ed. (Albany, NY: 1886), online book, http://galenet.galegroup.com (accessed May 16, 2006), 276–277 (emphasis added).

5. *Payne v. Western & Atl. R.R.*, 81 Tenn. 507: 519–520 (1884) (emphasis added).

6. Ibid., 543–544.

7. Andrew P. Morriss, "Exploding Myths: An Empirical and Economic Reassessment of the Rise of Employment At-Will," *Missouri Law Review* 59 (1994): 679–773.

8. Deborah A. Ballam, "Exploding the Original Myth Regarding Employment-at-Will: The True Origins of the Doctrine," *Berkeley Journal of Employment and Labor Law* 17 (1996): 91–130.

9. *Adair v. United States*, 208 U.S. 161 (1908); *Coppage v. Kansas*, 236 U.S. 1 (1915). See Lawrence E. Blades, "Employment-at-Will vs. Individual Freedom: On Limiting the Abusive Exercise of Employer Power," *Columbia Law Review* 67 (1967): 1416–1419, for a discussion of these cases and their effect on employment at will.

10. Werhane and Radin, *Employment and Employee Rights*, 55.

11. *National Labor Relations Act*, 29 U.S.C. § 157 and 29 U.S.C. § 158.

12. *Civil Rights Act of 1964*, 42 U.S.C. § 2000e-2.

13. See Werhane and Radin, *Employment and Employee Rights*, 59.

14. For a thorough review of exceptions based on off-work behavior, see Stephen D. Sugarman, "'Lifestyle Discrimination' in Employment," *Berkeley Journal of Employment and Labor Law* 24 (2003): 416–420.

15. Gilbert M. Roman, "Smoking Outside of Workplace Sparks New 'Civil

Rights' Laws," *Rocky Mountain News*, July 31, 1994, http://www.lexis-nexis
.com/ (accessed May 17, 2006).

16. Missouri Revised Statutes, §290.145, http://www.moga.state.mo.us/
statutes/c200-299/2900000145.htm (accessed May 17, 2006).

17. Effective analyses of the implied-contract and covenant-of-good-faith
exceptions are found in Charles J. Muhl, "The Employment-At-Will Doctrine:
Three Major Exceptions," *Monthly Labor Review*, January 2001, 3–11; Clyde
W. Summers, "Employment at Will in the United States: The Divine Right of
Employers," *Journal of Labor & Employment Law* 3 (2000): 65–86; and Werhane
and Radin, *Employment and Employee Rights*, 62–66. These three sources inform
my discussion of implicit agreement exceptions in this section.

18. *Roberson v. Wal-Mart*, 202 Ariz. 286 (2002). How big is Wal-Mart and
how often are they sued? A search for "Roberson v. Wal-Mart" using a legal
database search engine yields three different cases by that name since the mid-
1990s, involving three different Robersons in three different states. Change
"Roberson" to "Robertson" and four more cases, involving four different
Robertsons, show up.

19. Ibid., 293. The passages included here from the company's employment application and employee handbook are quoted from the Arizona Court
of Appeals ruling in the case. *Roberson v. Wal-Mart*, 202 Ariz. 286, 288–289.

20. Ibid., 296.

21. The classic formulation of the implied covenant is found in *Restatement
(Second) of Contracts* § 205 (1981). For an analysis of when and how it applies,
see Thomas A. Diamond and Howard Foss, "Proposed Standards for Evaluat-
ing When the Covenant of Good Faith and Fair Dealing Has Been Violated: A
Framework for Resolving the Mystery," *Hastings Law Journal* 47 (1996): 585–
633.

22. *Cleary v. American Airlines*, 111 Cal. App. 3d 443 (1980), 455.

23. Paul Falcone, "A Legal Dichotomy?" *HR Magazine*, May 1999, 110–
120.

24. Michael Kittner and Thomas C. Kohler, "Conditioning Expectations:
The Protection of the Employment Bond in German and American Law,"
Comparative Labor Law & Policy Journal 21 (2000): 290.

25. The U.S. Supreme Court in the late 1940s weighed in with a definition:
"The public policy of any state is to be found in its constitution, acts of the legislature, and decisions of its courts." *Building Service Union v. Gazzam*, 339 U.S.
532 (1949), 537.

26. My synopsis here of the history of the public policy exception draws on

a more extensive review found in Deborah A. Ballam, "Employment-at-Will: The Impending Death of a Doctrine," *American Business Law Journal* 37 (2000): 653–687.

27. *Noble v. City of Palo Alto*, 89 Cal. App. 47 (1928), 50–51.

28. *Petermann vs. International Brotherhood of Teamsters*, 174 Cal. Ap. 2d 184 (1959), 189 (emphasis added).

29. Muhl, "The Employment-At-Will Doctrine: Three Major Exceptions," 5.

30. *Palmateer v. International Harvester*, 421 N.E.2d 876 (1981), 878–879.

31. Blades, "Employment-at-Will vs. Individual Freedom," 1416.

32. Ibid., 1432–1433.

33. *Geary v. United States Steel Corp.*, 319 A.2d 174; Summers, "Employment at Will in the United States," 73.

34. Muhl, "The Employment-at-Will Doctrine: Three Major Exceptions," 4.

35. *Horn v. New York Times*, 100 N.Y.2d 85 (2003), 93.

36. Estimates of the size of the actual "at-will" American workforce are very difficult to come by given variations in state laws addressing exceptions to employment at will, and given no easy way to tally contractual exceptions. The Princeton, New Jersey-based National Workrights Institute estimates that three-fourths of all workers are employed at will. "Wrongful Discharge," legislative brief, National Workrights Institute, http://www.workrights.org/issue_discharge/wd_legislative_brief.html (accessed September 19, 2006). A San Francisco-based nonprofit organization called Workplace Fairness asserts that "most workers" are employed at will. *Here Today, Gone Tomorrow*, Workplace Fairness, http://www.workplacefairness.org/sc/protections.php (accessed September 19, 2006).

37. *Korb v. Raytheon*, 410 Mass. 581 (1991), 584.

38. *Drake v. Cheyenne*, 891 P.2d 80 (1995), 82.

39. *Novosel v. Nationwide Insurance Company*, 721 F.2d 894 (1983), 899. This case, concerning state law governing employment at will in Pennsylvania, was heard by a federal court sitting "in diversity" because of the multistate character of one of the parties. The federal court interprets and applies state law in such situations.

40. *Sarah Borse v. Piece Goods Shop, Inc.*, 963 F.2d 611 (1992).

41. A recent review and analysis of the law on whistleblowing in private-sector employment and its relation to employment at will is found in Frank J. Cavico, "Private Sector Whistleblowing and the Employment-at-Will Doc-

trine: A Comparative Legal, Ethical, and Pragmatic Analysis," *South Texas Law Review* 45 (2004): 543–645.

42. See Lewis D. Lowenfels and Alan R. Bromberg, "Implied Private Actions under Sarbanes-Oxley," *Seton Hall Law Review* 34 (2004): 775–806.

43. Jack Stieber, "Recent Developments in Employment-at-Will," *Labor Law Journal* 36 (1985): 558.

44. The multiplier is based on nonfarm employment growth reflected in statistics reported by the U.S. Bureau of Labor Statistics and reported in Betty W. Su, "The U.S. Economy to 2014," *Monthly Labor Review*, November 2005, 23. The overall civilian labor force estimate in the following sentence is from the same source.

45. Thomas C. Kohler, "The Employment Relation and Its Ordering at Century's End: Reflections on Emerging Trends in the United States," *Boston College Law Review* 41 (1999): 106–107.

46. John J. Donohue III and Peter Siegelman, "The Changing Nature of Employment Discrimination Litigation," *Stanford Law Review* 43 (1991): 985.

47. Jürgen O. Skoppek, "Employment-at-Will in Michigan: A Case for Retaining the Doctrine," Mackinac Center for Public Policy, http://www .mackinac.org/article.aspx?id=266 (accessed May 20, 2006).

48. Summers, "Employment at Will in the United States," 77.

49. Montana Code Annotated Title 39, Chapter 2, § 901–905 (2003). My comments on the law and how it works in practice are based on William L. Corbett, "Resolving Employee Discharge Disputes under the Montana Wrongful Discharge Act (MWDA), Discharge Claims Arising apart from the MWDA, and Practice and Procedure Issues in the Context of a Discharge Case," *Montana Law Review* 66 (2005): 329–404; Andrew P. Morriss, "How Montana Employers Got Rid of the Employment-at-Will Rule," *Labor and Employment Law* 34(3) (2006), https://www.abanet.org/labor/morriss_end-notes.pdf (accessed September 19, 2006).

50. *Buck v. Billings Chevrolet Inc.*, 248 Mont. 281–282 (1991). See also Donald C. Robinson, "The First Decade of Judicial Enforcement of the Montana Wrongful Discharge from Employment Act (WDEA)," *Montana Law Review* 57 (1996): 375–422.

51. Alan B. Krueger, "The Evolution of Unjust-Dismissal Legislation in the United States," *Industrial and Labor Relations Review* 44 (1991): 644–660.

52. Theodore J. St. Antoine, "The Model Employment Termination Act: A Fair Compromise," *Annals of the American Academy of Political and Social Science* 536 (1994): 96. For a thorough critique of the Model Act, see Kenneth A.

Sprang, "Beware the Toothless Tiger: A Critique of the Model Employment Termination Act," *American University Law Review* 43 (1994): 849–924.

53. See, for example, Richard A. Epstein, "In Defense of the Contract at Will," *University of Chicago Law Review* 51 (1984): 947–982; Jesse Rudy, "What They Don't Know Won't Hurt Them: Defending Employment-at-Will in Light of Findings That Employees Believe They Possess Just Cause Protection," *Berkeley Journal of Employment and Labor Law* 23 (2002): 307–367.

54. See, for example, Blades, "Employment-at-Will vs. Individual Freedom"; Summers, "Employment at Will in the United States"; Tara J. Radin and Patricia H. Werhane, "Employment-at-Will, Employee Rights, and Future Directions for Employment," *Business Ethics Quarterly* 13 (2003): 113–130.

55. This argument is fleshed out in Fred Magdoff and Harry Magdoff, "Disposable Workers: Today's Reserve Army of Labor," *Monthly Review* 55 (2004), http://www.monthlyreview.org/0404magdoff.htm (accessed October 18, 2006).

56. Jathan Janove, "Keep 'Em at Will, Treat 'Em for Cause," *HR Magazine*, May 2005, 111–117.

57. *Drake v. Cheyenne*, 891 P.2d 80 (1995), 83.

58. Janove, "Keep 'Em at Will, Treat 'Em For Cause," 117.

59. Jerre S. Williams, "The Twilight of State Action," *Texas Law Review* 41 (1963): 389.

60. Ballam, "Employment-at-Will: The Impending Death of a Doctrine," 687.

CHAPTER FOUR

1. Joe Kovacs, "Letter to the Editor Gets Man Fired," *WorldNetDaily*, June 18, 2004, http://www.worldnetdaily.com/news/article.asp?article_id=38996 (accessed July 31, 2006). The company, the athletic apparel maker Russell Corporation, said the man lost his job not because of his message but for identifying the company when speaking on a personal issue (the letter included a corporate email address, unintentionally, he says). As a private-sector employer, the company could have sacked him for either reason—the content of the letter or the identification of the firm—or for no reason at all.

2. *Pickering v. Board of Education*, 391 U.S. 563 (1968).

3. Alan Freeman and Elizabeth Mensch, "The Public-Private Distinction in American Law and Life," *Buffalo Law Review* 36 (1987): 237.

4. See Tara J. Radin and Patricia H. Werhane, "The Public/Private Distinction and the Political Status of Employment," *American Business Law Journal* 34 (1996): 248–249.

5. Robert P. Stephens, David Langdon, and Brady M. Stephens, "Payroll Employment in 2005: Recovery and Expansion," *Monthly Labor Review*, March 2006, 19–22.

6. *McAuliffe v. Mayor of New Bedford*, 155 Mass. 216 (1892), 220.

7. *Connick v. Myers*, 461 U.S. 138 (1983), 144.

8. *Adler v. Board of Education*, 342 U.S. 485 (1952), 492.

9. Ibid., 493.

10. Ibid., 508.

11. Ibid., 511.

12. *Wieman v. Updegraff*, 344 U.S. 183 (1952).

13. Ibid., 190–191.

14. *Shelton v. Tucker*, 364 U.S. 479 (1960), 490.

15. Geoffrey R. Stone, Louis M. Seidman, Cass R. Sunstein, Mark V. Tushnet, and Pamela S. Karlan, *The First Amendment*, 2nd ed. (New York: Aspen, 2003), 467.

16. *Keyishian v. Board of Regents*, 385 U.S. 589 (1967), 628–629.

17. Ibid., 605–606, quoting approvingly an earlier court of appeals ruling in this same matter: *Keyishian v. Board of Regents*, 345 F.2d 236 (1965), 239.

18. Paul Ferris Solomon, "The Public Employee's Right of Free Speech: A Proposal for a Fresh Start," *University of Cincinnati Law Review* 55 (1986): 452.

19. Some details of Pickering's situation, including recollections of those involved, are drawn from David L. Hudson Jr., *Balancing Act: Public Employees and Free Speech* (Nashville, TN: First Amendment Center, 2002), http://www.fac.org/pdf/firstreport.publicemployees.pdf (accessed May 26, 2006).

20. *Pickering v. Board of Education*, 391 U.S. 563 (1968), 575–578.

21. Hudson, *Balancing Act*, 9.

22. *Pickering v. Board of Education*, 391 U.S. 563, 564.

23. *Pickering v. Board of Education*, 36 Ill. 2d 568 (1967), 578.

24. *Pickering v. Board of Education*, 391 U.S. 563, 568 (emphasis added).

25. Ibid., 571–572.

26. *Thornhill v. Alabama*, 310 U.S. 88 (1940), 102.

27. For a review of the evolution and breadth of the public concern doctrine, see Cynthia L. Estlund, "Speech on Matters of Public Concern: The Perils of an Emerging First Amendment Category," *George Washington Law Review* 59 (1990): 1–55.

28. *New York Times Co. v. Sullivan*, 376 U.S. 254 (1964), 279–280.

29. *Perry v. Sindermann*, 408 U.S. 593 (1972).

30. *Mt. Healthy City School Dist. v. Doyle*, 429 U.S. 274 (1977).

31. *Doyle v. Mt. Healthy*, 670 F.2d 59 (1982).

32. Michael Wells, "Three Arguments against Mt. Healthy: Tort Theory, Constitutional Torts, and Freedom of Speech," *Mercer Law Review* 51 (2000): 598. Wells called *Mt. Healthy* "among the most important, and least discussed, cases in constitutional tort law" (p. 583) because of its role in defining the motives necessary to justify an adverse employment action. In the area of discrimination, the Civil Rights Act of 1991 replaced *Mt. Healthy*'s "but for" standard with a "motivating factor" standard. Previously, to prove illegal discrimination, a person had to show that he wouldn't have been fired but for his race (or sex or national origin, and so on). Under the new standard, he need only show that race was a motivating factor, even though there might have been other factors. 42 U.S.C. § 2000e-2(m). The new standard created within the Civil Rights Act applied to Title VII violations but not to First Amendment violations.

33. *Ayers v. Western Line Consol. School Dist.*, 555 F.2d 1309 (1977), 1312.

34. Ibid., 1319.

35. *Givhan v. Western Line Consol. Sch. Dist.*, 439 U.S. 410 (1979), 415–416.

36. *Connick v. Myers*, 461 U.S. 138 (1983), 141.

37. Hudson, *Balancing Act*, 20.

38. *Connick v. Myers*.

39. Ibid., 146.

40. Ibid., 147–148 (emphasis added).

41. Ibid., 149.

42. Ibid., 151–152, 153.

43. Ibid., 161.

44. Ibid., 170.

45. Estlund, "Speech on Matters of Public Concern," 12.

46. *Connick v. Myers*, 143.

47. Hudson, *Balancing Act*, 21.

48. D. Gordon Smith, "Beyond 'Public Concern': New Free Speech Standards for Public Employees," *University of Chicago Law Review* 57 (1990): 258.

49. Lawrence Rosenthal, "Permissible Content Discrimination under the First Amendment: The Strange Case of the Public Employee," *Hastings Constitutional Law Quarterly* 25 (1998): 557.

50. *McPherson v. Rankin*, 786 F.2d 1233 (1986), 1234.

51. Ibid., 1235.

52. Ibid., 1236.

53. *Rankin v. McPherson*, 483 U.S. 378 (1987), 387.

54. Ibid., 398.

55. *McPherson v. Rankin*, 1238.

56. *Rankin v. McPherson*, 393.

57. *Waters v. Churchill*, 511 U.S. 661 (1994).

58. Randy J. Kozel, "Reconceptualizing Public Employee Speech," *Northwestern University Law Review* 99 (2005): 1018.

59. *Board of County Commissioners v. Umbehr*, 518 U.S. 668 (1996).

60. *San Diego v. Roe*, 543 U.S. 77 (2004), 83–84.

61. *Roe v. San Diego*, 356 F.3d 1108 (2004).

62. Ibid., 1119–1121.

63. Ibid., 1123.

64. *Berger and Barhight v. Battaglia*, 779 F.2d 992 (1985).

65. *Tindle v. Caudell*, 56 F.3d 966 (1995).

66. *Garcetti v. Ceballos*, 126 S. Ct. 1951 (2006), 1960.

67. Ibid., 1965.

68. Ibid., 1965 n. 2.

69. Estlund, "Speech on Matters of Public Concern," 3.

70. Ibid., 38.

71. Rosenthal, "Permissible Content Discrimination under the First Amendment," 544.

72. Stanley Ingber, "Rediscovering the Communal Worth of Individual Rights: The First Amendment in Institutional Contexts," *Texas Law Review* 69 (1990): 55.

73. Joseph V. Kaplan and Edward H. Passman, *Federal Employees Legal Survival Guide: How To Protect & Enforce Your Job Rights*, 2nd ed. (San Francisco: Workplace Fairness, 2004).

74. Roberta Ann Johnson, *Whistleblowing: When It Works—and Why* (Boulder, CO: Lynne Rienner, 2003), 4.

75. *False Claims Act*, 31 U.S.C. § 3729.

76. Johnson, *Whistleblowing*, 9.

77. *Whistleblower Protection Act*, 5 U.S.C. § 2302(b)(8).

78. *LaChance v. White*, 174 F.3d 1378 (1999), 1381 [quoting *Alaska Airlines, Inc. v. Johnson*, 8 F.3d 791 (1993), 795] (emphasis added).

79. Government Accountability Project, "S. 494–H.R. 1317: Whistleblower Protection Act Amendments," http://www.whistleblower.org/template/page.cfm?page_id=146 (accessed May 29, 2006).

80. Ibid.

81. H.R. 1317 and S. 494, 109th Congress, THOMAS (Library of Congress), http://thomas.loc.gov/ (accessed December 23, 2006).

82. Stephen M. Kohn, *Concepts and Procedures in Whistleblower Law* (Westport, CT: Quorum, 2001), 1.

83. 5 U.S.C. § 2302(b)(3).

84. 18 U.S.C. § 600.

85. *Elrod v. Burns*, 427 U.S. 347 (1976).

86. *Branti v. Finkel*, 445 U.S. 507 (1980), 518.

87. *Rutan v. Republican Party of Illinois*, 497 U.S. 62 (1990).

88. *O'Hare Truck Service, Inc. v. City of Northlake*, 518 U.S. 712 (1996).

89. My discussion of the history of restrictions on political activities by government employees, including the Hatch Act, draws upon Scott J. Bloch, "The Judgment of History: Faction, Political Machines, and the Hatch Act," *Journal of Labor & Employment Law* 7 (2005): 225–277; see also Marcy S. Edwards, Jill Leka, James Baird, and Stefanie Lee Black, *Freedom of Speech in the Public Workplace* (Chicago: American Bar Association, 1998), 22–26.

90. James D. Richardson, *A Compilation of the Messages and Papers of the Presidents, 1789–1897* (1898), cited in Bloch, "The Judgment of History," 229.

91. *Ex Parte Curtis*, 106 U.S. 371 (1882), 373.

92. Ibid., 373–374.

93. Ibid., 376–377.

94. 5 U.S.C. § 1501

95. 5 U.S.C. § 7323 and 7324; codified in 5 C.F.R. § 733.103–106.

96. *United Public Workers v. Mitchell*, 330 U.S. 75 (1947); *United States Civil Service Commission v. Letter Carriers*, 413 U.S. 548 (1973).

97. *United States Civil Service Commission v. Letter Carriers*, 597.

98. William E. Reukauf, "Federal Hatch Act Advisory: Retirement of Campaign Debt," advisory letter, U.S. Office of Special Counsel, February 14, 2001, http://www.osc.gov/documents/hatchact/federal/fha-26.htm (accessed May 29, 2006).

99. *United States v. National Treasury Employees Union*, 513 U.S. 454 (1995).

100. *San Diego v. Roe*, 543 U.S. 77 (2004).

101. For a review of cases involving speech by police officers, see Edwards et al., *Freedom of Speech in the Public Workplace*, 135–139.

102. *Dahm v. Flynn*, 60 F.3d 253 (1994), 258.

CHAPTER FIVE

1. Cynthia L. Estlund, "Free Speech and Due Process in the Workplace," *Indiana Law Review* 71 (1995): 113.

2. *Jackson v. Metropolitan Edison Co.*, 419 U.S. 345 (1974), 351.

3. *Holodnak v. Avco Corp.*, 514 F.2d 285 (1975), 287.

4. Ibid., 290.

5. *Intel Corp. v. Hamidi*, 114 Cal.Rptr.2d 244 (2001), 253.

6. *George v. Pacific-CSC Work Furlough*, 91 F.3d 1227 (1996), 1230–1232.

The court in *George* drew upon the analytical framework described in *Lugar v. Edmondson Oil Co.*, 457 U.S. 922 (1982), 939.

7. *Burton v. Wilmington Parking Auth.*, 365 U.S. 715 (1961).

8. *Edmonson v. Leesville Concrete Co.*, 500 U.S. 614 (1991), 640.

9. Peter J. Duitsman, "The Private Prison Experiment: A Private Sector Solution to Prison Overcrowding," *North Carolina Law Review* 76 (1998): 2231.

10. Matthew W. Finkin, "Representation of Employees within the Firm: The United States Report," *The American Journal of Comparative Law* 54 (2006): 402.

11. James J. Brudney, "Isolated and Politicized: The NLRB's Uncertain Future," *Comparative Labor Law & Policy Journal* 26 (2005): 221–260.

12. 29 U.S.C. § 157 (emphasis added).

13. 29 U.S.C. § 158.

14. For a discussion of the congressional commentary on Section 7 before the passage of the NLRA, see Charles J. Morris, "NLRB Protection in the Nonunion Workplace: A Glimpse at a General Theory of Section 7 Conduct," *University of Pennsylvania Law Review* 137 (1989): 1681–1686.

15. *National Labor Relations Board v. Washington Aluminum Co.*, 370 U.S. 9 (1962), 14.

16. *Eastex, Inc. v. National Labor Relations Board*, 437 U.S. 556 (1978), 570.

17. Morris, "NLRB Protection in the Nonunion Workplace," 1685.

18. Cynthia L. Estlund, "Free Speech and Due Process in the Workplace," 118. See also Cynthia L. Estlund, "What Do Workers Want? Employee Interests, Public Interests, and Freedom of Expression under the National Labor Relations Act," *University of Pennsylvania Law Review* 140 (1992): 921–1004.

19. Ellen Dannin, "NLRA Values, Labor Values, American Values," *Berkeley Journal of Employment and Labor Law* 26 (2005): 229–230.

20. 29 U.S.C. § 158 (c).

21. Robert Wagner, 93 Cong. Rec. A895 (1947), cited in Kate E. Andrias, "A Robust Public Debate: Realizing Free Speech in Workplace Representation Elections," *Yale Law Journal* 112 (2003): 2429 n. 62.

22. Andrias, "A Robust Public Debate," 2420.

23. The discussion here of the transformation and politicization of the NLRB draws from Joan Flynn, "A Quiet Revolution at the Labor Board: The Transformation of the NLRB, 1935–2000," *Ohio State Law Journal* 61 (2000): 1361–1455; and James J. Brudney, "Isolated and Politicized: The NLRB's Uncertain Future," 243–252.

24. Brudney, "Isolated and Politicized: The NLRB's Uncertain Future," 248.

25. Flynn, "A Quiet Revolution at the Labor Board," 1452.

26. Jonathan P. Hiatt and Craig Becker, "At Age 70, Should the Wagner Act Be Retired? A Response to Professor Dannin," *Berkeley Journal of Employment and Labor Law* 26 (2005): 297.

27. Brudney, "Isolated and Politicized: The NLRB's Uncertain Future," 251, 259.

28. David C. Yamada, "Voices from the Cubicle: Protecting and Encouraging Private Employee Speech in the Post-Industrial Workplace," *Berkeley Journal of Employment and Labor Law* 19 (1998): 38–39.

29. David Brody, "Labor vs. the Law: How the Wagner Act Became a Management Tool," *New Labor Forum*, Spring 2004, cited in Dannin, "NLRA Values, Labor Values, American Values," 261.

30. Kenneth D. Walters, "Your Employees' Right to Blow the Whistle," *Harvard Business Review*, July-August 1975, 1–7.

31. Elletta Sangrey Callahan, Terry Morehead Dworkin, and David Lewis, "Whistleblowing: Australian, U.K., and U.S. Approaches to Disclosure in the Public Interest," *Virginia Journal of International Law* 44 (2004): 886–887.

32. Yamada, "Voices From the Cubicle," 38.

33. For a review and discussion of these variations, see Frank J. Cavico, "Private Sector Whistleblowing and the Employment-at-Will Doctrine: A Comparative Legal, Ethical, and Pragmatic Analysis," *South Texas Law Review* 45 (2004): 543–645. My overview here draws on Cavico's analysis.

34. N.Y. Labor Law § 740(2)(a).

35. *Schultz v. North American Insurance Group*, 34 F. Supp. 2d 866 (1999), 869.

36. Marc I. Steinberg and Seth A. Kaufman, "Minimizing Corporate Liability Exposure When the Whistle Blows in the Post Sarbanes-Oxley Era," *Journal of Corporation Law* 30 (2005): 448.

37. *Sarbanes-Oxley Act of 2002*, Public Law 107–204 § 806 (a), 116 Stat. 745, 803.

38. See, for example, Bruce Bartlett, "The Crimes of Sarbanes-Oxley," *National Review Online*, May 25, 2004, http://www.nationalreview.com/nrof _bartlett/bartlett200405250811.asp (accessed June 12, 2006); "The Trial of Sarbanes-Oxley," *Economist*, April 20, 2006, http://www.economist.com/ business/displaystory.cfm?story_id=6838442 (accessed June 12, 2006).

39. Larry E. Ribstein, "Market vs. Regulatory Responses to Corporate Fraud: A Critique of the Sarbanes-Oxley Act of 2002," *Journal of Corporation Law* 28 (2002): 43.

40. Alison Grant, "Whistleblowing in the Workplace: Law Offers Protec-

tions, but Risks Remain," *Plain Dealer*, February 2, 2003, G1, http://www.proquest.com/.

41. William K. Black, "The Moral Quandaries of a Government Whistle-blower," Markkula Center for Applied Ethics, Santa Clara University, http://www.scu.edu/ethics/publications/submitted/black/whistleblower.html (accessed September 20, 2006).

42. *Shovelin v. Central New Mexico Electric Cooperative, Inc.*, 850 P.2d 996 (1993).

43. New Mexico Statutes Annotated, § 3-8-78 (A).

44. 18 U.S.C. § 245 (b).

45. 38 A.L.R.5th 39, § 3.

46. 18 U.S.C. § 594; 18 U.S.C. § 597; Lisa B. Bingham, "Employee Free Speech in the Workplace: Using the First Amendment as Public Policy for Wrongful Discharge Actions," *Ohio State Law Journal* 55 (1994): 352–353 nn. 48–49.

47. California Labor Code § 1102.

48. *Fort v. Civil Service Commission*, 61 Cal.2d 331 (1964), 335.

49. Louisiana Revised Statutes 23 § 961 (emphasis added).

50. *Davis v. Louisiana Computing Corp.*, 394 So. 2d 678, La. Ct. App. (1981), 679.

51. Minnesota Statutes § 202A.135; 29 Delaware Code § 5110; Montana Code Annotated, § 2-18-620; Connecticut General Statutes § 2-3a.

52. Wal-Mart, "Voter Registration Drive Launched by America's Largest Private Company, Wal-Mart," Wal-Mart Facts.com, September 29, 2006, http://www.walmartfacts.com/articles/4479.aspx (accessed October 18, 2006).

53. Daniel Gross, "Wal-Mart Voters," *Slate*, October 6, 2006, http://www.slate.com/id/2151043/ (accessed October 18, 2006).

54. "State Voter Leave Laws," Time to Vote, http://www.timetovote.net/voter_leave_laws.html (accessed June 13, 2006).

55. Oklahoma Statutes § 26-7-101.

56. "Hectic Lifestyles Make for Record-Low Election Turnout, Census Bureau Reports," U.S. Census Bureau news release, August 17, 1998, http://www.census.gov/Press-Release/cb98-146.html (accessed June 13, 2006); Kelly Holder, "Voting and Registration in the Election of November 2004," *Current Population Reports*, U.S. Census Bureau, March 2006, http://www.census.gov/prod/2006pubs/p20-556.pdf (accessed June 13, 2006).

57. The award for most bizarre statute regulating off-work product consumption goes to Tennessee, where it is illegal to fire someone for "the use of an agricultural product not regulated by the alcoholic beverage commission

that is not otherwise proscribed by law." Tennessee Code § 50-1-304 (e). This was presumably aimed at tobacco use, but it appears to have the odd consequence of protecting workers from being fired for eating asparagus, while leaving them exposed to termination for drinking a diet soda (depending, of course, on how expansively a court wishes to interpret "agricultural product").

58. North Dakota Cent. Code § 14-02.4-03 and 14-02.4-08.

59. Colorado Rev. Stats. Ann. § 24-34-402.5.

60. New York State Consolidated Laws § 201-d.

61. California Labor Code § 96 (k).

62. Michelle R. Barrett, "'Lawful Conduct' in Amended California Labor Code 96: 'Lifestyle Discrimination' Provision or Restatement of Civil Liberties Protection?" *ASAP* (newsletter of Littler Mendelson, P.C., a California law firm), December 1999, http://library.findlaw.com/1999/Dec/1/128727.html (accessed June 14, 2006).

63. Michelle R. Barrett, interview with the author, June 16, 2006. For a review of early cases related to the California statute, see Marisa Anne Pagnattaro, "What Do You Do When You Are Not at Work? Limiting the Use of Off-Duty Conduct as the Basis for Adverse Employment Decisions," *Journal of Labor & Employment Law* 6 (2004): 646–652.

64. *Marsh v. Delta Air Lines*, 952 F. Supp. 1458 (1997), 1464.

65. *Hougum v. Valley Memorial Homes*, 1998 ND 24 (1998), 30.

66. Wisconsin Statutes § 111.321.

67. Eugene Volokh, "State Laws Potentially Protecting Employee Blogging," May 2, 2006, http://www.law.ucla.edu/volokh/empspeechstatutes.pdf (accessed June 13, 2006).

68. *Wiegand v. Motiva Enterprises*, 295 F. Supp. 2d 465 (2003), 466.

69. Connecticut General Statutes § 31-51q (emphasis added).

70. Joseph R. Grodin, "Constitutional Values in the Private Sector Workplace," *Industrial Relations Law Journal* 13 (1991): 24.

71. Martin B. Margulies, "Sherlock Holmes and Connecticut's Free Speech Statute," *Connecticut Bar Journal* 68 (1994): 456–459.

72. For a summary of more recent cases involving the Connecticut statute, see Pagnattaro, "What Do You Do When You Are Not at Work," 669–670.

73. Margulies, "Sherlock Holmes and Connecticut's Free Speech Statute," 458.

74. South Carolina Code Annotated § 16-17-560.

75. *Culler v. Blue Ridge Electric Cooperative*, 309 S.C. 243 (1992).

76. *Dixon v. Coburg*, 369 F.3d 811 (2004).

77. *Dixon v. Coburg*, 330 F.3d 250 (2003), 262.

78. Kingsley R. Browne, "Title VII as Censorship: Hostile-Environment Harassment and the First Amendment," *Ohio State Law Journal*, 52 (1991): 481–550; Eugene Volokh, "How Harassment Law Restricts Free Speech," *Rutgers Law Review*, 47 (1995): 563–576.

79. Suzanne Sangree, "Title VII Prohibitions against Hostile Environment Sexual Harassment and the First Amendment: No Collision in Sight," *Rutgers Law Review*, 47 (1995): 461–561; David Benjamin Oppenheimer, "Workplace Harassment and the First Amendment: A Reply to Professor Volokh," *Berkeley Journal of Employment and Labor Law* 17 (1996): 321–332.

80. Clyde W. Summers, "Worker Dislocation: Who Bears the Burden? A Comparative Study of Social Values in Five Countries," *Notre Dame Law Review*, 70 (1995): 1068.

81. Ron McCallum, "Plunder Downunder: Transplanting the Anglo-American Labor Law Model to Australia," *Comparative Labor Law & Policy Journal* 26 (2005): 383–389.

82. ILO, "Convention Concerning Termination of Employment at the Initiative of the Employer," International Labour Organization Convention 158, adopted June 22, 1982, http://www.ilo.org/ilolex/cgi-lex/convde.pl?C158 (accessed December 21, 2006), Articles 4 and 5.

83. ILO, "Convention Concerning Discrimination in Respect of Employment and Occupation" International Labour Organization Convention 111, adopted June 25, 1958, http://www.ilo.org/ilolex/cgi-lex/convde.pl?C111 (accessed December 21, 2006), Article 1.

84. Workplace Relations Act 1996 § 659 (2)(f), Attorney General's Department, Australian Government, http://www.comlaw.gov.au/ (accessed June 14, 2006).

85. Human Rights Act 1993 § 21 (j), New Zealand Human Rights Commission, http://rangi.knowledge-basket.co.nz/gpacts/public/text/1993/se/082se21 .html (accessed June 14, 2006).

86. Department of Justice, Equality and Law Reform, Government of Ireland, *Extending the Scope of Employment Equality Legislation: Comparative Perspectives on the Prohibited Grounds of Discrimination.* (Dublin: Stationary Office, 2004), 108.

87. The European Convention on Human Rights, Article 10, http://www .hri.org/docs/ECHR50.html (accessed June 14, 2006)

88. Lucy Vickers, *Freedom of Speech and Employment* (Oxford: Oxford University Press, 2002).

CHAPTER SIX

1. First Amendment Center, *State of the First Amendment 2005* (Nashville, TN: First Amendment Center, 2005), http://www.firstamendmentcenter .org/PDF/SOFA2005.pdf (accessed June 15, 2006); Charles M. Madigan, "Free Speech: Do Americans Really Believe in It?" *Chicago Tribune*, July 4, 2004, 1.

2. Chicago Tribune Poll conducted by Market Shares Corp. June 23–27, 2004, PollingReport.com, http://www.pollingreport.com/media.htm (accessed June 15, 2006).

3. Christopher Lee, "Noted with Interest," *Washington Post*, March 3, 2006, A15. Jumping on an easy opportunity to contrast civic with pop-cultural awareness, this survey found that 22 percent can name all five main characters in the animated television program *The Simpsons* and that 40 percent can name at least two of three judges on *American Idol*.

4. First Amendment Center, *State of the First Amendment 2005*, 14, 23.

5. Madigan, "Free Speech: Do Americans Really Believe in It?"

6. Not to mention Blasi, Bollinger, Kalven, Post, Redish, Scanlon, and Shriffin.

7. Zechariah Chafee, Jr., "Free Speech in War Time," *Harvard Law Review* 32 (1919): 958.

8. Cass R. Sunstein, *Democracy and the Problem of Free Speech* (New York: Free Press, 1993), 18. Legal historian David Rabban critiques Sunstein for "constantly invoking Madison but thinking more like John Dewey," the early-twentieth-century pragmatist philosopher who wrote in some detail about the relationship between free speech and the proper functioning of democracy. See David M. Rabban, *Free Speech in Its Forgotten Years* (Cambridge: Cambridge University Press, 1997), 389–390.

9. Owen M. Fiss, *The Irony of Free Speech* (Cambridge, MA: Harvard University Press, 1996), 3. Additional examples of the same basic distinction (with different labels) include Greenawalt's contrast between "consequentialist" and "non-consequentialist" approaches to expression; Kitrosser's distinction between "intrinsic" and "instrumental" theories of free speech value; and Lieberwitz's divide between "government process" and "self-development" models. Kent Greenawalt, "Free Speech Justifications," *Columbia Law Review*, 89 (1989): 119–155; Heidi Kitrosser, "Containing Unprotected Speech," *Florida Law Review* 57 (2005): 844; Risa L. Lieberwitz, "Freedom of Speech in Public Sector Employment: The Deconstitutionalization of the Public Sector Workplace, *U.C. Davis Law Review*, 19 (1986): 602–609.

10. Greenawalt, "Free Speech Justifications," 145–146.

11. J. S. Mill, *On Liberty* (Baltimore: Penguin, 1859/1974), 108.

12. Ibid., 110–111.

13. *Abrams v. United States*, 250 U.S. 616 (1919), 630 (emphasis added).

14. Robert C. Post, "Reconciling Theory and Doctrine in First Amendment Jurisprudence," *California Law Review* 88 (2000): 2366.

15. *Hustler Magazine, Inc. v. Falwell*, 485 U.S. 46 (1988), 52.

16. Alexander Meiklejohn, *Political Freedom: The Constitutional Powers of the People* (New York: Oxford University Press, 1948/1965), 79. Cass Sunstein, no slouch himself, called Meiklejohn "the greatest philosopher of the First Amendment." Cass R. Sunstein, "Free Speech Now," *University of Chicago Law Review*, 59 (1992): 301.

17. Meiklejohn, *Political Freedom*, 26. Meiklejohn later expanded his view of protected speech to include educational, scientific, literary, and artistic expression as long as it promotes knowledge that leads people to make better political decisions. Alexander Meiklejohn, "The First Amendment Is an Absolute," *Supreme Court Review* 1961 (1961): 256–267. The famously unsuccessful Supreme Court Justice nominee and long-time civil liberties provocateur Robert Bork offered an extreme version of Meiklejohn's argument—that the only speech that should be protected is the explicitly political, leaving out "scientific, educational, commercial or literary expressions as such." Robert H. Bork, "Neutral Principles and Some First Amendment Problems," *Indiana Law Journal* 47 (1971): 28. Bork eventually broadened his view of political speech to include scientific and moral debate but not artistic speech. Robert H. Bork, *The Individual, the State, and the First Amendment*, unpublished speech at the University of Michigan, cited in C. Edwin Baker, *Human Liberty and Freedom of Speech* (New York: Oxford University Press, 1989), 293 n. 6.

18. Sunstein, *Democracy and the Problem of Free Speech*, 18–23.

19. Ibid., 251.

20. *Buckley v. Valeo*, 424 U.S. 1 (1976), 49.

21. Owen M. Fiss, *Liberalism Divided: Freedom of Speech and the Many Uses of State Power* (Boulder, CO: Westview Press, 1996), 30.

22. Sunstein, *Democracy and the Problem of Free Speech*, 121–129.

23. *Chaplinsky v. New Hampshire*, 315 U.S. 568 (1942), 571–572. Three decades later, in overturning a man's disturbing-the-peace conviction for wearing a jacket bearing the words "Fuck the Draft" in a courthouse, the Supreme Court narrowed its tolerance for restrictions on offensive speech. *Cohen v. California*, 403 U.S. 15 (1971). In subsequent cases, the Court found prohibitions

on offensive language to be vague and overbroad and shifted its emphasis to the danger that a violent reaction is imminent. See Kent Greenawalt, *Fighting Words: Individuals, Communities, and Liberties of Speech* (Princeton, NJ: Princeton University Press, 1995), 50–53.

24. Baker, *Human Liberty and Freedom of Speech*, 5.

25. See David A. Strauss, "Persuasion, Autonomy, and Freedom of Expression," *Columbia Law Review* 91 (1991): 334–371; Thomas I. Emerson, *The System of Freedom of Expression* (New York: Random House, 1970); Martin H. Redish, "The Value of Free Speech," *University of Pennsylvania Law Review* 130 (1982): 591–645; Ronald Dworkin, "The Coming Battles over Free Speech," *New York Review of Books*, June 11, 1992, 55–64; Baker, *Human Liberty and Freedom of Speech*.

26. Steven Shiffrin, "The First Amendment and Economic Regulation: Away from a General Theory of the First Amendment," *Northwestern University Law Review*, 78 (1984): 1283; Emerson, *The System of Freedom of Expression*, 6–9.

27. Emerson, *The System of Freedom of Expression*, 8.

28. Baker, *Human Liberty and Freedom of Speech*, 47–48.

29. Rebecca L. Brown, "Liberty, the New Equality," *New York University Law Review* 77 (2002): 1497.

30. Baker, *Human Liberty and Freedom of Speech*, 15.

31. Ibid., 24.

32. Ibid., 59–60.

33. Ibid., 68. An interesting variation on Baker's brand of individualism is found in David Strauss's "persuasion principle" of free speech. Focusing on the moral position of the listener, Strauss argues that the important thing is how speech affects message recipients: "The government may not restrict speech because it fears, however justifiably, that the speech will persuade those who hear it to do something of which the government disapproves." The persuasion principle allows regulation of speech that works through subterfuge or other harmful means (such as inciting violence or egregious social disruption) but protects expression that involves nondeceptive, noncoercive persuasion. David A. Strauss, "Persuasion, Autonomy, and Freedom of Expression," 334.

34. Immanuel Kant, *Foundations of the Metaphysics of Morals*, trans. L. W. Beck (Indianapolis: Bobbs-Merrill, 1785/1969).

35. Kent Greenawalt, "Free Speech Justifications," *Columbia Law Review* 89 (1989): 120.

36. See, for example, Fiss, *Liberalism Divided*, 82–83.

37. Joshua Cohen, "Freedom of Expression," *Philosophy and Public Affairs* 22 (1993): 226.

38. Robert Post, "Meiklejohn's Mistake: Individual Autonomy and the Reform of Public Discourse," *Colorado Law Review* 64 (1993): 1120.

39. Susan J. Brison, "The Autonomy Defense of Free Speech," *Ethics* 108 (1998): 320.

40. Although early collectivist thought limited the reach of the First Amendment to political speech, contemporary versions are less restrictive. See, for example, Sunstein, *Democracy and the Problem of Free Speech*, 140.

41. Thomas I. Emerson, "Toward a General Theory of the First Amendment," *Yale Law Journal* 72 (1963): 907.

42. Sunstein, *Democracy and the Problem of Free Speech*, 141.

43. Shiffrin, "The First Amendment and Economic Regulation," 1283.

44. See, for example, Cynthia L. Estlund, "Working Together: The Workplace, Civil Society, and the Law," *Georgetown Law Journal* 89 (2000): 1–96.

CHAPTER SEVEN

1. Michael Higgins, "Did Fiery Essay Get Author Fired?" *Chicago Tribune*, August 18, 2005, http://www.proquest.com/ (accessed June 21, 2006).

2. J. Matt Barber, "'Intolerance' Will Not Be Tolerated! The Gay Agenda vs. Family Values," *The Conservative Voice*, December 17, 2004, http://www.theconservativevoice.com/article/1484.html (accessed June 21, 2006).

3. "Allstate Responds to Former Allstate Employee Allegations in Recent Press," Allstate, August 18, 2005, http://www.allstate.com/about/pagerender.asp?page=2005_08_18_allstate_responds.htm (accessed June 21, 2006).

4. Higgins, "Did Fiery Essay Get Author Fired?"

5. Ron Strom, "Allstate Terminates Manager over Homosexuality Column," *WorldNetDaily*, June 24, 2005, http://www.worldnetdaily.com/news/article.asp?ARTICLE_ID=44961 (accessed June 21, 2006).

6. Michael Higgins, "Allstate and Ex-Worker Settle Online-Essay Suit," *Chicago Tribune*, February 17, 2006.

7. Jim Brown and Jenni Parker, "Fund Created for Ex-Employee Who Openly Opposed Homosexual 'Marriage,'" AFA Online, December 6, 2005, http://headlines.agapepress.org/archive/12/afa/62005b.asp (accessed June 21, 2006).

8. Higgins, "Allstate and Ex-worker Settle Online-Essay Suit."

9. 42 U.S.C. § 2000e-2.

10. 29 U.S.C. § 623, 631; 42 U.S.C § 12112.

11. See, for example, Hawaii Revised Statutes § 378-2; North Dakota Cent. Code § 14-02.4-03.

12. U.S. Equal Employment Opportunity Commission, "Charge Statistics FY 1992 through FY 2005," January 27, 2006, http://www.eeoc.gov/stats/charges.html (accessed June 22, 2006).

13. CBS News survey based on telephone interviews with a national adult sample of 899, conducted April 6–April 9, 2006. Retrieved from the iPOLL Databank, The Roper Center for Public Opinion Research, University of Connecticut, http://www.ropercenter.uconn.edu (accessed June 23, 2006).

14. First Amendment Center, *State of the First Amendment 2005* (Nashville, TN: First Amendment Center, 2005), http://www.firstamendmentcenter.org/PDF/SOFA2005.pdf (accessed June 15, 2006), 13.

15. For example, *Equal Employment Opportunity Commission v. Sambo's of Georgia, Inc.*, 530 F. Supp. 86 (1981), 91.

16. Michael Luo, "M.T.A. Is Sued over Its Policy on Muslim Head Coverings," *New York Times*, October 1, 2004, late edition (East Coast), B4, http://www.proquest.com/ (accessed June 29, 2006); Carol Eisenberg, "MTA Faces New Complaints over Logo," *Newsday*, July 16, 2005, City Edition, A10, http://www.proquest.com/ (accessed June 29, 2006).

17. 42 U.S.C. § 2000e (j) (emphasis added).

18. *Trans World Airlines, Inc. v. Hardison*, 432 U.S. 63 (1977), 84.

19. *Cloutier v. Costco Wholesale Corp.*, 390 F.3d 126 (2004).

20. "The Church of Body Modification is a spiritual hub in which modified individuals around the world will find strength in sharing their spiritual encounters. The Church is a Church because when we modify our body, we have a deeper reason for what we are doing. We heal, live, grow strong, tell stories, etc. through our modifications. This is a common thread that pulls us together as a group to share our experiences with others who feel the same as we do." The Church of Body Modification, "Frequently Asked Questions," http://www.uscobm.com/faq.asp (accessed June 21, 2006).

21. *Cloutier v. Costco Wholesale Corp.*, 311 F. Supp. 2d 190 (2004), 191.

22. *United States v. Seeger*, 380 U.S. 163 (1965), 165–166.

23. *Walsh v. United States*, 398 U.S. 333 (1970).

24. 29 C.F.R. § 1605.1

25. *Thomas v. Review Bd. of Ind. Employment Sec. Div.*, 391 N.E.2d 1127 (1979), 1131.

26. *Thomas v. Review Bd. of Ind. Employment Sec. Div.*, 450 U.S. 707 (1981), 714–715.

27. Ibid., 716.

28. Ibid., 715.

29. *Brown v. Pena*, 441 F. Supp. 1382 (1977), 1384.

30. *Church of the Lukumi Babalu Aye, Inc. v. City of Hialeah*, 508 U.S. 520 (1993), 531.

31. For a detailed review of legal efforts to define religious belief, see Susannah P. Mroz, "True Believers? Problems of Definition in Title VII Religious Discrimination Jurisprudence," *Indiana Law Review* 35 (2005): 145–176.

32. *Daniels v. City of Arlington*, 246 F.3d 500 (2001).

33. Ibid., 504.

34. *Connick v. Myers*, 461 U.S. 138 (1983).

35. *Daniels v. City of Arlington*, 504.

36. *Tucker v. State of California Department of Education*, 97 F.3d 1204 (1996), 1210.

37. Ibid., 1216.

38. *Berry v. Department of Social Services*, 447 F.3d 642 (2006).

39. *Knight v. State of Conn. Department of Public Health*, 275 F.3d 156 (2001).

40. *Good News Club v. Milford Central School*, 533 U.S. 98 (2001): 112.

41. *Draper v. Logan County Public Library*, 403 F. Supp. 2d 608 (2003), 621.

42. See Thomas C. Berg, "Religious Speech in the Workplace: Harassment or Protected Speech?" *Harvard Journal of Law and Public Policy* 22 (1999): 974–975.

43. N.Y. Exec Law § 296, 10 (d) (1) (emphasis added).

44. *Workplace Religious Freedom Act of 2005*, 109th Congress, S. 677.

45. *Americans with Disabilities Act of 1990* (Pub. L. 101–336), 42 U.S.C. § 12111 (10).

46. This argument was raised by a University of Louisville law professor in testimony at a Congressional subcommittee hearing on the proposed bill. House Committee on Education and the Workforce, *Testimony of Samuel A. Marcosson*, November 10, 2005, http://www.house.gov/ed_workforce/hearings/109th/eer/wrfa111005/marcosson.htm (accessed June 23, 2006).

47. Camille A. Olson, *Testimony on the Workplace Religious Freedom Act of 2005 to the House Subcommittee on Employer-Employee Relations of the Committee on Education and the Workforce*, U.S. Chamber of Commerce, November 10, 2005, http://www.uschamber.com/issues/testimony/2005/051110workplace freedomact.htm (accessed June 22, 2006).

48. Laura W. Murphy and Christopher E. Anders, *ACLU Letter on the Harmful Effect of S. 893, the Workplace Religious Freedom Act, on Critical Personal and Civil Rights*, American Civil Liberties Union, June 2, 2004, http://www .aclu.org/religion/frb/162241eg20040602.html (accessed June 22, 2006).

49. *Meritor Savings Bank v. Vinson*, 477 U.S. 57 (1986).

50. *Harris v. Forklift Systems, Inc.*, 510 U.S. 17 (1993), 23.

51. U.S. Equal Employment Opportunity Commission, *Enforcement Guidance: Vicarious Employer Liability for Unlawful Harassment by Supervisors*, Notice #915.002, June 18, 1999, http://www.eeoc.gov/policy/docs/harassment.html (accessed June 29, 2006).

52. See, for example, Kingsley R. Browne, "Title VII as Censorship: Hostile-Environment Harassment and the First Amendment," *Ohio State Law Journal* 52 (1991): 481–550; Eugene Volokh, "What Speech Does 'Hostile Work Environment' Harassment Law Restrict?," *Georgetown Law Review* 85 (1997): 627–648; David Bernstein, *You Can't Say That! The Growing Threat to Civil Liberties From Antidiscrimination Laws* (Washington, DC: Cato Institute, 2003), 23–34.

53. Volokh, "What Speech Does 'Hostile Work Environment' Harassment Law Restrict?," 647.

54. *Robinson v. Jacksonville Shipyards, Inc.*, 760 F. Supp. 1486 (1991), 1535.

55. Ibid., 1542.

56. Bernstein, *You Can't Say That!*, 30.

57. For a mini-catalog of these and other workplace affronts, see Eugene Volokh, "Thinking Ahead about Freedom of Speech and Hostile Work Environment Harassment," *Berkeley Journal of Employment and Labor Law* 17 (1996): 305–310.

58. Eugene Volokh, "Freedom of Speech and Workplace Harassment," *UCLA Law Review* 39 (1992): 1816–1818.

59. Ibid., 1846.

60. Ibid., 1846–1847.

61. Jeffrey Rosen, *The Unwanted Gaze* (New York: Random House, 2000), 100–127.

62. *Peterson v. Hewlett-Packard Co.*, 358 F.3d 599 (2004), 607.

63. Suzanne Sangree, "Title VII Prohibitions against Hostile Environment Sexual Harassment and the First Amendment: No Collision in Sight," *Rutgers Law Review* 47 (1995): 528–532. See also Deborah Epstein, "Free Speech at Work: Verbal Harassment as Gender-Based Discriminatory (Mis)Treatment," *Georgetown Law Journal* 85 (1997): 658–667.

64. Sangree, "Title VII Prohibitions against Hostile Environment Sexual Harassment and the First Amendment," 546–547.

65. Ibid., 559. Concerns about the collision between harassment and free speech rest on a number of alarming anecdotes about employer censorship in the name of avoiding hostile-environment claims. Yale's Jack Balkin argues,

however, that the "horror stories" tend to "involve employer decisions that are overzealous, reflect traditional or puritanical sexual mores at odds with Title VII's promise of sexual equality, are products of mindless bureaucracy, or are plain idiotic." J. M. Balkin, "Free Speech and Hostile Environments," *Columbia Law Review* 99 (1999): 2318.

66. *Lyle v. Warner*, 38 Cal. 4th 264 (2006), 295.

67. Ibid., 284.

68. Mary Becker, "How Free Is Speech at Work?" *U.C. Davis Law Review* 29 (1996): 867.

69. *Robinson v. Jacksonville Shipyards, Inc.*, 1536.

70. *Federal Communications Commission v. Pacifica Foundation*, 438 U.S. 726 (1978), 748.

71. Volokh, "Freedom of Speech and Workplace Harassment," 1833 – 1840.

72. J. M. Balkin, "Legal Realist Approaches to the First Amendment," *Duke Law Journal* 1990 (1990): 423 – 424.

73. Theodore Kinni, "Faith at Work," *Across the Board*, November/December 2003, 15 – 20.

74. R. Charles Wilkin III, "What Is 'Appropriate' Workplace Speech?" *Oklahoma Employment Law Letter*, April 2001, http://www.lexis-nexis.com/ (accessed July 21, 2004).

CHAPTER EIGHT

1. Meg Spohn, "Dooced!," Megablog, December 16, 2005, http://www .megspohn.com/?p=288 (accessed July 6, 2006).

2. Meg Spohn, untitled entry, Megablog, May 24, 2004, http://www .megspohn.com/?p=212 (accessed July 6, 2006) (emphasis added and profanity partially redacted).

3. Meg Spohn, comment, Blogspotting, *BusinessWeek online*, December 28, 2005, http://www.businessweek.com/the_thread/blogspotting/archives/2005/ 12/is_blogging_a_f.html?campaign_id=rss_blog_blogspotting (accessed July 6, 2006).

4. Rob Smith, "Blogfired: Rob Smith," Morpheme Tales, January 20, 2005, http://morphemetales.blogspot.com/2005/01/blogfired-rob-smith.html (accessed July 5, 2006).

5. Acidman, "Fired for Blogging," Gut Rumbles, January 6, 2005, http:// gutrumbles.com/archives2/001641.php#001641 (accessed July 5, 2006).

6. Stephanie Armour, "Warning: Your Clever Little Blog Could Get You Fired," *USA TODAY*, June 15, 2005, Final Edition, 1B, http://www.lexis-nexis .com/ (accessed July 5, 2006); Evan Hansen, "Google Blogger Has Left the

Building," *CNET News.com*, February 8, 2005, http://news.com.com/Google +blogger+has+left+the+building/2100-1038_3-5567863.html (accessed July 5, 2006).

7. Mark Jen, "The Official Story, Straight from the Source," NINETY-NINEZEROS, February 11, 2005, http://99zeros.blogspot.com/2005/02/official-story-straight-from-source.html (accessed July 5, 2006).

8. Christine Negroni, "Fired Flight Attendant Finds Blogs Can Backfire," *New York Times*, November 16, 2004, Late Edition, C9, http://www.lexis-nexis .com/ (accessed July 4, 2006).

9. Naomi Branston, "What Are the Limits?," *Legal Week*, November 25, 2004, http://www.lexis-nexis.com/ (accessed July 4, 2006).

10. Ellen Simonetti, "Perspective: I Was Fired for Blogging," *CNET News .com*, December 16, 2004, http://news.com.com/I+was+fired+for+blogging/2010-1030_3-5490836.html (accessed July 4, 2006). Simonetti's blog, renamed "Diary of a Fired Flight Attendant," continued at http://queenofsky.journal space.com/.

11. Mike Tierney, "Ex-Flight Attendant Sues Delta Over Blog," *Atlanta Journal-Constitution*, September 8, 2005, home edition, 1E, http://www .lexis-nexis.com/ (accessed July 4, 2006).

12. Negroni, "Fired Flight Attendant Finds Blogs Can Backfire."

13. Todd Bishop, "Microsoft Fires Worker over Weblog," *Seattle Post-Intelligencer*, October 30, 2003, http://seattlepi.nwsource.com/business/146115 _blogger30.html (accessed July 5, 2006).

14. Michael Hanscom, "Of Blogging and Unemployment," eclecticism, October 27, 2003, http://www.michaelhanscom.com/eclecticism/2003/10/5 of_blogging_and.html (accessed July 5, 2006). The blog entry that got Hanscom sacked, "Even Microsoft Wants G5s," can be seen here: http://www.michael hanscom.com/eclecticism/2003/10/even_microsoft.html (accessed July 5, 2006).

15. Samuel Greengard, "The Virtual Pen Is Not Mightier Than the Ax, Fired Bloggers Find," *Workforce Management*, March 1, 2005, 74, http:// www.lexis-nexis.com/ (accessed July 5, 2006).

16. Eric Auchard, "Famed Microsoft Blogger Scoble Leaves for Startup," *Reuters*, Sunday, June 11, 2006, http://www.eweek.com/article2/0,1895,1975 266,00.asp (accessed July 6, 2006).

17. Robert Scoble, "Correcting the Record about Microsoft," Scobleizer, June 10, 2006, http://scobleizer.wordpress.com/2006/06/10/correcting-the -record-about-microsoft/ (accessed July 6, 2006).

18. Kevin Allison, "Microsoft's Scobleizer Blogs Out," *MSNBC.com*, June 12, 2006, http://msnbc.msn.com/id/13282299/ (accessed July 6, 2006).

19. David Sifry, "State of the Blogosphere, April 2006 Part 1: On Blogosphere Growth," Sifry's Alert (personal blog of the founder and CEO of Technorati), April 17, 2006, http://www.sifry.com/alerts/archives/000432.html (accessed July 5, 2006).

20. Amanda Lenhart and Susannah Fox, *Bloggers: A Portrait of the Internet's New Storytellers* (Washington, DC: Pew Internet & American Life Project, 2006), 22, http://www.pewinternet.org/PPF/r/186/report_display.asp (accessed August 23, 2006).

21. Leon Neyfakh, "Online Weblog Leads to Firing," *Harvard Crimson*, May 26, 2004, http://www.thecrimson.com/article.aspx?ref=502702 (accessed July 5, 2006).

22. Heather B. Armstrong, "Reasons the Asian Database Administrator Is So Fucking Annoying," dooce, February 4, 2002, http://www.dooce.com/archives/daily/02_04_2002.html (accessed July 5, 2006).

23. Heather B. Armstrong, "Collecting Unemployment," dooce, February 26, 2002, http://www.dooce.com/archives/daily/02_26_2002.html (accessed July 5, 2006).

24. Heather B. Armstrong, "About This Site," dooce, undated, http://www.dooce.com/about.html (accessed July 5, 2006).

25. *Urban Dictionary*, s.v. "dooce," http://www.urbandictionary.com/define.php?term=dooce (accessed July 5, 2006).

26. Janelle Brown, "Bitch, Bitch, Bitch," *Salon.com*, February 1, 2001, http://archive.salon.com/tech/feature/2001/02/01/vault/index.html (accessed September 12, 2006).

27. Carol T. Kulik, Molly B. Pepper, Debra L. Shapiro, and Christina Cregan, "The Electronic Water Cooler: Insiders and Outsiders Talk about Organizations on the Internet," paper given at the annual meeting of the Academy of Management, August 2006, Atlanta, GA.

28. See, for example, Felhaber, Larson, Fenlon, and Vogt, P.A., "Are Your Employees 'Blogging' You?" *Minnesota Employment Law Letter*, February 2006, http://www.lexis-nexis.com/ (accessed May 8, 2006); LeClair Ryan, "My employersucks.com: Why You Need a Blogging Policy," *Virginia Employment Law Letter*, July 2005, http://www.lexis-nexis.com/ (accessed July 6, 2006).

29. Felhaber, Larson, Fenlon, and Vogt, P.A., "Are Your Employees 'Blogging' You?"

30. LeClair Ryan, "Myemployersucks.com: Why You Need a Blogging Policy."

31. Felhaber, Larson, Fenlon, and Vogt, P.A., "Are Your Employees 'Blogging' You?"

32. Sun Microsystems, "Sun News—Sun Blogs," http://www.sun.com/aboutsun/media/blogs/policy.html (accessed July 7, 2006).

33. Susannah Fox and Mary Madden, "Generations Online," Pew Internet and American Life Project, December 2005, http://www.pewinternet.org/pdfs/PIP_Generations_Memo.pdf (accessed July 6, 2006).

34. Ibid.

35. Jen, "The Official Story, Straight from the Source."

36. Anna Bahney, "Interns? No Bloggers Need Apply," *New York Times*, May 25, 2006, E1.

37. Alan Finder, "When a Risqué Online Persona Undermines a Chance for a Job," *New York Times*, June 11, 2006, A1.

38. Amy Joyce, "Blogged Out of a Job," *Washington Post*, February 19, 2006, http://www.washingtonpost.com/wp-dyn/content/article/2006/02/18/AR2006021800131_pf.html (accessed July 6, 2006).

39. Ryan, "Myemployersucks.com: Why You Need a Blogging Policy."

40. Darren Garnick, "Thou Shalt Not Offend Your Boss with a Podcast," *Boston Herald*, August 10, 2005, Finance section, 30, http://www.lexis-nexis.com/ (accessed July 7, 2006).

41. Finder, "When a Risqué Online Persona Undermines a Chance for a Job."

42. Ibid.

43. Daniel J. Salove, "Law Professor Blogger Census (Version 5.1)," Concurring Opinions, October 5, 2006, http://www.concurringopinions.com/archives/2006/10/law_professor_b_6.html, (accessed October 7, 2006). In Salove's census, 83 of 309 law professors blogging in October 2006—over one-quarter—are faculty members at law schools ranked in the *U.S. News & World Report* top twenty law schools.

44. Henry Farrell, "The Blogosphere as a Carnival of Ideas," *Chronicle of Higher Education*, October 7, 2005, http://chronicle.com/free/v52/i07/07b01401.htm (accessed July 6, 2006).

45. Daniel W. Drezner, "Here Goes Nothing," Daniel W. Drezner blog, September 10, 2002, http://www.danieldrezner.com/archives/000623.html (accessed July 6, 2006).

46. Daniel W. Drezner, "So Friday Was a Pretty Bad Day," Daniel W. Drezner blog, October 8, 2005, http://www.danieldrezner.com/archives/002353.html (accessed July 6, 2006).

47. Daniel W. Drezner, "The Trouble with Blogs" *Chronicle of Higher Education*, July 28, 2006, B7, http://chronicle.com/free/v52/i47/47b00701.htm (accessed July 30, 2006).

48. Stanley Fish, "Conspiracy Theories 101," *New York Times*, July 23, 2006, Week in Review section, 13.

49. Robert S. Boynton, "Attack of the Career-Killing Blogs," *Slate*, November 16, 2005, http://www.slate.com/id/2130466/ (accessed July 6, 2006).

50. Ivan Tribble (pseudonym), "Bloggers Need Not Apply," *Chronicle of Higher Education*, July 8, 2005, http://chronicle.com/jobs/2005/07/2005070801c.htm (accessed July 6, 2006).

51. The Laurie Garrett episode is recounted in some detail here: James Grimmelmann, "Accidental Privacy Spills: Musings on Privacy, Democracy, and the Internet," *LawMeme*, February 19, 2003, http://research.yale.edu/law meme/modules.php?name=News&file=article&sid=938 (accessed July 7, 2006). Her email that sparked the episode can be seen here: http://lists.topica.com/lists/psychohistory/read/message.html?mid=1711891071&sort=d&start=4389 (accessed July 7, 2006).

52. beagle (posting for Laurie Garrett), comment on "Could This Be True?" MetaFilter, February 11, 2003, http://www.metafilter.com/mefi/23493 #437751 (accessed July 7, 2006).

53. Jared Sandberg, "Infamous Email Writers Aren't Always Killing Their Careers After All," *Wall Street Journal*, February 21, 2006, B1.

54. Ibid.

55. Alex Mindlin, "You've Got Someone Reading Your E-Mail," *New York Times*, June 12, 2006, C5, http://www.proquest.com/ (accessed July 7, 2006).

56. Pamela L. Moore, "Bank Fires 7 Workers in Misuse of E-mail," *Charlotte Observer*, August 27, 1999, 1A; Ellen Dedalius, "City Punishes 44 Workers over E-Mail Lewdness," *Tampa Tribune*, April 19, 2005, Metro section, 1, http://www.proquest.com/ (accessed July 7, 2006).

57. "Nearly 25 Percent of Corporate Email Is Personal in Nature," *CRM Today*, November 23, 2005, http://www.crm2day.com/news/crm/116495.php (accessed July 7, 2006).

58. Hewlett-Packard, *HP Standards of Business Conduct* (revised April 2005), 34, http://www.hp.com/hpinfo/globalcitizenship/csr/sbcbrochure.pdf (accessed July 7, 2006).

59. Pfizer, *Summary of Pfizer Policies on Business Conduct* (September 2003), 20, http://www.pfizer.com/pfizer/download/investors/corporate/business_conduct _policies_summary_2003.pdf (accessed July 7, 2006).

60. Joe Kovacs, "Kodak Fires Man over 'Gay' Stance," *WorldNetDaily*, October 24, 2002, http://www.worldnetdaily.com/news/article.asp?ARTICLE _ID=29394 (accessed July 7, 2006).

61. James Bandler, "Rights in Conflict," *Times Union*, November 18, 2001,

Life and Leisure section, C1, http://www.lexis-nexis.com/ (accessed July 7, 2006).

62. Ibid.

63. *Intel Corp. v. Hamidi*, 30 Cal. 4th 1342 (2003).

64. Ibid., 1365.

65. The credit for pointing out this bit of irony goes to Judy Olian, "Free Speech Meets Business Interest," *Scripps Howard News Service*, December 6, 2002, http://www.lexis-nexis.com/ (accessed July 7, 2006).

66. Howard Rheingold, *The Virtual Community: Homesteading on the Electronic Frontier*, revised edition (Cambridge, MA: MIT Press, 2000), 295.

67. Jack M. Balkin, "Digital Speech and Democratic Culture: A Theory of Freedom of Expression for the Information Society," *New York University Law Review* 79 (2004): 15.

68. Amy Joyce, "Free Expression Can Be Costly When Bloggers Bad-Mouth Jobs," *Washington Post*, Friday, February 11, 2005, A1, http://www.washingtonpost.com/wp-dyn/articles/A15511-2005Feb10.html (accessed July 6, 2006).

CHAPTER NINE

1. Jerry Unseem, "Match Game," *Fortune*, November 18, 2002, http://www.proquest.com/ (accessed March 14, 2005).

2. For a review of some of this history of management thought, see William G. Scott, "The Management Governance Theories of Justice and Liberty," *Journal of Management* 14 (1988): 286–290. See also Richard L. Daft, *Organization Theory and Design*, 8th ed. (Mason, OH: Thomson, 2004).

3. For a review and reanalysis of multiple studies of the effects of participation, see John A. Wagner III, "Participation's Effects on Performance and Satisfaction: A Reconsideration of Research Evidence," *Academy of Management Journal* 19 (1994): 312–330.

4. Glenn R. Carroll and Albert C. Teo, "On the Social Networks of Managers," *Academy of Management Journal* 39 (1996): 421–440.

5. Elizabeth Wolfe Morrison and Frances J. Milliken, "Organizational Silence: A Barrier to Change and Development in a Pluralistic World," *Academy of Management Review* 25 (2000): 706–725.

6. Frances J. Milliken, Elizabeth W. Morrison, and Patricia F. Hewlin, "An Exploratory Study of Employee Silence: Issues That Employees Don't Communicate Upward and Why," *Journal of Management Studies* 40 (2003): 1462–1465.

7. Morrison and Milliken, "Organizational Silence," 717–721.

8. Scott, "The Management Governance Theories of Justice and Liberty," 286.

9. Ibid., 287.

10. Les Christie, "Bad Attitudes in the Workplace," *CNNMoney.com*, September 6, 2005, http://money.cnn.com/2005/08/24/pf/workplace_morale/index .htm (accessed July 20, 2006).

11. Chester I. Barnard, *The Functions of the Executive* (Cambridge, MA: Harvard University Press, 1938).

12. See, for example, Gerald S. Leventhal, "The Distribution of Rewards and Resources in Groups and Organizations," in *Advances in Experimental Social Psychology*, vol. 9, ed. Leonard Berkowitz and Elaine Walster (New York: Academic Press, 1976), 91–131.

13. John Thibaut and Lauren S, Walker, *Procedural Justice: A Psychological Analysis* (Hillsdale, NJ: Erlbaum, 1975).

14. See Jason A. Colquitt, Donald E. Conlon, Michael J. Wesson, Christopher O. Porter, and K. Yee Ng, "Justice at the Millennium: A Meta-Analytic Review of 25 Years of Organizational Justice Research," *Journal of Applied Psychology* 86 (2001): 425–445.

15. For a review of findings in this area, see Mary A. Konovsky, "Understanding Procedural Justice and Its Impact on Business Organizations," *Journal of Management* 26 (2000), 489–511. See also Colquitt and others, "Justice at the Millennium."

16. Konovsky, "Understanding Procedural Justice," 495–497.

17. E. Allan Lind, Ruth Kanfer, and P. Christopher Earley, "Voice, Control, and Procedural Justice: Instrumental and Noninstrumental Concerns in Fairness Judgments," *Journal of Personality and Social Psychology* 59 (1990): 952–959.

18. These and related social consequences of organizational justice emerge from Allen Lind and Tom Tyler's "group-value model" of procedural justice. See, for example, Tom R. Tyler, "The Psychology of Procedural Justice: A Test of the Group-Value Model," *Journal of Personality and Social Psychology* 57 (1989): 830–838; Tom R. Tyler, Peter Degoey, and Heather Smith, "Understanding Why the Justice of Group Procedures Matters: A Test of the Psychological Dynamics of the Group-Value Model," *Journal of Personality and Social Psychology* 70 (1996): 913–930.

19. Scott, "The Management Governance Theories of Justice and Liberty," 287.

20. In a law review article focused mainly on the intersection between due process and free speech at work, Cynthia Estlund concluded that "a universal requirement of just cause and fair process would provide crucial support and

'breathing room' for the existing free speech rights of public and private employees." Cynthia L. Estlund, "Free Speech and Due Process in the Workplace," *Indiana Law Review* 71 (1995): 151.

21. For an analysis of the prevalence of these codes in the world's largest corporations, and an assessment of their content, see Muel Kaptein, "Business Codes of Multinational Firms: What Do They Say?" *Journal of Business Ethics* 50 (2004): 13–31.

22. Paula Desio, *An Overview of the United States Sentencing Commission and the Organizational Guidelines* (Washington, DC: United States Sentencing Commission, 2004), http://www.ussc.gov/TRAINING/corpover.PDF (accessed July 21, 2006).

23. A survey conducted in 2002 found that 68 percent of the largest U.S. companies (those within the world's two hundred largest) had business codes. See Kaptein, "Business Codes of Multinational Firms," 18. An earlier estimate from the late 1990s found that 78 percent of large U.S. firms had codes of ethics. See Gary R. Weaver, Linda Klebe Trevino, and Philip L. Cochran, "Corporate Ethics Programs as Control Systems: Influences of Executive Commitment and Environmental Factors," *Academy of Management Journal* 42 (1999): 41.

24. Kaptein, "Business Codes of Multinational Firms," 22–24.

25. We examined every available code for the 50 largest firms on the list, and sampled 10 percent of the remaining 450 firms on the list for inspection of their codes. This analysis was originally performed using the Fortune 500 list published in 2004 and updated using the list published in 2006. For the list, see "Fortune 500 Ranking of America's Largest Corporations," *Fortune*, April 17, 2006, http://money.cnn.com/magazines/fortune/fortune500/full_list/ (accessed July 22, 2006).

26. The Boeing Company, *Ethical Business Conduct Guidelines*, April 2005, 9, http://www.boeing.com/companyoffices/aboutus/ethics/ethics_booklet.pdf (accessed July 23, 2006).

27. AT&T, *AT&T Code of Conduct*, February 2004, 6, http://www.att.com/ir/pdf/code_conduct.pdf (accessed July 23, 2006).

28. ConocoPhillips Company, *Code of Business Ethics and Conduct*, February 2005, 4, http://www.conocophillips.com/NR/rdonlyres/C57758DE-739A-4840-97BE-D47474B17991/0/3183980EthicsBooklet205Rev.pdf (accessed July 23, 2006).

29. Ryder System, *Principles of Business Conduct and Ethics*, http://www.ryder.com/inv_portal_principles.html (accessed July 23, 2006).

30. AmerisourceBergen, *Code of Ethics and Business Conduct*, June 2004, 5,

http://media.corporate-ir.net/media_files/IROL/61/61181/corpgov/code_of_ethics1.pdf (accessed July 23, 2006).

31. Target Corporation, *Business Conduct Guide*, April 2004, 3, http://media.corporate-ir.net/media_files/irol/65/65828/corpgov/business_conduct_guide.pdf (accessed July 23, 2006).

32. See, for example, "Workplace Privacy," *Electronic Privacy Information Center*, July 21, 2006, http://www.epic.org/privacy/workplace/ (accessed July 23, 2006).

33. Wal-Mart, *Statement of Ethics*, January 2005, 12, http://media.corporate-ir.net/media_files/IROL/11/112761/corpgov/Statement_Of_Ethics.pdf (accessed July 23, 2006).

34. "Electronic Media," *Corporate Compliance Policy Manual*, Tenneco Inc., February 2003, http://www.tenneco.com/governance/documents/compliance/electronic_media.pdf (accessed July 23, 2006).

35. Target, *Business Conduct Guide*, 7.

36. Hewlett-Packard Company, *HP Standards of Business Conduct*, April 2005, 32, http://www.hp.com/hpinfo/globalcitizenship/csr/sbcbrochure.pdf (accessed July 24, 2006).

37. Verizon Communications, *Connecting through Integrity: Our Code of Business Conduct*, 2001, 23, http://www22.verizon.com/about/careers/codeofconduct.pdf (accessed July 24, 2006) (emphasis added).

38. Cardinal Health, *Ethics Guide*, 2003, 26, http://www.cardinal.com/careers/why/EthicsGuide.pdf (accessed July 24, 2006) (emphasis added).

39. The Walt Disney Company, *Standards of Business Conduct*, 9, http://corporate.disney.go.com/corporate/conduct_standards.html (accessed July 24, 2006).

40. See, for example, Federal Election Commission, "Quick Answers to PAC Questions," http://www.fec.gov/ans/answers_pac.shtml (accessed July 24, 2006).

41. Tim Reason, "Office Politics: Banned from Making Political Donations, Companies Harvest Them from Employees Instead," *CFO Magazine*, July 1, 2004, http://www.cfo.com/article.cfm/3014831 (accessed July 24, 2006).

42. ConocoPhillips, *Code of Business Ethics and Conduct*, 21.

43. The Coca-Cola Company, *The Code of Business Conduct*, June 2006, 23, http://www2.coca-cola.com/ourcompany/pdf/business_conduct_codes.pdf (accessed July 24, 2006).

44. Reason, "Office Politics."

45. Ibid.

46. "We believe an avowed homosexual is not a role model for the values

espoused in the Scout Oath and Law." Boy Scouts of America, "Boy Scouts of America Sustained by United States Supreme Court," news release, June 28, 2000, http://www.scouting.org/media/press/2000/000628/index.html (accessed September 25, 2006).

47. United Way of the Bay Area, "Frequently Asked Questions," http://www.uwba.org/about/faqs.html (accessed September 25, 2006).

48. Joel S. Hirschhorn, "Democracy's Arrow," *CommonDreams.org*, February 7, 2005, http://www.commondreams.org/views05/0207-22.htm (accessed July 25, 2006).

49. Kelley Holland, "How Office Politics and Real Politics Can Mix," *New York Times*, October 8, 2006, SundayBusiness section, 3.

50. James Hoopes, *False Prophets: The Gurus Who Created Modern Management and Why Their Ideas Are Bad for Business Today* (Cambridge, MA: Perseus, 2003), xvi.

51. Ibid., 276.

52. Rob Olmstead, "Woman Wins Free Speech Suit against COD," *Chicago Daily Herald*, News section, 3, June 18, 2004, http://www.lexis-nexis.com/ (accessed June 15, 2006).

CONCLUSION

1. Thomas I. Emerson, *The System of Freedom of Expression* (New York: Random House, 1970), 9.

2. Walter Lippmann, "The Indispensable Opposition," *Atlantic Monthly*, August 1939, 190.

3. Bennett J. Tepper, "Consequences of Abusive Supervision," *Academy of Management Journal* 43 (2000): 178–190.

4. Lawrence Soley, *Censorship, Inc.: The Corporate Threat to Free Speech in the United States* (New York: Monthly Review Press, 2002), 253. See also William A. Wines and Terence J. Lau, "Can You Hear Me Now? Corporate Censorship and Its Troubling Implications for the First Amendment," *DePaul Law Review* 55 (2005): 119–167.

5. David W. Ewing, "Who Wants Employee Rights," *Harvard Business Review*, November-December 1971, 22–35 and 155–160.

6. David W. Ewing, "Free Speech from Nine to Five," *The Nation* 218 (1974): 756.

7. Ibid.

8. Kenneth D. Walters, "Your Employees' Right to Blow the Whistle," *Harvard Business Review*, July–August 1975, 34.

9. Ibid.

10. Jay W. Forrester, "A New Corporate Design," *Industrial Management Review*, Fall 1965, 14.

11. Erwin Chemerinsky, "More Speech Is Better," *UCLA Law Review* 45 (1998): 1639.

12. The term "democratic culture" as used here is law professor Jack Balkin's. See Jack M. Balkin, "Digital Speech and Democratic Culture: A Theory of Freedom of Expression for the Information Society," *New York University Law Review* 79 (2004): 33–38.

13. See, for example, C. Edwin Baker, *Human Liberty and Freedom of Speech* (New York: Oxford University Press, 1989); Martin H. Redish, "The Value of Free Speech," *University of Pennsylvania Law Review* 130 (1982): 591–645; David A. Strauss, "Persuasion, Autonomy, and Freedom of Expression," *Columbia Law Review* 91 (1991): 334–371; Emerson, *The System of Freedom of Expression*.

14. Patricia H. Werhane, *Persons, Rights, & Corporations* (Englewood Cliffs, NJ: Prentice-Hall, 1985), 7.

15. Lucy Vickers discusses market factors that define employer rights to suppress free speech at some length in her excellent book on free speech and employment in the United Kingdom, and I draw upon her arguments here. See Lucy Vickers, *Freedom of Speech and Employment* (Oxford: Oxford University Press, 2002), 28–36.

16. *Dartmouth v. Woodward*, 17 U.S. 518 (1819), 636.

17. For a brief account of the four-hundred-year history of the corporation as a business form, see Joel Bakan, *The Corporation: The Pathological Pursuit of Profit and Power* (New York: Free Press, 2004), 5–27.

18. *First National Bank of Boston v. Bellotti*, 435 U.S. 765 (1978), 804–805.

19. See John J. McCall, "A Defense of Just Cause Dismissal Rules," *Business Ethics Quarterly*, 13 (2003): 164.

20. Ibid., 158–159.

21. Richard A. Epstein, "In Defense of the Contract at Will," *University of Chicago Law Review* 51 (1984): 982.

22. *Rankin v. McPherson*, 483 U.S. 378 (1987), 388.

23. On the history and nature of civil society, see Adam B. Seligman, *The Idea of Civil Society* (Princeton: Princeton University Press, 1992).

24. Alexis de Tocqueville, *Democracy in America*, vol. 1, chap. 12, 1835, also available online at http://xroads.virginia.edu/~HYPER/DETOC/toc_indx .html (accessed July 29, 2006).

25. Ibid.

26. See William A. Galston, "Civil Society and the 'Art of Association,'" *Journal of Democracy* 11 (2000): 65.

27. Robert D. Putnam, *Bowling Alone: The Collapse and Revival of American Community* (New York: Simon & Schuster, 2000).

28. Cynthia Estlund develops this point at length in her excellent recent book exploring connections between workforce demography, workplace interaction, and democratic society. Cynthia Estlund, *Working Together: How Workplace Bonds Strengthen a Diverse Democracy* (Oxford: Oxford University Press, 2003).

29. James S. Coleman, "Social Capital in the Creation of Human Capital," *American Journal of Sociology* 94 Supplement (1988): S95–S120. See also Robert D. Putnam, "Bowling Alone: America's Declining Social Capital," *Journal of Democracy* 6 (1995): 66–67.

30. On the subject of time Americans spend at work, see Patricia Wallace, *The Internet in the Workplace: How New Technology Is Transforming Work* (Cambridge: Cambridge University Press, 2004), 55–57.

31. See, for example, Robert Huckfeldt and John Sprague, *Citizens, Politics, and Social Communication* (Cambridge: Cambridge University Press, 1995); Robert Huckfeldt, Paul Allen Beck, Russell J. Dalton, and Jeffrey Levine, "Political Environments, Cohesive Social Groups, and the Communication of Public Opinion," *American Journal of Political Science* 39 (1995): 1025–1054; Diana C. Mutz, "The Consequences of Cross-Cutting Networks for Political Participation," *American Journal of Political Science* 46 (2002): 838–855; M. Stephen Weatherford, "Interpersonal Networks and Political Behavior," *American Journal of Political Science* 26 (1982): 117–143.

32. Ada W. Finifter, "The Friendship Group as a Protective Environment for Political Deviants," *The American Political Science Review* 68 (1974): 607–625.

33. Richard Sobel, "From Occupational Involvement to Political Participation: An Exploratory Analysis," *Political Behavior* 15 (1993): 349.

34. Linn Van Dyne, Soon Ang, and Isabel C. Botero, "Conceptualizing Employee Silence and Employee Voice as Multidimensional Constructs," *Journal of Management Studies* 40 (2003): 1359–1392.

35. Alexander Meiklejohn, "The First Amendment Is an Absolute," *Supreme Court Review* 1961 (1961): 257.

36. Alice H. Eagly and Shelly Chaiken, *The Psychology of Attitudes* (Fort Worth, TX: Harcourt Brace Jovanovich, 1993).

37. Elisabeth Noelle-Neumann, "The Theory of Public Opinion: The

Concept of the Spiral of Silence," in *Communication Yearbook 14*, ed. J. Anderson (Newbury Park, CA: Sage, 1991), 259.

38. Timur Kuran, *Private Truths, Public Lies* (Cambridge, MA: Harvard University Press, 1995), 19.

39. Montana Code Annotated Title 39, Chapter 2, § 901-905 (2003). See also William L. Corbett, "Resolving Employee Discharge Disputes under the Montana Wrongful Discharge Act (MWDA), Discharge Claims Arising apart from the MWDA, and Practice and Procedure Issues in the Context of a Discharge Case," *Montana Law Review* 66 (2005): 329-404; Theodore J. St. Antoine, "The Model Employment Termination Act: A Fair Compromise," *Annals of the American Academy of Political and Social Science* 536 (1994): 96.

40. Cynthia L. Estlund, "Free Speech and Due Process in the Workplace," *Indiana Law Review* 71 (1995): 137.

41. This is admittedly easier said than done: Changes to common law are more likely to evolve than abruptly arise and may or may not involve clear, well-defined principles that are easily applied in practice. Accordingly, their consequences for the ensuing exercise of employee free-speech rights are somewhat unpredictable.

42. California Labor Code § 1102.

43. Louisiana Revised Statutes 23 § 961.

44. North Dakota Cent. Code § 14-02.4-03 and 14-02.4-08.

45. Connecticut General Statutes § 31-51q; South Carolina Code Annotated § 16-17-560.

46. *Connick v. Myers*, 461 U.S. 138 (1983), 146.

47. Gary Peller and Mark Tushnet, "State Action and a New Birth of Freedom," *Georgetown Law Journal* 92 (2004): 789.

48. *Shelton v. Tucker*, 364 U.S. 479 (1960), 485–486.

49. Erwin Chemerinsky, "Rethinking State Action," *Northwestern University Law Review*, 80 (1985): 503–557.

50. Charles A. Reich, "The Individual Sector," *Yale Law Journal* 100 (1991): 1429.

51. Jeffrey Rosen, *The Unwanted Gaze* (New York: Random House, 2000), 100–127. See also Eugene Volokh, "Freedom of Speech and Workplace Harassment," *UCLA Law Review* 39 (1992): 1816–1818.

52. The origin of this aphorism is elusive. A 1996 essay by sociologist Robert N. Bellah credits journalist James Fallows with having made the remark "some years ago." Robert N. Bellah, "The Neocapitalist Employment Crisis," *Christian Ethics Today*, August 1996, http://www.christianethicstoday.com/Issue/007/Issue_007_August_1996.htm (accessed July 30, 2006).

Index

About the Author

Bruce Barry is Professor of Management and Sociology at Vanderbilt University, where he teaches courses on power and influence in organizations, business and society, negotiation, and the sociology of media and technology.

His research on behavior at work, including negotiation, power, and justice, has appeared in many scholarly journals and volumes. He also writes about business ethics, workplace rights, and public policy issues at the intersection of business and society. He is co-author of three books on negotiation that are widely used in courses at universities worldwide.

Barry is a past president of the International Association for Conflict Management, and a past chair of the Conflict Management Division of the Academy of Management. He is a member of the editorial boards of the journals *Business Ethics Quarterly*, *Work and Occupations*, and *Negotiation and Conflict Management Research*.

Barry is president of the board of directors of the American Civil Liberties Union of Tennessee and is a contributing writer for the *Nashville Scene* (a weekly alternative newspaper).

He lives in Nashville, Tennessee.

ABOUT BERRETT-KOEHLER PUBLISHERS

Berrett-Koehler is an independent publisher dedicated to an ambitious mission: Creating a World that Works for All.

We believe that to truly create a better world, action is needed at all levels—individual, organizational, and societal. At the individual level, our publications help people align their lives with their values and with their aspirations for a better world. At the organizational level, our publications promote progressive leadership and management practices, socially responsible approaches to business, and humane and effective organizations. At the societal level, our publications advance social and economic justice, shared prosperity, sustainability, and new solutions to national and global issues.

A major theme of our publications is "Opening Up New Space." They challenge conventional thinking, introduce new ideas, and foster positive change. Their common quest is changing the underlying beliefs, mindsets, and structures that keep generating the same cycles of problems, no matter who our leaders are or what improvement programs we adopt.

We strive to practice what we preach—to operate our publishing company in line with the ideas in our books. At the core of our approach is *stewardship*, which we define as a deep sense of responsibility to administer the company for the benefit of all of our "stakeholder" groups: authors, customers, employees, investors, service providers, and the communities and environment around us.

We are grateful to the thousands of readers, authors, and other friends of the company who consider themselves to be part of the "BK Community." We hope that you, too, will join us in our mission.

A BK CURRENTS BOOK

This book is part of our BK Currents series. BK Currents books advance social and economic justice by exploring the critical intersections between business and society. Offering a unique combination of thoughtful analysis and progressive alternatives, BK Currents books promote positive change at the national and global levels. To find out more, visit www.bkcurrents.com.

Be Connected

VISIT OUR WEBSITE

Go to www.bkconnection.com to read exclusive previews and excerpts of new books, find detailed information on all Berrett-Koehler titles and authors, browse subject-area libraries of books, and get special discounts.

SUBSCRIBE TO OUR FREE E-NEWSLETTER

Be the first to hear about new publications, special discount offers, exclusive articles, news about bestsellers, and more! Get on the list for our free e-newsletter by going to www.bkconnection.com.

GET QUANTITY DISCOUNTS

Berrett-Koehler books are available at quantity discounts for orders of ten or more copies. Please call us toll-free at (800) 929-2929 or email us at bkp.orders@aidcvt.com.

HOST A READING GROUP

For tips on how to form and carry on a book reading group in your workplace or community, see our website at www.bkconnection.com.

JOIN THE BK COMMUNITY

Thousands of readers of our books have become part of the "BK Community" by participating in events featuring our authors, reviewing draft manuscripts of forthcoming books, spreading the word about their favorite books, and supporting our publishing program in other ways. If you would like to join the BK Community, please contact us at bkcommunity@bkpub.com.